*f*P

ALSO BY ERIC BOEHLERT

Lapdogs: How the Press Rolled Over for Bush

BLOGGERS ON THE BUS

How the Internet Changed Politics and the Press

ERIC BOEHLERT

FREE PRESS

NEW YORK LONDON TORONTO SYDNEY

*f*P

Free Press
A Division of Simon & Schuster, Inc.
1230 Avenue of the Americas
New York, NY 10020

First Free Press hardcover edition May 2009

FREE PRESS and colophon are trademarks of Simon & Schuster, Inc.

For information about special discounts for bulk purchases,
please contact Simon & Schuster Special Sales at 1-866-506-1949
or business@simonandschuster.com.

The Simon & Schuster Speakers Bureau can bring authors to your live event.
For more information or to book an event, contact the Simon & Schuster Speakers
Bureau at 1-866-248-3049 or visit our website at www.simonspeakers.com.

Designed by Level C

Manufactured in the United States of America

10 9 8 7 6 5 4 3 2 1

Library of Congress Cataloging-in-Publication Data

Boehlert, Eric.
    Bloggers on the bus : how the internet changed politics and the press /
by Eric Boehlert.
        p.   cm.
    1. Internet in political campaigns—United States.   2. Internet—Political aspects—
United States.   3. Press and politics—United States.   4. Presidents—United
States—Election—2008.   5. United States—Politics and government—2001–
6. Political campaigns—United States.   I. Title.
JK2281.B643 2009
324.973'0931-dc22   2009007371

ISBN-13: 978-1-4165-6010-4
ISBN-10:   1-4165-6010-6

For Tracy

CONTENTS

INTRODUCTION

Chronicling the 1972 presidential campaign, Timothy Crouse's landmark book, *The Boys on the Bus,* exposed how the political press really functioned, and in the process he helped give birth to modern-day journalism. With a sharp eye for detail and an outsider's disdain for conformity, the young *Rolling Stone* writer explored how a handful of supremely confident, cigarette-smoking and bad-tie-wearing journalists who rode the back of campaign buses (and airplanes) were really the ones who framed the story—who set the agenda—for the unfolding White House race.

Dishing healthy doses of gossip and painting compelling character sketches, while also bluntly critiquing their campaign work, Crouse detailed the rise of "pack journalism" and the incestuous press culture that fueled it: "They all fed off the same pool report, the same daily handout, the same speech by the candidate; the whole pack was isolated in the same mobile village."

For most readers who had never given much thought to the (mostly) male band of reporters behind the news, and who couldn't name more than one or two Beltway journalists, Crouse's insider account came as a revelation. Published at a time when political journalists didn't seek out celebrity status and didn't clog up untold hours of TV time listening to themselves talk, *The Boys on the Bus* introduced a new era in political reporting and ushered in the notion of journalists as newsmakers themselves. In fact, Crouse's book helped make media stars of a whole generation of influential insiders who for decades afterward maintained a viselike grip on crafting Beltway conventional wisdom, insiders like David Broder of the *Washington Post,* Jack Germond of the *Baltimore Sun,* and the legendary reporter Johnny Apple of the *New York Times.*

Back in 1972 the key to getting the story right, to capturing the campaign, was being on the bus. "Because travel is the soul of this business," Apple told Crouse. "You gotta be there because you can't do it all by telephone."

But over time the bus morphed into a bubble as campaign operatives increasingly limited access to candidates, and even to senior aides, to the point where the bus riders became among the least well-informed about the day's unfolding developments. With the arrival of the Internet age, the bus looked more and more like a horse and buggy.

Describing a surreal scene of approaching antiquity during the 2008 campaign, as journalists filed dispatches from a Barack Obama rally, Howard Kurtz of the *Washington Post* wrote, "Before the Democratic nominee took the podium, the text of his speech arrived by BlackBerry. The address was carried by CNN, Fox and MSNBC. While he was still delivering his applause lines, an *Atlantic* blogger posted excerpts."

The outdated campaign bus had broken down. Worse, over the years not only had its media passengers slavishly maintained the same pack-driven approach that Crouse bemoaned decades earlier, but the political press had become increasingly unserious, with an almost nonstop devotion to campaign tactics, process, and trivia.

Fed up, liberal bloggers adopted the Internet as their bus. Fueled by high-speed cable modems, they didn't claim to be objective or to uncover the insider, tactical minutiae that the mainstream media obsessed over. But during the 2008 race, by communicating directly with their audience and deputizing their readers ("the people formerly known as the audience," as the blogger Jay Rosen put it), bloggers helped democratize the process by sapping the mainstream media of some of its previous, oracle-like control over the campaign narratives. The Internet, as Barack Obama demonstrated in 2008, offered a way for candidates to go around the traditional Beltway media and communicate directly with voters.

During the White House run, the blogs created user-generated content that periodically altered the course of the campaign. They forced two televised debates to be canceled, infuriating Fox News in the process. They vetted Sarah Palin better than the GOP had. They pushed back against shoddy journalism and unleashed blogswarms on offensive cable commentators who diminished Democratic candidates. And they bedeviled the Republican candidate, Sen. John McCain, at nearly every turn, using an array of online tools to confuse the slow-footed candidate whose Republican Party, still in love with AM talk radio, seemed oblivious to the political revolution unfolding online.

The recent rise of the liberal blogosphere, or the netroots, as it's also known, has unfolded at an extraordinary pace. "Already, the netroots are the most significant mass movement in U.S. politics since the rise of the Christian right more than two decades ago," marveled Jonathan Chait in the pages of the centrist *New Republic* magazine. "What they have accomplished in just a few years is astonishing." Indeed, by late 2008 the readership at the flagship liberal site Daily Kos was roughly equivalent to that of America's most-read newspaper, *USA Today*.

Bill Clinton cleared his calendar to host a private, two-hour lunch at his Harlem office with prominent liberal bloggers just prior to his wife's White House campaign push. And the Huffington Post's Sam Stein was called on to ask a question at Barack Obama's first presidential press conference in February 2009. A political and media transformation was unfolding in plain sight.

And yet there hasn't been enough serious public attention paid to the netroots phenomenon, which is I why decided to write *Bloggers on the Bus*. Inspired by Crouse's book, although I'm in no way comparing my work with his pioneering effort, I believe the uniquely twenty-first-century phenomenon of the netroots ought to be documented. I want to pull back the curtain a bit so readers can appreciate in more detail, and with a more nuanced understanding, the revolution taking place, as well as the unlikely participants leading it: students, housewives, attorneys, professors, musicians. A fan of the liberal blogosphere, I hoped the 2008 White House campaign would provide an illuminating backdrop to highlight the extraordinary gains of the netroots, as well as allow me to document the inevitable missteps and growing pains that all movements experience as they experience adolescence.

Along with detailing how the netroots influenced and altered the road to the White House, I want to shed more light on the people behind the blogosphere. So often depicted in the mainstream press as faceless, interchangeable parts ("Bloggers reacted angrily . . ."), I wanted to find out more about the people who reinvented all kinds of election and newsroom rules. Who were these amateur citizen journalists? Why did they blog? How did they amass so much power in such a short period and with so little money and resources behind them? How did this band of ragtag activists help elect a new Congress in 2006 and a new president in 2008?

For years those types of questions had continued to pile up, and I kept waiting for somebody in the press to answer them. Bloggers, forever obsessed with what's next and averse to look back even at the previous week, weren't going to devote much of their time to reflect on the larger netroots movement. Neither did journalists show much interest in netroots history. Over the years they had occasionally, and rather reluctantly, acknowledged liberal bloggers. But they showed almost no desire to detail, in depth, the blogosphere's rise or spotlight the new media stars it was producing. As a matter of fact, I was the first person to even ask some of the A-list bloggers profiled in this book for extended interviews about the rapid growth of the netroots and their own role in the online insurrection.

Back in 1994, when the emerging stars of right-wing talk radio helped Republicans gain control of Congress, AM hosts were toasted in the press as being wildly influential. They even scored a *Time* magazine cover feature. By contrast, when liberal bloggers helped Democrats win back the House in 2006, there was mostly radio silence from media elites. The same media indifference followed Obama's victory two years later; the press showed no interest in toasting the bloggers.

This silence was odd because traditionally there are few assignments journalists relish more than writing about other writers. Crouse's *The Boys on the Bus* had ushered in the era of political journalists as celebrities, which only intensified with each passing decade. NBC's week-long, flood-the-zone coverage of Tim Russert's death in 2008 simply confirmed that fact. Perhaps driven by feelings of competitive jealousy for the fresh generation of citizen journalists and their newfound clout, or maybe fueled by contempt for the bloggers who so effectively critiqued the Beltway media's often shoddy work, the traditional press mostly kept its distance and chose not to shine a spotlight on the new writers and activists. That is, when the press wasn't being openly contemptuous of the bloggers. A *New York Times* writer once expressed his "half-sickening feeling" at the realization that the news agenda was being set by a "largely unpaid, T-shirt-clad army of bloggers."

Instead, the press clung to its outdated caricatures, portraying bloggers as polarizing, amateurish extremists, downplaying their concrete achievements, and reluctant to tell the personal stories behind the creation of the blogosphere, the unlikely professional odysseys bloggers often took before securing leadership positions within the vibrant political community. How reluctant? As of January 2009, the normally media-obsessed *Washington Post* still has not published, ever, a single feature profile of an A-list liberal blogger.

The media's indifference is even more baffling considering that the story of the blogosphere is a remarkably fertile and personal one, the kind journalists usually love to tell, and filled with an almost endless collection of unlikely biographies of online pioneers who rose from complete obscurity to the forefront of a game-changing media movement. If journalists had bothered to take the time, they would have discovered that the netroots was occupied with all kinds of improbable actors, such as Chris Bowers, the former Temple University English professor who, in the early part of the decade, found himself habitually hunched over his laptop between classes, reading everything he could find online. Bored with the freshman composition and literary theory courses he was teaching and plagued by nightmares about returning to the classroom for another semester, the young bearded professor with wire-rim glasses and long hair tucked behind each ear started leaving reader comments on Daily Kos. That fledgling online site was launched in 2002 by an army vet named Markos Moulitsas Zuniga, who at the time was stuck at a Web-development firm helping corporate clients he despised. Often noisy, contentious, and brawling with his snide and argumentative attacks, Markos, as he is universally known online, quickly gave voice to the howls of protest on the Left during the Bush administration. At Daily Kos, Bowers finally found the community, and the political voice, he'd been searching for. "I just threw myself in politics," he told me.

Soon Bowers's life revolved around blogging. He loved the free Internet connection at work so much that he often slept on his office floor so he'd have an entire night's worth of uninterrupted blogging. In fact, he'd learned the hard way the importance of a solid online connection. In his Philadelphia apartment on Election Eve 2004, moments after he had hit the *send* button to post a long, detailed breakdown of the final campaign polling data on the landmark liberal site MyDD, he lost his cable and Internet connection. He hadn't paid his electricity bill, now $145 overdue. His apartment lost power with disturbing regularity, actually.

He later developed a physical tic, shaking if he remained offline for more than two hours. If he didn't post anything for an eight-hour stretch during the day, Bowers's friends and family assumed something was wrong.

"I blog, therefore I am," he wrote.

In November 2006 an exhausted Bowers appeared in a YouTube clip that showed him slumped on a couch and staring into his friend Matt Stoller's video camera, explaining the harsh realities of being a political blogger: "If you have no children, no one to support, and no career ambitions, then you too can become a full-time progressive blogger, as long as you're wiling to do nothing else in your entire life."

Bowers later amended the list to include other key job qualifications:

If you don't care about having a social life.
If you don't mind being viciously attacked dozens of times every day.
If you don't have a wide range of interests in life.
If you don't mind paying for your own health insurance.
If you don't like taking vacations.
If a one-bedroom apartment in West Philly is your idea of high living.

Did Democratic politicians and their consultants embrace every blogger idea and initiative? Hardly. But they paid attention. And compared to the wilderness years between 2001 and 2004, compared to how the liberal voice had been completely silenced at the turn of the decade, when the

Democratic Party retreated into an ineffectual fetal position, the rise of the blogs represented a huge achievement. And Bowers just had to be part of it.

That's how the progressive blogosphere was born. Creative people like Bowers were drawn to it because it represented a much-needed release valve for the pent-up political frustration so many Democrats and liberals had felt throughout the late 1990s and into this decade. For them, blogs represented small-scale places where people could stand up to the onslaught of conservative misinformation that had fueled Bill Clinton's impeachment, the Florida recount in 2000, and the rush to war with Iraq. It was where citizens could at least *try* to launch a new form of participatory democracy online. At first they just blogged in hopes of retaining their sanity as they watched the Bush Doctrine unfurl and liberals being attacked as unpatriotic while the government cut taxes on its most wealthy citizens and waged a costly, unprecedented war over nonexistent WMDs.

The liberal blogosphere, made up of lots of funny-sounding anchors— Firedoglake, Hullabaloo, FiveThirtyEight, the Field, AmericaBlog, Shakesville, Eschaton, Crooks and Liars, Suburban Guerrilla—represents perhaps the most unplanned, un-thought-through media and political movement in modern America. Liberal bloggers changed politics and the press in a way that no other left-leaning movement had done in decades. But it really did just happen.

Early on, the netroots movement was built with very little coordination and no money. There were no memos, no outlines, no projections, and certainly no budgets. No nothing. (Only later did coordination begin to surface.) It grew organically and grew out of a deep-seated frustration with the direction the country was taking. It became an accidental empire as bloggers served as a conduit to the grassroots. The bloggers talked to people who talked to people, and collectively they amassed real political power by raising hell together.

It was an accidental empire because the pent-up dissatisfaction among liberals just happened to peak at the exact moment the Internet knocked down barriers of entry for public discussion. It was accidental because the key players who helped bring the liberal blogosphere to life represented the most unlikely cast of characters imaginable. Most brought with them no experience in politics or journalism. None of them ever dreamed that their online essays, posted in an effort to keep themselves sane, would ever represent career options, or that White House candidates would one day come courting.

Collectively, bloggers expanded well beyond the traditional role of journalist or commentator; they tossed aside the mantle of objectivity that the boys on the bus had worn for decades. Instead, bloggers raised money, trained leaders, forged vibrant online communities, picked candidates, fostered participation, forged coalitions among existing special interest groups, launched policy initiatives, produced original reporting, called bullshit out on the press, and occasionally, and out of sheer force of will, attached a spine to the Democratic Party, which for much of the decade had been too nervous, too spooked by the pro-war GOP, to acknowledge its proud progressive past. They literally kept the lights on during a very dark period. "Without the netroots, Democrats would not be in the position we are in today," U.S. Senate Majority Leader Harry Reid announced after the Party's sweeping congressional wins in 2006. "It's as simple as that."

Many of the bloggers wrote better, more succinctly and more passionately, than most high-paid newspaper columnists. They were more politically astute than TV's paid Beltway pundits, although they were rarely invited to be part of the televised round-table discussions, and they were just as powerful as labor leaders when it came to igniting key issues within the Democratic Party. They even put on better presidential debates: the blogger-sponsored candidate forum in 2007 turned out to be far more substantive than any of the cable television debates that followed.

Growth and influence came at an astonishing clip. Four years earlier, desperately trying to push Sen. John Kerry across the White House finish line, the nascent blogosphere represented the campaign oddity, the proverbial new kids with their newly minted press credentials and their laptops stuck up in the nosebleed section at the Democratic National Convention in Boston. By 2008 they starred as a main attraction. Camped out inside the bloggers-only Big Tent, a two-story, corporate-sponsored 8,000-foot pavilion just blocks from the Convention in downtown Denver, hundreds of bloggers chilled on couches in the New Media Lounge, watched news updates on flat-screen TVs, and feasted on free WiFi, back massages, smoothies, and beer while CBS's Katie Couric came by with a camera crew to interview *them.*

Sure, arch enemy Bill O'Reilly still compared liberal bloggers to the Ku Klux Klan and the Nazi Party. (Bloggers chuckled every time he did.) But O'Reilly was probably just angry that so many conservative bloggers, blinded by their pursuit of half-baked conspiracy theories over the years, had failed to emerge as a political force on their own. After all, the goose chases related to Barack Obama—he was born in Kenya!—took up months of the bloggers' time in 2008. There was simply nothing on the Right that matched the passion, or the proven results, of the liberal netroots.

Indeed, beginning on November 3, 2004, the day after Bush won re-election, the netroots became focused on electing a Democratic president. For four years the blogs worked toward that goal. "In their role as a central conduit of political information and opinion, they will calibrate, amplify, and disseminate the messages and themes that shape people's beliefs and bolster their convictions, providing the impetus for organizing, fundraising and GOTV [getting out the vote]," wrote the netroots guru Peter Daou. "And on November 4, 2008, eight long years of doing battle against the excesses of the Bush presidency will come to a triumphant conclusion."

A triumph, yes, but the White House campaign also revealed deep growing pains in the liberal blogosphere. The rupture emerged during the Democratic primary season, when the normally tightly knit community was torn apart by a venomous civil war between online supporters of Barack Obama and those of Hillary Clinton. The months-long showdown left deep, lasting scars, especially among some netroots veterans, who were aghast at the sexist language lobbed at Clinton from within the progressive community.

Flexing all kinds of new muscles built up between 2004 and 2008, the netroots did everything it could to get Obama and Democrats elected: Media Matters for America played the role of relentless watchdog; the Huffington Post built a gigantic bulletin board; the all-star think tank sponsored by the Center for American Progress critiqued Republican policies; and ActBlue served as the money hub for candidates. A new generation of creative operatives enthralled by the historic possibilities of Obama's run was fostered and promoted. But Obama himself often failed to return the online love. Bloggers, even the majority of Obama supporters, had to wrestle with the nominee's standoffishness toward the netroots and its love of unambiguous progressive politics. Embracing the campaign rhetoric of bipartisan unity, Obama's team focused more on the revolutionary fund-raising and Facebook-style social-networking possibilities the Internet held, and less on the brand of scrappy liberal politics the blogosphere embraced.

That political disconnect prompted some painful introspection throughout the campaign and into Obama's early days as president. Had the blogosphere simply been cast aside by a new team of centrist Democrats? Had bloggers failed to secure a pledge from Obama that he'd govern as a liberal before showering him with support, before giving him the netroots endorsement, during the primary season?

It's impossible to know whether the 2008 campaign represented the netroots' pinnacle in terms of passion and influence, or if it has lasting power and this election season was just the first of many when liberal bloggers will forcefully help to shape the parameters of political debate. What is clear is that in 2008 bloggers took the campaign bus down a very different route.

BLOGGERS ON THE BUS

one

FOX NEWS AND "WTF?"

Sitting behind a cluttered, horseshoe-shaped desk in his Culver City, California, office just beyond downtown Los Angeles, the filmmaker Robert Greenwald felt sick to his stomach after he clicked on a Huffington Post headline in February 2007. As he scanned the dispatch announcing that Nevada Democrats had teamed up with Fox News to cosponsor a debate among the Party's presidential hopefuls, Greenwald hoped the article was some sort of gigantic typo.

He didn't want to believe that Democrats had joined forces with Fox News to help voters pick the next president. He didn't want to imagine that any Democrat in a leadership position thought it was a wise, strategic media move to team up with Fox News. And he winced at the idea of Democrats helping to legitimize Rupert Murdoch's all-news channel.

For Greenwald, the unholy alliance was personal. A prolific Hollywood television producer and director with 55 mostly dramatic television titles to his credit, Greenwald in his early retirement years had produced his own second act as a partisan and persuasive anti-Bush and antiwar documentary filmmaker. He had also set his sights on Fox News and helped unmask the GOP-friendly outlet with his 2004 documentary *Outfoxed: Rupert Murdoch's War on Journalism,* the most telling portions of which were told by former Fox News employees who detailed how the self-proclaimed fair-and-balanced news network remained unabashedly movement-oriented and explained that its main focus was to promote and advance the Republican agenda at the expense of Democrats.

In fact, at the time Greenwald read about the just-announced Nevada debate, he and his team of young filmmakers at Brave New Films, led by twentysomething cofounder Jim Gilliam, were already in the process of pulling together Fox News clips that unfairly attacked Barack Obama as he prepared to enter the presidential race. The project was initiated after Fox News's January 2007 smear campaign suggested that while growing up in Indonesia, Obama had been raised a Muslim and attended a radical Islamic madrassa as a young boy. "This is huge!" exclaimed Fox News host Steve Doocy at the prospect of a Democrat with possible ties to jihad.

Yet just weeks after the Obama offensive, Nevada Democrats were celebrating their new Fox News affiliation for the planned debate to be held on August 14 in Reno. Nevada Sen. Harry Reid, the de facto leader of the state's Democratic Party, boasted, "This is more great news for Nevada. I'm happy FOX News will be a partner for the August presidential debate." Fox News President and CEO Roger Ailes personally expressed delight with the debate plans.

"That was clearly a calculated move on his part to try to reinforce the 'fair and balanced' nonsense," Greenwald told me. "The fact that the Nevada Democrats had taken the bait was despairing to me."

Those same alarms were going off all over the liberal blogosphere when news spread about the planned debate. "My immediate reaction was, 'What the fuck are Democrats doing?' Which is a common reaction for me," recalled the blogger Matt Stoller. He got the news from a reader's email that contained a link to a February 16 Mediabistro.com item about the just-announced Fox News debate. An agenda-setting blogger who spent his undergrad years at Harvard writing for the campus *Lampoon* humor magazine, Stoller threw himself into the progressive movement after the Iraq war was launched and became something of an online wunderkind, displaying a behind-the-scenes gift for organizing and agitating. Out front, Stoller distinguished himself as an influential blogger, known for his aggressive left politics, his distrust of Hillary Clinton (soon replaced by his distrust of Barack Obama), and his disdain for weak-kneed compromise. When he read about the proposed Fox News debate, Stoller did what he always does: he blogged it. The headline for Stoller's first of many angry posts about the Fox News partnership read simply, and in its entirety, "WTF?"

For Stoller and others, the remedy was obvious: bloggers had to get the debate canceled. So began the unlikely media showdown between a group of mostly amateur lefty activists camped out online and the mighty Fox News, the highest rated cable news outlet in the country, reaching tens of millions of households each day.

Fox News never had a chance.

By the time the media brawl concluded, bloggers, in an unprecedented move, got not one but two Fox News–sponsored debates knocked off the campaign schedule, which clearly cost Fox in the ratings department when the Democratic primaries unfolded in early 2008 as must-see TV. The move allowed CNN to surpass Fox as the cable go-to destination for political news. The skirmish also put Fox News on notice that online progressives, brandishing new communication tools, were done being pushed around, and that if leaders of the Democratic Party were too timid to wage open warfare with Rupert Murdoch's conservative news outlet, then the netroots would do it for them.

To bloggers, having Fox News cohost a Democratic debate made as much sense as having it moderated by Rush Limbaugh or cosponsored by the *National Review.* All three dealt in GOP attack-style politics. In other words, Fox News was not a news outlet to partner with, to put out self-congratulatory press releases with the way the Nevada Democrats had done. Fox News needed to be discredited.

The point of the media pushback was to begin chipping away in a serious, consistent manner at Fox News's reputation. Bloggers wanted to move the debate beyond the question of whether the news operation was fair and balanced and instead pose the more pressing question of whether Fox News was even a genuine news organization.

Bloggers wanted to badly dent the Fox News brand.

COMPLACENT DEMOCRATIC POLITICIANS who avoided picking fights had adopted a "go along, get along" strategy with Fox News, hoping that if they were nice and cooperative, then Fox News would be nice and cooperative in return. That strategy didn't work. In 2004 a study conducted by the Center for Media and Public Affairs found that during the height of the presidential campaign, just 13 percent of Fox News panelist comments about Democratic candidate Sen. John Kerry were positive, compared to 50 percent positive for Bush.

There was a reason that four years after launching, the archives at Media Matters for America, the liberal watchdog group, contained more than 4,500 entries under "Fox News," as the group diligently documented each bout of misinformation. That was simply how Fox News operated. And sure enough, the all-news channel kicked off its White House coverage in early 2007 by embracing a discredited, anonymous report from a dubious right-wing news source claiming that Obama, while growing up in Indonesia, had attended a radical Islamic school as a 6-year-old.

Bolstered by the electoral success of 2006, when more Democrats ran openly as progressives and won back control of the House and Senate, bloggers figured it was time to take the fight right to Fox News, dragging nervous Democrats along, if need be. Now functioning as a skeptical Party ally, the netroots decided to make Democratic leaders choose between their activist base and Fox News.

The issue of the debate itself would serve as the battering ram, even though Fox News's candidate face-off, in and of itself, was rather meaningless. Bloggers didn't really care about the actual debate, and certainly were not scared about what kinds of questions the Fox News moderators would pose to the Democrats. Bloggers were more concerned about the other 364 days of the year and how Fox News would benefit from the legitimacy attached to cosponsoring a Democratic debate, and how Fox would use that authority to attack more Democratic candidates if given the chance.

AT THE CENTER of the quixotic Fox News campaign was the Internet odd couple of Robert Greenwald and Jim Gilliam at Brave New Films. Slightly undersized and in his sixties, Greenwald grew up in a liberal New York City Jewish family and admits to being a late adapter to the Internet. Gilliam, by contrast, is in his twenties and hovers at six feet, nine inches tall. (He looks like the Smashing Pumpkins' lanky lead singer, Billy Corgan, but even taller.) Home-schooled by his evangelical parents, Gilliam grew up listening to Rush Limbaugh and attending church several times a week. A self-taught computer whiz, he started posting his online diary nearly a decade ago, long before most people had ever heard of blogging.

What the odd couple had in common, though, was a desire to drive Fox News out of the mainstream of American media, as well as their understanding that the power of posting short films online was one of the best ways to accomplish that goal. They realized that people could go online and read about how unfair and unbalanced Fox News was, but when they *saw* it in video form it was far more powerful. Greenwald and Gilliam shared another common trait, one many netroots players claimed: prior to the September 11 terror attacks, neither man paid much attention to politics, and they certainly never gave serious thought to devoting their work to a political cause.

During the 1990s, Greenwald was immersed in his filmmaking and Gilliam was busy cashing in on the dot-com boom as a tech guru. The terror attacks jolted both men. Specifically, the rightward, pro-war lurch that America took convinced them that it was time for a career change, time to walk away from filmmaking and lucrative start-ups and instead use their talents to counter what they saw as the dangerous and destructive path the country was taking. Now, just a few short years later, they were at the forefront of the netroots' muscular expansion. In the spring of 2007 Fox News found that out the hard way.

THE TWO MEN work in a nondescript, one-floor office building—a converted motel, actually—in Culver City, across a busy boulevard from a looming Sony Pictures outpost. A horseshoe-shaped structure where starlets and studio executives used to meet discreetly during another era, the row of old motel rooms now serves as offices for Greenwald's Brave New Films team. To get from office to office, employees don't stroll down an indoor hallway; instead, they open their doors onto the motel's courtyard, which remains intact, and walk across the sun-splashed patio to meet with colleagues. (Hey, it's L.A.)

A 63-year-old with boyish enthusiasm, his reading glasses perched atop his mostly hairless head, Greenwald could fit right in on any leafy college campus as an unassuming member of the political science department. A born storyteller, he attended Antioch College and the New School for Social Research and had a commitment to social justice instilled in him at a young age by his parents. Raised in New York City and born into a family of psychiatrists (even his siblings became shrinks), Greenwald embraced the theater and began directing plays in the 1970s before migrating to Los Angeles, where he directed plays at the Mark Taper Forum, the Lincoln Center of Los Angeles.

Once he arrived on the West Coast, Greenwald realized that he was no good at being an employee and that if he didn't start his own business he would soon be fired. So he set up his own television production company and quickly became a master of the true-life television tale, tackling major stories such as Hiroshima, Love Canal, the Pamela Smart murder case in New Hampshire, the Munich Olympics massacre, and Enron, as well as topical issues such as alcoholism, divorce, patricide, teenage pregnancy, eating disorders, and AIDS.

Perhaps the most memorable effort was Greenwald's turn as director of the 1980s domestic violence TV classic, *The Burning Bed,* in which Farrah Fawcett transformed herself from one of Charlie's glamorous crime-fighting Angels into a swollen and battered wife. A ratings phenomenon in 1984, *The Burning Bed* was seen by 40 million viewers. His most forgettable effort? Directing the 1980 film *Xanadu,* a kitsch classic starring Olivia Newton-John as a roller-skating Greek muse. "If you look at *Xanadu* very closely you'll see the political impact of the leg warmers," Greenwald joked years later. When *Xanadu* was turned into a successful Broadway musical in 2007, Greenwald took his son to see it. The boy turned to his father after the final curtain call and said, "Sorry, Pop, but that was way better than the movie."

By 2000 Robert Greenwald Productions had produced nearly 50 films and boasted a bookcase full of awards. That year the *New York Times* referred to Greenwald as "one of the most respected producers in television." But 18 months later, following the terrorist strike of September 11, Greenwald was desperate for a career change.

The father of four, Greenwald was shocked and alienated at how the country had moved after 9/11 from pain and fear to rage and revenge. He started looking for ways to get involved. He had previously scratched his activist itch in 2001, when the filmmakers Richard Ray Perez and Joan Sekler came calling in search of help as they tried to finish their documentary about the chaotic 2000 Florida recount. Greenwald invited them to work in some extra offices he had. Greenwald had recently purchased a new, simple editing machine, a Final Pro Cut, which represented the new generation in editing and cost just a fraction of the older, six-figure models. He offered Final Pro Cut to the duo to see if they could make a movie on it. They did, and Greenwald saw his future. He loved the process of making documentaries, the creativity of the editing room. So the next time he had a current events idea for a film, instead of trying to force it into the commercial world, which had become uninviting due to media consolidation and the political atmosphere in the country, he decided to try to do it as a documentary.

In quick succession, Greenwald's muckraking, Bush-bashing *Un* trilogy was rolled out: *Unprecedented: The 2000 Presidential Election* (2002), *Uncovered: The War on Iraq* (2003), and *Unconstitutional: The War on Our Civil Liberties* (2004).

It was *Uncovered,* about the faulty intelligence that led the United States to war, that cemented Greenwald's commitment to a new generation of film: the grassroots political documentary. He called it people-powered film. The first screening of *Uncovered* got him hooked for good. It took place in Santa Monica on November 11, 2003, just six months after Bush's infamous "Mission Accomplished" declaration aboard the USS *Abraham Lincoln;* there was still a large degree of war frenzy in the culture and Greenwald didn't know if anybody would show up to see his low-budget film. As he approached the Laemmle Theatre on Second Street in Santa Monica, two blocks from the Pacific Ocean, he saw hundreds of people queued up out front.

His initial reaction was, "Oh shit, we've made a mistake. There's a film premiering there tonight." It didn't occur to him that they were there for *Uncovered.* The screening was sold out. Greenwald had made a lot of movies over the years; some were good and some were not; some people liked them and some did not. But after *Uncovered,* people came up to him and said, "Thank you for making this movie." That was the turning point for him. Nobody before had ever thanked him for making a movie.

Opinionated and aggressive, Greenwald's timely guerrilla films (short shooting schedules, small budgets) had a clear agenda. They were also factually sound and represented responsible journalism. His films became the blogosphere's de facto movie studio, echoing the issues and arguments being made online. They were also backed by a revolutionary distribution network that utilized the netroots community.

That's what propelled *Outfoxed: Rupert Murdoch's War on Journalism,* which put Greenwald on the mainstream documentary map in 2004. In a partnership with MoveOn.org, Greenwald released *Outfoxed* on DVD over the Internet and sold more than 100,000 copies in three weeks at $10 a disk. The headline for the *Outfoxed* review that ran in Rupert Murdoch's *New York Post* was "FAIR AND BALANCED, THIS DOC'S NOT." By the time his company released *Wal-Mart: The High Cost of Low Price* in 2005, 10,000 volunteer screenings were hosted in schools, living rooms, churches, and community centers, 7,000 in the first week of release. Traditional theatrical distribution was of little interest to Greenwald and his team.

Early on, Greenwald relied on donors and also took out personal loans to cover the production costs and then hoped DVD sales would recoup the expenditures. For his 2006 film, *Iraq for Sale: The War Profiteers,* he directly asked thousands of supporters for money up front to help pay for the production. That way the moviemaker wouldn't be beholden to skittish donors who sometimes had second thoughts about the crusading nature of his films. (He lost a big donor midway through making a Wal-Mart documentary.) The initial plea, emailed April 23, was sent to people who had ordered his DVDs in the past. The proposed budget for *Iraq for Sale* was $750,000. Within 10 days the email blast generated $267,892 in pledged funds. Inside Greenwald's Brave New Films offices, the pledge request became affectionately known as the "$200,000 email."

The concept of the direct donor plea came from Greenwald's young Brave New Films cofounder, Jim Gilliam. He got the idea while lying in bed and battling a life-threatening illness. Again.

• • •

LIKE HIS BOSS, Gilliam propelled himself into progressive politics after 9/11. He even quit his job as chief technical officer for the search engine Business.com, where he made a healthy six-figure salary. Not bad for a single guy in his twenties with no college degree. Gilliam taught himself everything he knew about computers, which was a lot. In the 1990s he served as a principal software engineer for the search engine pioneer Lycos.

Prior to 9/11 Gilliam had been oblivious to politics. He paid no attention to the tumultuous Florida recount and didn't even vote for a president until 2004. But after the terrorist attacks and the subsequent drums of war began to bang louder, he looked for a career change, wanting to do something more meaningful. He didn't know exactly what he wanted to do with his life, he just knew that it didn't include making money for people who were already rich.

Just weeks after the terrorist attacks, Gilliam was sitting in the back row of a darkened Los Angeles movie theater watching *The Glass House,* a forgettable thriller. A catastrophic event had just occurred in America and Gilliam had no idea why. He didn't know the first thing about Al Qaeda and couldn't even describe President Bush's foreign policy. He had purposefully blocked that stuff out for years—politics, news, all of it. Now, still shaken by the terrorist attacks, Gilliam searched for his response. What should he *do*? It was while sitting there in the dark watching *The Glass House* that he had an epiphany: he had to quit his job. It was the only way he could clear his head and figure out his plan of action.

The urgency was driven by Gilliam's earlier bouts with cancer and the feeling that he was supposed to accomplish something with his life. Yes, he had mastered the role of computer start-up wunderkind. But now he felt he needed to focus his energies, his smarts, his passion, not to mention his postcancer borrowed time, on something besides inflating the dot-com bubble. "Am I going to use this for good, or for evil?" he asked himself.

But how to put his talents to use? Still searching for a long-term path in the summer of 2003, Gilliam participated in a MoveOn exercise among members: to interview another MoveOn colleague in their area code, find out what that person felt were the top priorities for the country, and then report back to MoveOn, which was always taking the temperature of is members. Gilliam's interview subject turned out to be a Hollywood producer. A few days later the producer forwarded Gilliam a "help wanted" email that Greenwald had sent out to associates looking for a researcher willing to work on an antiwar documentary for very little pay. Within days Gilliam had joined the staff researching *Uncovered,* which was completed and released just 12 weeks later.

Gilliam used his computer wizardry to figure out a way to streamline the film's production by downloading video clips of Bush right from the White House website, which had the best collection of Bush's misstatements about the war. At the time of *Uncovered'*s production there was no YouTube or any other free video-hosting site, and most news clips posted online were streamed, which meant they were designed specifically so users could not copy or alter them. Without that online library of clips, Brave New Films producers, if they were not able to capture specific video clips themselves via TiVo, had to request clips from the White House or from traditional news outlets such as NBC News. It was a process that could take weeks, if the requests were honored at all.

To get around those roadblocks, Gilliam and his team hacked their way through production by grabbing Microsoft Windows' streaming video and learning how to edit it. They were able to stream clips to their hard drive but then had to send the clips to a television, record them on VHS tape, and edit from there: New School meets Old School. Gilliam loved that the finished *Uncovered* product shipped out in October and featured one TV clip that was broadcast less than 30 days earlier, an amazing accomplishment for a documentary.

It's true that Gilliam was a self-taught computer whiz and a dedicated blog reader and was getting his best progressive information online from Daily Kos and MyDD. But he quickly concluded that the most effective way to alter the national conversation was through film. That's how Americans communicate best; that's what we respond to. Gilliam understood that instinctively from his evangelical upbringing and his days studying at

Jerry Falwell's Liberty University. "You go to Liberty, and they literally have Evangelicalism 101, which is really just sales," Gilliam told me. "They teach you how to reach people on their level. And I spent a lot of time drawing those parallels on how to take what I learned about one of the greatest movements that America's ever seen, which is the evangelical movement, which is incredibly well-funded and organized and has strong infrastructure with churches everywhere, and . . . take those principles and spread a different gospel." The gospel of liberalism.

When not attending Liberty convocations three times a week, Gilliam was obsessed not with computer programming, but with the idea of getting computers to talk to each other. He camped out in Liberty's fledgling computer lab, which was where he spent much of his freshman year and where he knew most of the faculty. Soon he helped bring the Internet to Liberty campuswide and created the university's first website. Then he got sick and everything changed. It was in March 1996 when bouts with cancer began to overwhelm Gilliam and his family. The medical emergencies sparked soul-searching about life and politics.

After suffering during his freshman year with what doctors first assumed was bronchitis, Gilliam was diagnosed with lymphoblastic lymphoma, a rare and extremely aggressive form of non-Hodgkin's lymphoma. Incredibly, two weeks later, while he was in chemotherapy, Gilliam's mother, Kathy, was diagnosed with the even more rare adrenal cancer. She had a large tumor removed but died later that year.

In December 1996 Gilliam was declared cancer-free. But just seven months later he returned to the hospital and was again diagnosed with cancer, this time with acute lymphoblastic leukemia. Following chemo, more radiation, and a bone-marrow transplant, in November 1997, for the second time in 12 months, Gilliam was pronounced healthy.

By then he'd left Liberty U. far behind, not bothering to get a degree. Instead, he cashed in on the Internet start-up boom, first with Lycos, then with eCompanies and Business.com. "It's what I called my ticket out of the [fundamentalist] ghetto," he joked. That's when he started asking more of life's questions, which sparked his transformation into a progressive.

"My mother died, and then I got cancer again, and basically that gets you to wake up. So it wasn't like I was sitting there and all of a sudden my political views changed," he explained. "I became a little more conscious of things. And over time, over the next few years, I actually started reading things. I actually learned what evolution was. At home, I didn't know that. At home I wasn't investigating and questioning the things that I had been told. It was after the cancer that I really started to."

There was also the simple fact that Gilliam was wired from birth to be inquisitive. That, plus his love of the Internet, where seemingly every question could be asked and answered in an instant, meant it was only a matter of time before he punctured the evangelical bubble that surrounded him growing up.

But Gilliam had one more medical hurdle to face. Hard at work in 2005 on Greenwald's Wal-Mart exposé, Gilliam began to feel lethargic and experienced shortness of breath from simply climbing a flight of stairs. The condition became gradually worse, but Gilliam assured himself that he was simply out of shape. When a friend pressed him about why he didn't go see a doctor, however, he admitted that it was because he didn't want to know the truth. That truth came in July 2005, when his doctor told him his condition looked serious. Worse news came in September: his lungs were scarred from the cancer treatment he had undergone years earlier to battle leukemia. He suffered from postradiation fibrosis and needed a transplant of both lungs before they stopped working completely.

After 18 anxious months of waiting, at 9:40 a.m. on February 1, 2007, UCLA Medical Center called with the news that a lung match had been found. Within minutes, Gilliam was in a car with his family, speeding up I-405 to the hospital. Within two hours of getting the call he was in surgery, where doctors cut open his chest, removed the old, damaged lungs, and sewed new lungs to his airway. Twenty-five days later he was released from the hospital. Four weeks after that he walked two-thirds of a mile on his own. And 10 weeks after the transplant Gilliam returned to work at Brave New Films.

Looking back, Gilliam figures his medical bills have cost insurance companies between $3 and $4 million. Sitting on a couch in his uncomfortably warm, sun-drenched office at Brave New Films (the couch was in case Gilliam had to lie down and rest during the day), he reflected on his unlikely decade-long journey from evangelical student to progressive movement pioneer. He was convinced that his medical battles dictated his path. "It's a cliché, but if it doesn't kill you it will make you stronger," he told me. "I would not be doing anything that I'm doing now if I hadn't gotten cancer. It takes some kind of traumatic, big event to get you to re-evaluate your basic assumptions. The big event for me was getting cancer and reevaluating a lot of assumptions about what I wanted to do with my life. Nine-eleven made me reevaluate whether . . . what I was doing was good or bad. The lung transplant made me reevaluate whether my time is even more limited now, and what can I do that will make the three- to four-million-dollar investment worthwhile?"

THE TRAUMATIC EVENTS of 9/11 had also jolted Greenwald into a career change, from TV producer to antiwar documentarian. But as 2007 unfolded, Greenwald wondered if there was another, more immediate way for him to spread a progressive message. Although he and his team of editors had been amazingly productive, churning out half a dozen documentaries in less than four years, Greenwald was looking for a way to turn around films even more quickly so they could have a more immediate impact. He had been spending more time online reading the blogs and seeing how fast the news cycle was accelerating. A flood of new progressive documentaries were being made, particularly about Iraq, and he was looking for a new niche, a way to stay ahead of the curve, or at least stay even with it.

He wanted to have quick-strike capability. He wanted something that would go viral.

"From a social change point of view, I started to analyze whether there were other ways to be helpful," said Greenwald, sitting by a large bay window of his Culver City office. He kept thinking back to the mock Halliburton commercials Brave New Films had posted online at YouTube in connection with the *Iraq for Sale* release in 2006. The clips landed more than 60,000 views in a single week without anyone ever promoting them. It was Greenwald's "Holy shit!" moment.

In early 2007 the Fox News madrassa smear of Obama had caught the attention of Greenwald, the veteran Fox News critic. "I just got pissed off and said, 'This is insane, and we cannot let this happen to another Democratic candidate.'" He decided to make a short montage of clips, peeled right off Fox News, to give viewers an up-close look at the cable channel's slanted ways. He kept the rapid-fire video to two and a half minutes because advertising research had shown that anything longer made people bookmark the videos for future viewing rather than clicking the *play* button right away. Thus began the *Fox Attacks* series—"They distort. We reply"—with its first installment, *Fox Attacks: Obama*. Within six months the *Fox Attacks* clips had been viewed 2.5 million times.

At the same time that Greenwald began responding to the madrassa smear, the controversy erupted over the Nevada Democratic Party and Fox News cosponsoring a debate, and Greenwald knew he had the perfect hook for his new *Fox Attacks* video. The clip would include a petition for viewers to sign (300,000 quickly did), stating that "Fox is a mouthpiece for the Republican Party, not a legitimate news channel" and urging that the debate be dropped.

This was a new type of counteroffensive. To make their point, progressives didn't have to buy TV time or spend tens of thousands of dollars on full-page newspaper ads. Greenwald and his team didn't need to create a whole new documentary and spend weeks shipping out DVDs. The editors at Brave New Films simply collected offensive snippets about Obama off Fox News and put the video compilation online, where it was rapidly, and widely, distributed. All in a matter of days.

BY ITSELF, THOUGH, Greenwald's video clip wouldn't be enough to get the debates scratched from the campaign's summer schedule. So MoveOn began emailing 2,500 members daily, asking them to contact the Nevada Democratic Party and urge that the debate be canceled. At the same time, bloggers were raising hell about the issue. Days later, on March 6, John Edwards's campaign announced that the North Carolina Democrat would not participate. Fittingly, the statement was sent first to bloggers, including Markos at Daily Kos and the Talking Points Memo media writer Greg Sargent. The next day the Nevada blog Reno Discontent posted a letter from Tom Collins, the chairman of the Nevada Democratic Party, who still hoped to salvage the debate. Collins suggested that a local progressive voice be added to the moderator mix.

Christiane Brown from Reno talk station KFJK was tapped as that possible progressive voice. But the talk show host wanted no part of it. "I was on the line with someone from Fox and they were trying to convince me that this would be great exposure for me," she said. She viewed the invitation as an obvious token gesture. Plus, her callers were furious about the proposed partnership with Fox News: "They were saying things like, 'I'm never giving money to the Democratic Party again. I can't believe this, I'm done with them.' The phone was ringing off the hook. We couldn't answer all of the calls, and even after the show was over people were still calling about this issue."

Rather than assuage activists' concerns, Collins's attempted compromise just made them angrier. MoveOn organizers jacked up the number of daily calls to the Nevada Democratic Party from 2,500 to 50,000 a day, just so Party officials got the message. And they did. Then, on the evening of March 7, the Carson City Democratic Central Committee passed a resolution by a count of 40 to 2 that proclaimed:

WHEREAS, Fox News is not a neutral source of news—it's a right-wing mouthpiece like Rush Limbaugh that smears Democrats and spreads blatantly false information; and

WHEREAS, we believe that Democrats need to fight back against Fox News and the right-wing smear machine in the 2008 election cycle—not enable it.

BE IT RESOLVED, the Carson City Democratic Central Committee opposes the proposal to let Fox News host a Democratic presidential debate and strongly urges the Nevada Democratic Party to drop that proposal.

The next day Sen. Harry Reid agreed to a conference call with key bloggers, including Matt Stoller, Markos, and Hugh Jackson of the local Las Vegas Gleaner. During the 20-minute confab, Markos mentioned that in the most recent straw poll held at Daily Kos, Reid's favorable ratings among readers had dropped nearly 40 points. After the uncomfortable call was over he reportedly told his aides, "Fix this."

The Nevada Democratic Party's prized debate with Fox News was doomed. But little did Reid or his aides know that the mess would quickly resolve itself, courtesy of Roger Ailes. A bear of a man, Ailes provided progressives with an enormous target. A former hardball Republican media consultant who helped engineer Richard Nixon's 1968 political resurrection, Ailes also scripted Ronald Reagan's 1984 debate comeback and rescued George Bush Sr.'s floundering presidential campaign in 1988. Ailes had also served as the producer of Rush Limbaugh's failed television show.

Fast-forward to the night of March 8, 2007, when the Fox News chairman accepted that year's First Amendment Leadership Award at the annual Radio & TV News Directors Foundation Awards dinner at the Ritz-Carlton Hotel in Washington, D.C. He opened his remarks with some partisan jabs. One was about how Bill Clinton wanted his wife to remain on the campaign trail so he could fool around with other women. Another tapped into Obama-sounds-like-a-terrorist: "And it is true that Barack Obama is on the move. I don't know if it's true that President Bush called Musharraf and said, 'Why can't we catch this guy?'"

By sunrise Ailes's wisecrack had unleashed a new round of online rebukes. For Nevada Democrats desperately searching for a way out of their Fox News quagmire, Ailes's quip descended from the skies like a gift. On March 9 Senator Reid informed Fox News, "In light of his [Ailes's] comments, we have concluded that it is not possible to hold a Presidential debate that will focus on our candidates and are therefore canceling our August debate."

That's when key Fox News players, in front of and behind the cameras, went bonkers. Frustrated for weeks that they had no leverage in the unfolding debate within the Democratic Party about whether or not to go forward with the proposed alliance, the channel's executives erupted with rage when they were finally, and unceremoniously, dumped.

On the air, Fox News pundit Mort Kondracke claimed that the netroots campaign to cancel the debate amounted to "junior-grade Stalinism." The afternoon host John Gibson also invoked Stalin, as well as Trotsky. And Bill O'Reilly claimed that the network's online debate opponents "use propaganda techniques perfected by Dr. Joseph Goebbels, the Nazi minister of information. They lie, distort, defame, all the time."

This came from Ailes himself: "The candidates that can't face Fox, can't face Al Qaeda. And that's what's coming." (Did that mean Fox News was the equivalent of Al Qaeda?) Bloggers were thrilled that the CEO of the most successful cable news channel couldn't resist becoming publicly embroiled in the debate over the debates; they knew they'd struck a nerve within Rupert Murdoch's empire.

The Fox News brand had been dented.

two

"VOTE DIFFERENT"

When he picked up the phone at Blue State Digital, the left-leaning communications firm in Washington, D.C., in late March 2007 and heard the distinctive Greek accent of Arianna Huffington leaping through the other end of the receiver, Philip de Vellis knew the day would end badly. The 33-year-old graphics tech pro realized immediately, instinctively, why Huffington was calling, and he knew it had nothing to do with the job interview de Vellis had had at the Huffington Post several months back, when he was looking for work.

The unsolicited call came in response to that day's article in the Style section of the *Washington Post*. Headlined "Watching Big Sister; '1984' Takeoff on YouTube Is a Sign of Why 2008 Won't Be Like 2004," the piece chronicled the first media phenomenon of the still-young campaign season. Dubbed "Vote Different" and posted anonymously on YouTube on March 5, 2007, the buzz-worthy mash-up clip had ingeniously taken Apple computer's famous Orwellian "1984" ad and interspersed it with clips off Hillary Clinton's official site to turn Clinton into the authoritarian, Big Brother figure droning on to the masses.

The original Apple ad famously depicted a dystopian world where bleak workers wearing drab, oversize uniforms move listlessly through their robotic workday while passively absorbing the Big Brother messages delivered from the droning giant screen that hovers above them at all times: "We are one people with one resolve, one cause." A blonde female track-and-field athlete sent to break the chains of monotony then sprints ahead of the riot police and defiantly throws a hammer into the projection screen.

In the twenty-first-century version, the detached head of Senator Clinton addresses the inert masses—"I intend to keep telling you exactly where I stand on all of the issues"—and it is her image that explodes, shattering the politics-as-usual that Clinton had come to represent for many Democrats. The Apple ad in 1984 served as an apt metaphor of the upstart Macintosh user fighting against a conformist establishment, IBM. The Clinton version fit nicely into the larger netroots cultural push for a more genuinely participatory system of campaigning.

By late March "Vote Different" emerged as the first full-fledged press happening of the White House run and had been viewed more than a million times. By the summer of 2008 it had been clicked on more than 5 million times, the equivalent of $10 million worth of free TV time. The *Washington Post* described the YouTube effort as "a brilliant piece of agit-prop, expertly produced." *Newsweek* called it "stunning." Both Democratic frontrunners publicly discussed the mysterious clip that took less than five hours to create. "It combines some of the strongest elements of technology, politics, and bottom-up empowered political campaigning into one brilliant example," wrote the blogger Adam Conner.

Not only visually arresting, the clip also seemed to capture the promise of the decentralized approach to politics and campaigning that the Internet offered. It represented a media landscape where everyday supporters, thanks to YouTube's minimal barrier to entry, could effectively, albeit temporarily, set the agenda of the national debate, even during a presidential run. No PACs were needed; no TV time had to be purchased; and no famous bylines had to be attached to the creative product.

In this brave new world, passionate activists operating outside the confines of traditional campaigns had the power to shape the narrative. And they could be *creative.* They could break away from the Beltway consultant-approved script for making safe but effective campaign commercials. In other words, "Vote Different" represented the democratization of the campaign process through user-generated media. It also illustrated how the Internet had changed the campaign rhythms of the mainstream media, how the gatekeepers, rather than dictating the terms of the coverage, were sometimes forced to react to and respond to grassroots efforts unfolding online.

By late March 2007 the media mob had moved on from the *what* and *why* part of the "Vote Different" story to the *who:* Who had created the clip? Who was the digital whiz kid who set tongues wagging by seamlessly transforming the former first lady into Big Sister? Did the Obama campaign commission it? A mischief-making Republican? One blogger even suggested that Arianna Huffington herself had created the clip.

Answer: It was de Vellis.

He wanted his role to remain anonymous for professional reasons, but on the morning of March 21, on the way to work, he knew the chances of remaining in the shadows were growing slim. When he got off the D.C. city bus on 16th Street near the White House and started his walk to Blue State Digital, located just a few blocks away, de Vellis passed a *Post* vending machine and saw a screen grab of "Vote Different" on the front page, hyping the Style section article inside about the viral phenomenon. De Vellis, who almost never paid for the *Post* (he read it for free online), purchased the daily and smiled.

"That's pretty cool," he said to himself, following up with a second internal message: "Oh shit."

He loved that the viral video became hugely popular and helped spread his idea that the Obama campaign represented much needed change within the Democratic Party. The clip had long ago eclipsed any life span he could have mapped out for it when he banged out the mash-up video on his Mac laptop on the first Saturday of that month. But as it became increasingly popular and attracted widespread media attention, de Vellis knew pressure would mount to uncover the unknown creator. A creature of the Internet himself, and a longtime blogging fan, he knew that online legions were ready to pounce, just relishing the challenge of unmasking an anonymous player who refused to be indentified.

Walking down 16th Street that morning in the nation's capital, de Vellis retraced the steps he had taken weeks earlier in posting the video and pushing it out onto the Internet. Had he left any fingerprints behind? He worried only about an email exchange he'd had with Micah Sifry, the editor of techPresident.com, who had inquired about the video for an article he was writing. The emails from de Vellis had been anonymous and sent from a separate email account. Still, he was nervous that the correspondence might have provided some clues about his identity or how to track him down.

Then, at three o'clock, when Huffington's phone call came through to Blue State Digital, de Vellis realized he was "fucked," as he later put it. Huffington called because after challenging her staffers to uncover the anonymous creator, to solve this media whodunit, and after being briefed on the results of their investigation, she was convinced that de Vellis was the man behind "Vote Different." In her signature rapid-fire style, Huffington told de Vellis that she knew for a fact he had created the clip and that the Huffington Post wanted to report the story.

De Vellis, though, wondered if she were bluffing, if Huffington *thought* he was the creator and just wanted him to admit it, handing her a good scoop for her site. (It turned out that the actual pool of people with the digital videomaking expertise as well as campaign background necessary to pull off a clip like "Vote Different" was pretty shallow.) He made a couple of quick attempts to parry with Huffington and asked if they could go off the record. But that phrasing only got the attention of his nearby officemates at Blue State Digital, who were not accustomed to staffers dealing with reporters calling into the shop.

De Vellis had imagined that this conversation would eventually take place and had decided that if he were ever asked directly about the clip, he'd simply confess. He remembered that the author Joe Klein got in trouble back in the 1990s for denying that he had written the campaign book *Primary Colors* as Anonymous. De Vellis didn't want to make the same mistake.

Concerned that Huffington would publicly float his name even if he denied ownership of the clip, de Vellis admitted that he had created "Vote Different." Her only request was that he blog his coming-out announcement at the Huffington Post. He agreed, and by 7 p.m. had posted his item: "Hi. I'm Phil. I did it. And I'm proud of it." But before ending his call with Huffington that afternoon he told her he'd need a grace period of a few hours.

First de Vellis had to go get fired.

• • •

IT MADE SENSE that as a kid growing up in Los Angeles, de Vellis became transfixed by Apple computers, a West Coast creation, and Democratic politics, which dominated the Golden State. The Apple IIc was his first PC at the age of nine (128k of RAM!). He still remembers the summer between second and third grade, when he watched Walter Mondale get nominated on TV at the 1984 Democratic National Convention.

After majoring in history at UCLA, de Vellis worked several years doing freelance postproduction work on documentaries and for television commercials. In 2003 he caught the Howard Dean bug and soon moved east to Washington, in pursuit of politics full time. He got a job with Wal-Mart Watch, the progressive group that shadowed the retail giant.

In 2006 de Vellis became the Internet communications director for Sherwood Brown's successful Senate campaign in Ohio. Blue State Digital in Washington came next, where he had an up-close view of the unfolding White House race just as it got out of the gates in 2007.

Not that de Vellis could pick a White House winner. Every four years he fell for insurgent Democrats like Bill Bradley and Howard Dean, only to watch them get mowed down by the Party establishment, and then he watched the safe Democratic nominee lose in the general election anyway. He saw warning signs everywhere of a repeat performance in the 2008 race, and he didn't want that to happen. In February 2007, when he attended the Democratic National Committee's annual winter meeting and saw the candidates address the crowd of Party insiders and activists, he got that sinking feeling again.

Something about Hillary Clinton's appearance annoyed him. He sensed an air of royalty about it, the way Democrats in attendance seemed to be filing by as if to kiss her hand. Excited about the Democratic primary race, de Vellis wanted it to be a real contest, not a coronation. If Clinton won fair and square, he'd proudly support her in November 2008. But he didn't want it to be a case of Party insiders ultimately making the decision to gang up on Obama, or of the all-powerful Clintons exerting their control over the Party apparatus.

He also didn't like Clinton's Web chats, her much-hyped online "conversations" at the outset of her campaign in which the candidate vowed to listen to the concerns of everyday Americans. De Vellis watched the forums and thought they looked staged and as if the participants had been prescreened. Corporate propaganda, he thought. Rather than breaking down new campaign barriers, Clinton was just paying lip service to the Internet. Instead of initiating an honest, two-way conversation with voters, with the netroots, she just used the Internet to create the illusion of one.

At the time, de Vellis didn't know if Obama was up to the tall campaign task, or whether he had the fortitude to navigate the difficult trail ahead. He didn't even know if Obama represented the best candidate. But he wanted him to at least have a shot. He didn't want to see Obama's candidacy strangled in the crib the way campaigns of previous insurgent Democrats had been.

He figured that somebody, preferably an everyday citizen, should make a statement about how the old political machine no longer held all the power and that Obama was supported by a new kind of activist base, that Clinton represented the entrenched Democratic establishment and change was badly needed, and that the Web community would not be satisfied being talked to by candidates having pretend conversations. At least that was the idea de Vellis wanted to convey when he sat down with his Mac laptop inside his Columbia Heights apartment in Washington, opened up his Final Cut Studio editing package, and started working on his "Vote Different" clip.

The idea of hijacking the famous Apple ad had popped into his head a few days earlier. It was an iconic commercial and one that he remembered from his Apple-fanatic youth. Directed by the Hollywood hit-maker Ridley Scott (*Blade Runner, Alien*), "1984" was immediately heralded by ad critics as Madison Avenue's most inspiring TV sales pitch ever. With the upstart Apple computer brand (now Apple Inc.) targeting the established computer giant IBM (aka Big Blue) as the oppressive Big Brother, the cinematic gem featured deeply political, albeit nonpartisan, themes.

At the commercial's unveiling in the fall of 1983 before an auditorium of rapturous Apple worshippers, CEO Steve Jobs, hyping the pending arrival of the Macintosh home computer in January, demanded to know,

"Will Big Blue dominate the entire computer industry? The entire information age?" Cries of "No!" could be heard from the revival-like crowd. "Was George Orwell right about 1984?"

With that, the hall went dark, the commercial played, and the Apple faithful went nuts, giving a one-minute standing ovation to a commercial. Of course, it wasn't just a commercial. The spot represented a clarion call-to-arms for a new way of thinking and living for Apple devotees who saw their desktops as far more than tools to help them work efficiently. Six presidential cycles later, the commercial's central message about the last best hope for the future found new meaning when attached to the insurgent Obama campaign.

After finding a digital version of the "1984" ad online, which Apple produced in 2004, when it updated the spot to show the heroine wearing an iPod, de Vellis saw the thematic possibilities immediately. He saw in his mind's eye how easy it would be to execute since the transformation required replacing just a few bits of imagery. That turned out to be the key to the spot's quick execution as well as its creative success: altering as little as possible from the original spot. The process he used to seamlessly cut and paste the Clinton videos onto "1984" is called corner pinning; it allows editors to stretch or shrink or skew images when they're repositioned by each of their four corners.

So yes, de Vellis had the idea, but he wasn't sure he'd actually do it. Lots of creative ideas floated into his head, only to remain there, dormant for weeks and months. Plus, the situation with his employer was problematic. If his bosses at Blue State Digital, which enjoyed close ties to the Obama campaign, found out he had publicly commented on the campaign, let alone uploaded a scathing anti-Clinton mash-up video, he'd be fired. It was a risky, renegade effort to launch for somebody who had just started a new job, his dream job, actually, at the hot Blue State Digital media shop.

Tugging at him was the alluring prospect of marrying the two dream megabrands of Apple and Obama and doing it on YouTube. He knew that would create big buzz. If careful when posting it anonymously, he would never be connected to the clip. So de Vellis started culture-jacking Apple's "1984."

"I just happened to have some free time that day and decided, fuck it, I'll go ahead and do it. It didn't take long. It was almost like I was in a trance," recalled de Vellis many months later, in the summer of 2008. He was sitting in a conference room at a video postproduction house in Arlington, Virginia, where he was helping to finish a new batch of TV spots for local Democratic candidates. In the wake of "Vote Different," he had landed a plum VP job at a Washington political advertising firm.

At the end of his clip, he included the address BarackObama.com, since that seemed like the most logical direction to point viewers who wanted to help the campaign. Mimicking the on-screen scroll of the original Apple ad, "Vote Different" ended with the message "On January 14th the Democratic primary will begin. And you will see why 2008 won't be like '1984.'"

It took him four or five hours at the most. The next morning he looked at it again, made a couple of minor changes, and then uploaded it to YouTube. To post the 74-second clip, he needed to create an account; the name ParkRidge 47 just came to him. Park Ridge, Illinois, was Clinton's birthplace in 1947.

When the YouTube clip eventually surged past 1 million views it got praised as a brilliant case of viral marketing. In truth, all de Vellis did was ask a friend to seed the video via emails to the blogger Josh Marshall at Talking Points Memo and to an editor at the Huffington Post to see if they would post it. By 5 p.m. on March 5, both of them did post it, and the video did the rest.

De Vellis began obsessively checking in with Technorati, the blogcentric search engine, to see which bloggers had posted links to his YouTube creation. Within the first 48 hours, the clip had been viewed more than 100,000 times and had become an instant hit within the netroots. It struck a nerve among those calling for more interactivity and genuine outreach from candidates. For two weeks the video enjoyed solid, exponential, word-of-mouth growth, and every now and then an unsuspecting friend would email de Vellis a link to "Vote Different," and De Vellis would email back saying that he really liked the clever mash-up clip.

Apple could have stepped in at any time and gotten the clip yanked from YouTube for copyright infringement. De Vellis wouldn't have protested. But Apple stayed out of it. Technically, because the clip featured the official Obama campaign logo on the hammer thrower's shirt, the candidate, too, citing copyright infringement, could have demanded that YouTube take down the video. Obama did not.

Two weeks after debuting, the clip's viewership leveled off. Considering the endless number of amateur videos that got uploaded daily (hourly even) in hopes of making a big cultural impact, in hopes of creating a buzz, "Vote Different" clearly qualified as a success and de Vellis assumed the run had ended. That's when the traditional media belatedly took notice of the clip and its influence, and "Vote Different" became a blockbuster.

It was Carla Marinucci, the political writer for the *San Francisco Chronicle,* and her front-page article on March 18 that fueled the mass media phenomenon. Calling the clip a "watershed moment" and "perhaps the most stunning and creative attack ad" of the campaign, Marinucci quoted a campaign expert who compared the two-week-old "Vote Different" ad to Lyndon Johnson's "Daisy" campaign commercial from 1964, arguably the most famous campaign spot in U.S. history. (That quickly pulled ad featured a young girl pulling the petals off a daisy one by one, only to be startled by the distant explosion of an atomic bomb.)

In an earlier campaign Marinucci's article would have been read by California subscribers, and that would have been the extent of its influence. But in 2007 the article quickly surfed the Internet rapids and got picked up not only by bloggers but by the widely read Yahoo News, which spread word of "Vote Different" all over the Internet. That helped send YouTube views of the clip past the one million mark. Then Matt Drudge linked to Marinucci's piece and posted a link to the YouTube video. AOL picked up the story as well, which produced a ton of views, and cable news channels were chattering about the video. CNN anchors and reporters discussed the clip 14 different times in March, and Fox News aired the clip in its entirety at least five times in just one day. Soon the big network outlets got onboard. *Good Morning America* called it "a presidential campaign ad that is creating a lot of buzz." On March 21 came the *Washing-*

ton Post Style feature, which in the Beltway comes with an unofficial seal of approval, meaning that everyone in the media and politics now agreed that de Vellis's mash-up had become a very big deal.

A little too big, as it turned out, for Blue State Digital.

The firm was founded in 2004 by four former members of Howard Dean's Internet team. They had met daily that spring at a coffee shop on P Street in Washington, trying to figure out their next move after their quixotic Dean for America Internet-fueled campaign hit empty. Their company quickly grew into a liberal hot shop and seemed a natural fit for the upstart White House candidate advertising change, and an Internet-friendly campaign, for 2008.

Blue State Digital built the Internet foundation for Obama's campaign. In fact, one of the firm's founders, 27-year-old Joe Rospars, took a leave from Blue State to work directly at Obama headquarters in Chicago. All of this meant that a sizable controversy was about to break when word got out on March 21 that somebody at Blue State had created the Clinton hit clip on YouTube. True, the firm had nothing to do with de Vellis's free-lance work, and de Vellis, to protect them, had never mentioned it to his coworkers. But it still looked bad for the candidate running on change and who pledged to soften the tone in Washington to be the beneficiary of the season's most talked-about attack ad that equated his opponent to Big Sister, portrayed her supporters as obedient automatons, and culminated with a huge hammer being thrown into the former first lady's face.

After de Vellis informed his suddenly very nervous Blue State Digital boss, Macon Phillips, that he was the creator of "Vote Different," Macon notified the firm's partners and powwowed via conference call to map out their response. De Vellis offered to quit, worried that if Blue State fired him they might catch flak from the creative community for stifling work-place freedom. But the bosses told him that he couldn't quit until they checked with the company lawyer. Then they told him he was fired. This was fine with de Vellis; he knew all along that if his YouTube identity leaked out he'd have to sacrifice his job.

Not that he was happy about it. A new apartment and no job was not his favorite budgetary formula. But when the news broke about his You-Tube identity—and the news flashes were everywhere: "The presidential campaign of Sen. Barack Obama, D-Ill., was rocked by revelations Wednesday night" was the breathless ABC News dispatch—his chief concern was not being portrayed in the press as some kind of Karl Rove, dirty trickster character. He wanted to protect his reputation and to make sure people in the political world still trusted him. To do that, he needed to ignore the story and not give it any oxygen. That meant that even though producers from the *Today* show kept calling for weeks, pleading for de Vellis to come on the program to talk up his clip, he turned them down. He shunned the media requests that poured in because he knew that talking about the video would only hurt Obama; it would only encourage people to speculate about whether his campaign had had any involvement with the viral phenomenon. Besides, the clip had already accomplished more than de Vellis ever thought it would, so there was no need to talk it up on *Today*.

And to be honest, if he'd known all the headaches "Vote Different" would cause the Obama campaign in terms of questions about its possible association, de Vellis wouldn't have posted the video in the first place. It just got out of control, which of course is what going viral is all about: content careening around the Internet without a pilot to steer it. That's the thrill.

For de Vellis personally, his experiment in grassroots participation was a success and affirmed his faith in Obama's new brand of bottom-up, participatory politics. Six weeks later, out in Los Angeles, another diehard grassroots Obama supporter made headlines with his own online expression of reverence for the Illinois Democrat. But unlike de Vellis, that supervolunteer didn't come away heartened by Obama's message of change. He came away feeling squashed.

three

WHOSE SPACE?

Just as Joe Anthony headed out the door of his Los Angeles apartment in the late afternoon, the phone rang and he circled back inside to answer the call. It was only Wednesday, but the first week of May 2007 had already been an extraordinary and tumultuous one for Anthony. When he picked up the phone and a voice on the other end announced, "We have Senator Barack Obama for you," Anthony's week became even more surreal.

The low-key, 28-year-old paralegal with no previous experience in politics or media, and certainly without deep donor pockets, got called at home, unannounced, by the rock-star famous White House hopeful who just wanted to check in and make sure Anthony knew that all his hard work was appreciated at Obama headquarters and by the candidate himself.

If the call had come one week earlier the star-struck Anthony probably would have been too stunned to even talk to his political hero. Obama had inspired him to become immersed in politics like never before and to devote nearly all his free time to helping the candidate win converts online. But by that Wednesday in May, in the wake of the week's previous acrimony, in the wake of the broken promises and the headlines that had bounced around the Internet detailing the very public split Anthony had suffered with the Obama campaign, the supervolunteer was too exhausted and deflated to enjoy his rare one-on-one conversation with the rising Democratic star.

The conversation did not last long, and when Anthony complained about how the campaign had treated him, Obama did not offer an apology. Instead, he stood by his staffers who had tangled with Anthony and thanked the volunteer for his hard work in creating an Obama MySpace fan page that had become an online phenomenon in 2007 and funneled tens of thousands of new supporters in Obama's direction. Anthony's MySpace initiative highlighted the extraordinary support the candidate enjoyed online and tapped in to a social-networking potential for politics that most people hadn't even considered at the time.

Anthony was surprised by the call, but not shocked. He had a feeling that Obama might reach out to him. Still, standing in his bare Los Angeles apartment, it was weird to think that an obscure activist like himself would end up on Obama's radar and be viewed as important enough for the candidate himself to call at home to try to smooth over any hard feelings. The Internet really had democratized elections, Anthony thought.

So yes, Anthony appreciated the gesture. And he blogged it, of course: "TC from Barack Obama (!!!)." But no, the hard feelings did not wash away. In fact, just hours after Obama cordially said good-bye, the next chapter in Anthony's battle with the campaign unfolded online and those hard feelings quickly inflamed into rage.

Just like the YouTube clip that Philip de Vellis independently created on behalf of Obama and that helped the candidate at a crucial early stage of the campaign, the pro bono work Anthony quietly did out of his apartment became an election season sensation as well. Once again, an unknown supervolunteer and strident Obama supporter managed to alter, however slightly, the dynamics of a national campaign by harnessing the power of voter-generated media. Or in this case, by creating "the MySpace political success story of the year," as the Huffington Post crowned Anthony's creation.

But whereas the "Vote Different" chapter of the campaign highlighted the eye-popping creativity that unsung volunteers were capable of when inspired by Obama, and how that unsolicited, and unrestricted, ingenuity helped boost his campaign, the Anthony chapter captured the dark side of what happened when a volunteer collided with the professional mechanics of a presidential campaign still eager to exert control over key online structures, not merely to coordinate them.

In other words, it was the story of what happened when a volunteer got squashed.

"I DON'T EVER want to work with a political campaign, and I probably won't, thanks to that situation," said Anthony, hanging out in his Los Angeles apartment. He was recounting the Obama saga, which still sometimes felt as though it had happened to somebody else. With a pale oval face and mostly bald head, Anthony, wearing jeans and a T-shirt, looked like he'd fit right in as a fan at an English soccer match. But his flat, friendly accent gave away his midwestern American roots.

Back in 2007 Anthony was consumed with election news, feverishly updating his Obama MySpace page with the latest campaign headlines. But now, 12 months later, he didn't even pay for cable to watch the news channels. Instead, a rabbit-ear antenna hung from his television.

You know somebody is an optimist when his goal is to get auto-centric Los Angelenos to bike to work each day. That's where Anthony now devotes his activist impulse: the Los Angeles County Bicycle Coalition. He even became a bicycling mentor, helping new L.A. cyclists map out safe routes through a city that seems to pride itself on its lack of friendly bike paths. (Anthony had been hit by a car on the L.A. streets, but he just bounced back up and kept riding his bike.) In fact, the centerpiece of Anthony's small living space on the second floor of a two-story apartment complex in the Silver Lake neighborhood was a restored 1986 Trek 500 Tri-Series 10-speed bike, purchased off Craigslist for $300. It hung proudly on the living room wall. In the summer of 2008 he sold the Trek in favor of an early 1970s Raleigh Super Course bike. Anthony just likes the way the old bikes ride. He built that into what he called his commuter/grocery-getter because by August, he had sold his car and used his bike for most of his transportation needs. Anthony is committed to doing his part to making a lasting change.

It was that optimist's streak that Obama tapped into during his soaring prime-time speech at the Democratic National Convention in July 2004. Taken aback by the positive vibe from the charismatic politician who represented a refreshing, inspiring break from his same old-same old Demo-

cratic Beltway forebears John Kerry and Hillary Clinton, who offered to
him so little personal appeal, Anthony researched Obama's career and became deeply intrigued. When the topic of Obama came up between Anthony and his best friend late in 2004, Anthony announced that he would
start an unofficial MySpace fan page for Barack Obama. His poker pals
thought he was nuts and ribbed him mercilessly, tagging him as a dork for
volunteering to be a MySpace cheerleader for some obscure politician.

In 2004 such a premise *was* humorous because most politicians didn't
have social-networking ties. MySpace was where young fans built pages
for their favorite celebrities or indie rock bands, and where people went to
build alter egos for themselves. It wasn't a place for serious organizing
around politics or elections. At least not yet. But Anthony sensed a potential, not only in Obama the candidate, but in the enormous MySpace
community. He didn't see why members of the emerging social-networking
community couldn't, or wouldn't, use the sites and links to learn about
presidential hopefuls.

Anthony had a MySpace profile of his own and had created one for his
buddy's band. Now he decided to create one for Barack Obama. With that
Anthony grabbed the soon-to-be-golden Web address of myspace.com/
barackobama. Over time, as his Obama profile grew, Anthony told pals
that his initiative was working, that people were emailing him (serious)
questions about Obama. They were making contributions to the campaign, putting digital Obama banners on their own sites, telling friends
about the candidate, and registering to vote.

For a couple of years, maintaining the Obama profile represented very
little work. Friend requests from MySpace community members who
wanted to be associated with Anthony's profile would trickle in and Anthony would okay them one by one. He added information and news
headlines about Obama to the MySpace profile. Then in late 2006, when
the chatter about a possible Obama White House run intensified, the
MySpace traffic spiked.

By early 2007 Obama had nearly 30,000 friends at MySpace, far more
than any other White House hopeful on the social-networking site. Each
request had to be okayed personally by Anthony since he officially oversaw the profile. With a presidential announcement pending, Anthony

knew Obama's MySpace profile would explode in popularity. By being first on the site to promote Obama, Anthony's profile had become a de facto starting point for thousands of curious voters who Googled "Obama" or searched MySpace and ended up at Anthony's Obama profile.

Suddenly his poker pals weren't laughing anymore. Instead, they showed up at his place to play cards wearing their own Obama T-shirts. Each time the host folded a hand early, he'd go over to his Mac to check emails and accept more friends for Obama. On February 10 Obama made his White House intentions official and Anthony, with the help of a handful of Obama's dedicated MySpace friends who were feeding the profile page headlines, scrambled to post fresh content as the candidate kicked off his historic White House bid.

In March, after *Newsweek* mentioned Obama's MySpace profile, Anthony became inundated with tens of thousands of new friend requests. Suddenly, maintaining the profile as official moderator had become an all-consuming pursuit. Just accepting all the friends, sometimes thousands each day, became a monumental task.

At the time, MySpace allowed profile managers to accept a maximum of 10 friends at a time. So Anthony devised a way to accept the endless stream of requests with his toes. He set up his laptop computer on the floor of his apartment and then just tap, tap, tap, and with each toe stroke he welcomed a batch of 10 new friends to Obama's unofficial MySpace fan page.

By mid-March Anthony had logged in approximately 70,000 friends. Then MySpace launched the Impact Channel on its site, designed to focus attention on the presidential race. Because the Obama team still did not have an official MySpace presence, the campaign, unbeknown to Anthony, told MySpace to use Anthony's page as the candidate's go-to social-networking source. Thirty thousand new friends quickly requested access. After the profile was featured on the MySpace homepage as part of the "Cool New People" box, Anthony's profile rocketed to 140,000 friends and counting.

Anthony felt completely vindicated. All the hard work had been worth it. Plus, the Obama campaign had reached out to him that winter, which also validated his efforts. He couldn't believe he was having an impact on the race. He was thrilled about the prospect of actually turning new voters on to Obama and his campaign for change. But his MySpace workload was definitely piling up. After the Obama campaign staffers initiated contact in March, Anthony was in touch with them every day for two months, often at all hours of the day. He'd still be up at 2 a.m. answering campaign emails even though he had to be awake for work in five hours. And the increasingly frequent communications with the campaign were scheduled for right in the middle of his workday. He had the coolest boss in the world who allowed him all sorts of on-the-job flexibility so he could maintain Obama's profile. But still. "I worked my ass off like you could not believe," he told me.

The demands of maintaining the profile multiplied faster than Anthony could handle. An option at that point was to slack off and not shower the profile with so much attention. He would have *loved* to ignore those never-ending friend requests for just a few days. But as long as the profile he created represented Obama's largest presence on MySpace, Anthony felt he had to keep it in top form and up-to-the-minute fresh, for the sake of the candidate and his campaign. The responsibility was taking its toll, though. "Just the stress of it was freaking me out. I was barely sleeping. It was such an overwhelming situation," he said.

Increasingly, as the campaign called him with more and more requests, Anthony began to feel cheated. His work was strictly volunteer, but his contacts at the campaign were getting paid, were benefiting from the MySpace profile, and they stood to become wealthy political consultants if Obama won.

"I'm the most minimalistic person. I ride a bike to work three times a week," said Anthony, showing some hints of lingering anger. "My apartment is very plain. I'm not a person who cares about money. But I am a person of principle, and I did not like the idea that I was killing myself and they were getting paid for it."

In April it became clear that the Obama team wanted to take control of Anthony's profile and to fold it, and its 160,000 friends, into the campaign's online operation. Yes, the campaign was all for empowering its online activists and supporters with their from-the-ground-up initiatives.

"If you really want grass-roots participation, then you have to give folks at the grass roots some autonomy to do this in their own way," Obama's media advisor David Axelrod told *Rolling Stone* during the campaign. But it just didn't make sense to have a twentysomething supervolunteer they'd never even met exercising control over such an important asset, Obama's biggest MySpace profile. Not for a campaign that had big plans to revolutionize the way candidates used social-networking sites to connect to and inspire supporters.

Also, the campaign had freaked out in March when *Newsweek* pointed out that on Anthony's MySpace profile, Obama's ethnicity got described as "Other" and his religion as "Christian-other." (Anthony quickly corrected both miscues.) Campaign strategists wanted control of the profile, but was it theirs to take? And why didn't the Obama team just hire Anthony and have him continue to oversee the burgeoning profile as it was officially integrated into the campaign? Or at least make him a consultant and have him continue to contribute from Los Angeles? Strategists at Obama's headquarters made it clear that they weren't interested in hiring someone to just sit around and accept MySpace friends all day, which Anthony took as an insult.

Why didn't the campaign just start its own MySpace page? Anthony would have been happy with that, even welcomed it. If the campaign christened its own profile, than Anthony could have slacked off maintaining his Obama fan page without feeling guilty. He raised that possibility with the campaign several times.

In fact, that's what the Hillary Clinton campaign ended up doing. During the primaries Anthony got to know the volunteer who started up the first Clinton MySpace profile (which always lagged behind Obama friendswise, Anthony liked to point out). Anthony found out that the Clinton campaign contacted the supporter, flew him to campaign headquarters, and talked about giving him a job on staff. In the end, that didn't work out; the Clinton campaign simply created its own official MySpace profile and the two coexisted peacefully online. Anthony would have been thrilled with that kind of arrangement. He would have been happy to ease up on the gas and let the Obama campaign's own MySpace profile pass him by. He pushed for it, in fact. But the Obama campaign didn't want to start from scratch. It wanted the 160,000 friends on the profile that Anthony had created.

Anthony understood that, but he wasn't just going to give away what he'd worked on for two and a half years. It wasn't fair to him and it wasn't fair to the netroots community that had turned the MySpace profile into a success. He wanted to see some proof that the campaign valued online activists and saw them as more than just potential donors. Plus, Obama's online strategists in Chicago, most of whom were younger than Obama, were getting paid to build the candidate's online presence, and specifically to enlarge his social-networking footprint, whereas Anthony worked for free. That just did not sit right with the paralegal.

During an April 25 conference call with the campaign, Anthony says it was Chris Hughes, who was in charge of Obama's social networking, who first raised the idea of buying the MySpace profile. He suggested that the campaign could pay Anthony a one-time, largely symbolic fee to document the profile's transfer in ownership from Anthony to Obama headquarters. MySpace officials were consulted and signed off on the idea of a one-time payment, if that's what the two sides agreed to. Then again, Hughes also suggested that Anthony could just turn over the profile at no cost at all, and in exchange the campaign would put together a media package to salute him for all the work he'd done.

Anthony wasn't interested in getting lots of attention. But a one-time fee? He was stumped. How would he quantify what the site was worth, either to him or to the campaign? He didn't know where to turn for help in answering that riddle. There is one big difference between Anthony and de Vellis, the two grassroots online pioneers of 2007. Whereas de Vellis felt a certain ease within the world of big-time Democratic politics because he'd worked on campaigns and knew people at the Democratic Party and in the press, Anthony was a complete novice with virtually no contacts and very few places to turn for counsel. He'd attended a couple of L.A.-area peace marches over the years, but that was about the extent of his political involvement. Yet suddenly he found himself dealing directly with presidential campaign operatives, and often with nobody to turn to for advice. He'd get off the phone with Barack Obama or he'd finish a conversation with his aides and he'd go to a poker game, where his buddies were more interested in talking about the latest episode of *24*. They felt bad for Anthony and all the stress he was feeling, but they didn't know what to say or what advice to offer.

Truth was, Anthony had traveled far beyond his comfort zone. Music, not politics, was his lifelong passion. He started playing guitar as an eight-year-old and had joined bands while growing up in Youngstown, Ohio. He studied music at Youngstown State University and then moved out to the L.A. area at the turn of the decade where he got his first job in a law office. Quiet and reserved by nature, Anthony maintained a small, close circle of friends and was uncomfortable in any kind of spotlight. He didn't even use his last name while moderating the MySpace profile (it was always just "Joe"), and it never dawned on him to post his photo on the site. The less people knew about him the better was how he felt about his role as Obama's booster.

As the deadline neared for the "symbolic amount" to ask for, Anthony went for a walk up and down Silver Lake Boulevard, pinched between the neighborhood's namesake reservoir to the west and the hulking I-5 bypass to the east. He thought about how much his time was worth, considering his hourly wage as a paralegal, and he thought about the likelihood that many of those 160,000 Obama friends on the MySpace profile he created had donated money to the candidate's coffers. He tried to determine what amount would send the signal that the Obama team took the netroots and the MySpace community seriously. It was Anthony's boss who suggested that he create an itemized list to show the campaign the amount of time he spent on the site. Don't just throw a number out there, his boss said. Try to quantify it for the Obama team.

He finally came up with his tally: $39,000 plus a cap of $10,000 for any advertising money the Obama campaign had spent on the MySpace profile.

To a lot of people who later read about the details, $49,000 didn't seem like a very "symbolic" figure; it seemed like a very large chunk of change from a guy trying to cash in on Obama mania. But was it really so much money for a White House campaign? When campaigns purchase mailing lists of names to contact prior to Election Day, they often pay as much as five dollars per name for snail mail addresses and one dollar for email addresses. At the rate Anthony suggested, the campaign would have paid just 32 cents for each MySpace friend of Obama's. Then again, the campaign couldn't really confirm how many of those 160,000 friends were even eligible to vote.

Anthony stayed up all night writing his proposal and then emailed it to the campaign. After Chris Hughes read it the next morning he sent word back that he wasn't expecting a proposal. Anthony thought the response was weird, since Hughes was the one who had suggested the one-time fee. Hughes said he'd have to check with others in the campaign and that he'd get back to Anthony, who thought, fine, it would all work out.

But days passed and then more than a week and still no word about the proposal. Anthony continued to work closely with the campaign to maintain the MySpace profile. Finally, after several postponed meetings, a conference call was held on May 1, and Anthony was told that the campaign had been shocked by his $49,000 proposal. Besides, it just didn't have that kind of money. Budgets had been set and Obama's new media division just couldn't write a check for $49,000 for unplanned expenses.

There was no counteroffer. Obama aides didn't like the image of a major campaign haggling over money with a volunteer. "Literally if they had said, 'We'll give you ten thousand dollars,' I would have said, 'Okay, whatever.' I just wanted to know that they at least valued all the time that I had put into it," said Anthony. "But that didn't happen. I knew it was bullshit that they didn't have any money."

Instead, he got an email from Hughes, who said he was sorry to hear that Anthony had decided to delete the Obama profile and that it was a shame all his hard work had to go to waste. *Delete the profile?* Anthony had no intention of deleting the profile, and said so. He stressed that if the profile did get shut down it wouldn't be his doing.

That the Obama campaign itself could delete the profile was a possibility. According to MySpace's terms of use agreement, politicians, athletes, celebrities, and other public figures had the right to their own name; because Anthony's profile appeared in Obama's name, the candidate could have asked MySpace to pull the plug on it at any time. Anthony thought that would have been insulting to the 160,000 people who requested to be Obama's friend. Plus, by deleting the profile, the campaign would lose the vital information about his MySpace friends.

When Anthony got home from work after exchanging emails with the campaign, he logged on to the Obama profile and braced himself for the possibility that it had been erased. Instead, he was stunned to discover that, thanks to a high-level intervention from some MySpace executives who granted Obama aides access to the profile without Anthony's permission, the campaign had locked Anthony out of his own site. And while he was locked out, the campaign had posted bulletins on Anthony's Obama profile redirecting its 160,000 friends to sign up at Obama's brand-new "official" social-networking site. (Ironically, Obama, the Internet candidate, was practically the last presidential hopeful to create his own official MySpace profile.)

"I was just absolutely in shock," said Anthony. "They essentially stole my work. I was pissed."

THE STORY QUICKLY detonated online: "Obama's MySpace Mayhem," read one Internet headline. Early in the election season the netroots community was extremely sensitive to any sign of major campaigns trying to steamroll or muscle out online volunteers. Anthony's story seemed to capture just such a case. The backlash against the Obama campaign was fierce, with prominent bloggers chastising Obama's team for treating a supervolunteer in such a shabby manner. "Shitting on your biggest supporters is generally not a wise thing to do," wrote Markos at Daily Kos. Atrios at Eschaton noted that for a White House run, $50,000 represented "chump change."

The next day, still trying to make sense of the lockout, Anthony received the surprise phone call from Obama himself. The outreach made him feel a little better, and if the story had ended there Anthony might have remained an Obama supporter in 2008. But on the same day as the Obama phone call, at about 4 p.m. West Coast time, the campaign's new media director, Joe Rospars, cross-posted an open letter on MyDD and

Daily Kos. "Our MySpace Experiment" was an attempt to answer online critics by spelling out the campaign's version of events surrounding the MySpace saga.

Anthony had gotten a heads-up that the blog post was coming and had been assured by the campaign that if there was anything in it that needed to be changed they'd be happy to accommodate him. So though he still fumed about being locked out of his Obama profile, he wasn't anxious or nervous about the explanation the campaign would post online. But when he sat down in his apartment, fired up his Mac, clicked on the item, and started to read it, he went numb.

Two things about the campaign's public explanation for seizing control of the profile stunned Anthony. First, it claimed that people visiting the profile thought they were dealing directly with the Obama campaign. Anthony thought that was absurd, given the prominent disclaimer he'd posted online. Second, it suggested that Anthony had tried to hold the campaign hostage by refusing to give it the password to the MySpace profile until his five-figure proposal was accepted. "We asked Joe what was needed to restore access, and subsequently we received the list of itemized financial requests that have been discussed elsewhere," Rospars wrote. Left out of the explanation was the fact that the campaign itself had asked for the financial requests.

Nonetheless, the pendulum began to swing online. Suddenly, more and more readers and commenters saw Anthony as the bad guy, an opportunist trying to milk the Obama campaign for a big payday.

"There was a huge friggin' gap that they left out, which conveniently made me look really, really bad," said Anthony. "But still, people ran with it, and if you search my name on Google there are still negative comments about me on every blog on the Internet. 'Joe Anthony is a loser.' 'Joe Anthony is scum.' 'He's just a greedy jerk.' Somebody on Democrats.org called me a felony extortionist. You know, I would like to do more with my life. What if I go for a job interview and they Google me? Nobody's going to hire me. I know it seems silly, but it was my vision to see that the profile become a success, because I knew it could be. And it did! Not only did I not get credit for it but I got negative shit written about me all over the Internet."

Regarding the issue of the profile's password, Anthony did pass it along to the campaign, but just a couple of times, he said. Truth was, for weeks he had been changing the password nearly every day in an effort to thwart hackers who lurked online, trying to create havoc on the high-profile Obama site. He occasionally provided the updated password to the campaign, but for the most part he simply made whatever profile changes Obama aides requested, so exchanging the password wasn't really necessary. Then, as talks progressed toward formalizing the relationship with the campaign, Anthony thought it was wise to hold off on relaying the updated password until a deal had been completed. It just made sense. Plus, he discovered that according to the MySpace user terms, the creator of a profile was the only person who should have the password. To protect himself, he did not pass it around. When the campaign was without the password, Anthony continued to tweak the profile and post bulletins or anything else the campaign asked for. Now the campaign suggested that Anthony's refusal to hand over the password was akin to a ransom threat.

Furious, the supervolunteer immediately called up the campaign and fired off emails demanding that they change the post. But despite earlier assurances, the campaign refused. "We went back and forth. I'm a very mild-mannered guy, but I was pissed, and I'm sure I was probably yelling at them by that point," said Anthony. "It takes a real lot to make me lose my temper. But my temper was lost."

When did Anthony realize he'd have to post a rebuttal to the campaign's blog? "Oh, I don't know," he said. "Maybe after I got the one-thousandth email attacking me."

He posted an extensive reply to the campaign, emphasizing that the Chicago Obama headquarters, not he, had requested the one-time payment notice. With that revelation, the pendulum online swung again, this time back in Anthony's favor. It is amazing that, thanks to the Internet, a lone volunteer activist working out of his one-bedroom apartment enjoyed the same size megaphone as the multimillion-dollar Obama campaign in terms of getting out his side of the unfolding story.

Chris Hughes called and spoke to Anthony one final time. Hughes assured him that everything would be taken care of and that the campaign would post a new message online that would clear up everything. Relieved, Anthony thanked Hughes profusely.

Then he saw the subsequent post.

The campaign notice, published on the new, official Obama MySpace profile, thanked Anthony for his hard work, announced that it wanted to dispel any negative rumors about the volunteer, and then urged Obama supporters to not attack Joe Anthony directly for his actions.

"'My actions'? I was like, thanks a lot. That only led people online to attack me *more*," Anthony told me. He wrote Chicago right away with a you've-got-to-be-kidding-me-with-this-blog note, but there wasn't much else he could do. The campaign issued no more comments or explanations regarding the saga that it wanted to see quickly fade.

The decision had been made internally within the Obama campaign that Anthony's MySpace profile needed to be controlled no matter how bad the transfer process looked. Campaign aides also did not want to set a precedent of paying large sums to volunteers, thereby opening the door to all sorts of requests and demands for compensation every time a supporter created something of value. The campaign certainly never intended for things with Anthony to end in such a messy way. But once the relationship with him fell apart, the Obama team had to absorb the hits and keep moving forward.

Writing at techPresident.com, the high-profile hub covering the nexus between politics and the Internet, Micah Sifry seemed to capture the online vibe when he scolded the campaign for the way Anthony was treated: "I certainly would like to hear from the Obama campaign how they justify what they did, which—given the lack of any real apology for their mistakes—seems the height of expedience and rationalization, rather than anything honorable." The Obama campaign declined to offer any further explanations.

MONTHS LATER, ON February 5, 2008, Anthony faced a dilemma. He was registered to cast a ballot in the California Democratic primary for president. There was just no way he could vote for Hillary Clinton, but he couldn't generate much enthusiasm for Obama, the candidate who had once inspired him to launch a MySpace phenomenon in 2007.

On a personal level, Anthony still had deep affection for Obama, and he saw the obvious potential he represented. But the bitterness over the MySpace battle lingered. Watching the campaign haul in hundreds of millions of dollars in new donations didn't help ease the pain for Anthony, who was told in 2007 that the Obama campaign couldn't spare $49,000 to cover the expenses of his work.

Plus, it was grating to read all the praise Obama received during the campaign for tapping into the Internet, for cultivating grassroots activism, for creating a new, participatory model of democracy. Anthony had a tough time hearing all the hosannas after the Obama campaign didn't act very interested in cultivating his grassroots effort.

"I just couldn't bring myself to vote for him," said Anthony, who stayed home on primary day.

four

THE ACCIDENTAL EMPIRE

"Is this thing on?" Duncan Black tapped into his keyboard, blogging his netroots introduction late at night on April 17, 2002. Minutes later, the 30-year-old economics professor mocked the venture and the mighty pull of his new, all-powerful website: "I wonder how long it will be until literally dozens of people are reading this on an almost monthly basis." Two days later, flashing the droll sense of humor that would become his online trademark, Black wondered, "100 visitors already? You *like me,* you *really like me!*"

Unhappily employed by the University of California at Irvine, Black turned to the Internet for politics in an increasingly desperate attempt to find a voice that echoed his own progressive views, views he didn't see expressed, let alone embraced, in the mainstream. His sense of invisibility had been growing for years.

To Black, it was madness the way the media "debated" the run-up to war with Iraq and managed to very often ignore the antiwar point of view. Instead, he saw two camps represented by the pundits: the war is awesome versus the war is necessary but I'd probably do it differently. The viewpoint that had been completely edited out of the media debate, as well as the viewpoint Black proudly subscribed to, was "This war is just a really stupid idea. Period." That's how Black felt at the time. It didn't seem to be a fringe perspective; he figured lots of mainstream Americans agreed with him. Not that he could see or hear them in the media, which was why his sense of powerlessness had become palpable. The shouting-at-the-TV routine got old pretty quickly. Maybe he could submit some op-ed pieces to newspapers? By that point, though, Black was beyond trying to make dry academic cases. He wanted to scream a bit more loudly than befitted a young tenure-track economics professor. So where was he going to turn?

The Internet. And Black wasn't alone.

Blogging's semiofficial birth date is December 23, 1997, when the online diarist and computer programmer Jorn Barger decided to keep a daily log of links to favorite items he read as he surfed the Internet. These were articles and posts about his intellectual pursuits, which included politics, culture, books, and technology. The online roundup was dubbed a "weblog," quickly shortened to "blog." By 2008 more than 100 million blogs populated the Internet worldwide.

A lot of the early blogging revolved around gadgets and gossip. Mickey Kaus and Andrew Sullivan are two political writers who quickly embraced the blogging form. The movement liberals, though, in the form of Howard Dean cheerleaders, didn't arrive online until 2002. Led by Jerome Armstrong, who started up the pioneering site MyDD, and soon followed by Daily Kos, launched by Markos, a former MyDD reader, the two liberal hubs sparked the creation of the larger liberal netroots movement. In fact, according to the linguistics detective William Safire, it was Armstrong who first coined the term "netroots" to describe the emerging, people-powered online political community. "O.K., so Dean is still polling 1 to 4 percent nationally, so what. Look at the netroots," Armstrong blogged on December 18, 2002.

The terms "blogosphere" and "netroots" are often used interchangeably, although technically there's a difference. The blogosphere represents the specific online space where the blogs congregate and readers tune in and light up sites with comments and diaries. The blogosphere, though, is a subset of the larger online netroots community, which includes bloggers as well as other online-based liberal activist outposts, such as MoveOn, Media Matters for America, and Think Progress.

When Black ventured online in early 2002, most of the political sites he found were either conservative, fake libertarian, or I-used-to-be-a-liberal-but-now-we-really-need-to-go-to-war-with-Iraq sites. He was discouraged: another new medium was taking off, a medium that the traditional press was paying attention to, and already conservatives dominated. Then Black had a thought: "I'll be the liberal."

That's how small the blogosphere was in early 2002; the liberal slot was still there for the taking. So in April, Black created his blog and dubbed it Eschaton, named after a WWIII-type simulation game played in David Foster Wallace's 1996 landmark novel, *Infinite Jest*. He posted under the name Atrios, an obscure reference to an unseen character in the Yasmina Reza play *Art*—so obscure that Black misspelled the character's name. And yes, at the time he had a mild obsession with faint literary references.

Back then, he hid behind anonymity because he was still on the staff at UC Irvine, and then at Bryn Mawr College in Philadelphia, which he joined in the summer of 2002. Black knew the Internet had a long memory and he wasn't sure he wanted his name permanently attached to his online musings. He also didn't want to appear to be shoving ideology down his students' throats either, and he didn't want them to see him as a professional Bush basher.

Black never thought of himself as a writer. He didn't ponder long and hard about his prose or worry about how to make a sentence more powerful or pleasing. Many of his blog posts were fewer than 10 words long, including headline. He didn't chew over elections incessantly the way Armstrong and Markos did. Instead, Black was the guy who, day in and day out, helped point the community toward important stories and issues. He served as an early blogosphere aggregate, somebody who posted lots of links each day and included minimal topspin. Rather than being an outlet for commentary, Eschaton served as a clearinghouse for the online liberal Zeitgeist. It became, as one reader put it, "liberal-Democrat central."

The model Black used for what the blog would sound like was a PG-13 version of the Howard Stern radio show, not the T & A part of Stern's shtick, but the running jokes and themes, a cast of heroes and villains, and weird nicknames and inside jokes. Almost none of it was ever explicitly explained to newcomers tuning in to Stern for the first time, but listeners got sucked in and wanted to know what everybody was talking about. When they did, they felt part of that world. That's how Black saw his blog.

He also wanted to push, in a purposefully impolite way, the idea that there was something seriously, almost structurally wrong with the Beltway media, both with its lapdog Bush coverage and its factually challenged reporting of everyday events. Liberals had been critiquing the press for years, but Black wanted to help move that discussion away from university journals and make it much more immediate. He wanted to lace it with an incredulous, "WTF?" attitude.

The snark and sarcasm at Eschaton came in thick doses. The funny part was that the smart-aleck, ballbusting persona of Atrios online was nothing like Black offline, who in person is exceedingly shy and unassuming, with a perpetually sleepy look on his face. He's the guy at the cocktail party who hovers on the outer circles of the room, speaking quietly, with a glass of red wine always in his hand and who enjoys discussing mass transit. The discrepancy between the online and offline personalities actually became a bit of a problem after Black lifted his cloak of blogger anonymity in 2004, because when readers met him in person they expected him to lay out the punch lines. They expected him to be funny, like Atrios. But he was never that person in person.

He didn't really set out to create an alter ego, a voice that was not like his. That just sort of happened. (Something about online anonymity seems to bring out the caustic side in people.) But he did set out to create a specific voice for his Atrios handle, a biting inflection that Black thought was missing from the liberal repertoire. In the mainstream media, especially on television, the liberal chair in a debate usually got filled either by an NPR, hand-wringing, three-sides-to-every-issue type of person, or by a professional Beltway centrist insider who didn't even represent liberalism.

There were no aggressive, in-your-face combative liberal representatives on TV, or ones who dished out talking points with a devilish love of irreverence. Black saw signs of that emerging online. He saw the *Nation* writer Eric Alterman not taking any shit as a daily blogger for MSNBC, where he outlined the absurdity of war with Iraq months before it began. Black wanted to add to that aggressive progressive posturing, as well as be part of the high factual and intellectual standards that Alterman was setting for the emerging blogosphere. He wanted to help build that into a booming online chorus.

"I'm completely amazed at what happened," said Black six years after Eschaton's launch. Black's duplex apartment in Center City Philadelphia, where he lives with his professor wife, still has the feel of an extended, postcollege existence; it's bare and simple and with a tower of DVDs and CDs prominently featured in the living space. But what sets Black apart from most other bloggers is the stack of papers resting on the windowsill, paperwork for the mortgage to the four-floor apartment located seven blocks away that he and his wife are in the process of purchasing. In other words, Black makes a decent living from blogging, which means he represents something of a netroots anomaly. Black's income comes from advertising revenue generated from his highly trafficked site, as well as his job as a senior fellow at the progressive think tank Media Matters for America.

"It's all very strange when you sit back for a few seconds and think about what [the blogosphere] has become," said Black. "The fact that in some ways it's become institutionalized and has become so mainstream. And the fact that congressional staffers worry about what bloggers say. What blogs on the left have managed to do is stitch together a kind of coherent running narrative from the liberal perspective, which wasn't there before. There's a connective tissue that we kind of provide: this network, this web, between institutions, which didn't have a way of listening to each other before."

Black himself represents the perfect example of somebody who, if it weren't for the open door of the Internet, never would have become engaged in the political process in any kind of meaningful way. He just wasn't on that career track. After growing up in Australia, New Mexico, Minnesota, Switzerland, Pennsylvania, Utah, and then back to Pennsylvania to the Philadelphia suburbs, Black, whose dad worked for computer companies and liked to move around, figured he'd be an accountant when he headed off to Indiana University of Pennsylvania, the affordable land grant school located at the other end of the Keystone State, northeast of Pittsburgh.

His dad steered him away from accounting and toward economics, a natural for a kid who grew up in a house where C-SPAN always seemed to be broadcasting in the background. And so from his first days as an undergraduate in 1989 to the day he walked away from being a professor in

2004 in order to blog full time, Black studied economics. He studied at IUP and at Brown University, where he earned his Ph.D., and he taught at the London School of Economics before landing at UC Irvine.

But by 2002 economics wasn't enough. Black wanted to become more directly involved in the political process, and a blog, Eschaton, was his shot. At least it would provide a forum to express his anger and frustration and allow him to openly mock the press and Republicans, a tactic that remained key to his sanity.

He was shocked when Paul Krugman name-dropped Atrios in his influential *New York Times* column in late 2002. Even before he saw Krugman's piece that morning, he knew something was up because when he turned on his computer a dozen new emails had arrived overnight from readers. At the time, this represented an eruption of interest. (By 2008, Black would log 12 reader emails every 10 minutes, getting buried in 800 missives every day.) The Krugman column helped spike Eschaton's Web traffic as curious *Times* readers checked out the "Internet commentator" Krugman referenced.

At the end of 2002 Eschaton had been dubbed Best Blog by liberal readers across the Internet, many of whom now made Eschaton their home.

ONE OF ESCHATON'S earliest denizens, known simply as Digby, showed up one month after Eschaton went live. Black was so impressed with the elegantly angry posts Digby composed in his comment section that he often pulled them out and posted them, in full, right on the homepage. They were that good.

Digby wrote voluminous reader feedback comments where most other messages were between 20 and 30 words long. Readers began urging Digby to start a separate blog because the intricate essays, those not rescued by Black and posted on the homepage, were being wasted in a comment thread. Digby offered up remarkably insightful and fluid political analysis, but it went mostly unnoticed in Black's unlit basement.

On January 1, 2003, on the heels of the Democrats' crushing November midterm losses and driven to distraction by the political and media discourse she felt was careening out of control as the war with Iraq loomed closer and closer, Digby put her New Year's resolution into action and launched her blog that very day. She called it Hullabaloo because she liked the causing-a-commotion ring to the name. She posted a photo of Howard Beale in his "I'm mad as hell and I'm not going to take it anymore" moment from *Network* to capture the creeping madness she felt oozing out of the Bush White House and from the Beltway press corps.

"The Internet became available just as American politics turned batshit crazy," recalled Digby. She stood at the counter of her snug, one bedroom, rent-controlled apartment in the liberal bastion of Santa Monica, which sits in the cool ocean breeze shadow of downtown Los Angeles. It's where, every night, she and her husband took the same six-block walk down Ashland Avenue at dusk to Ocean View Park to watch the Pacific sunsets.

Not surprisingly for a news junkie like Digby, the television dominates the living space and can be seen from all angles of the apartment. With no sound on, CNN was broadcasting on the morning I visited. Like Black, who was surprised at what his blog had accomplished and what it helped spark, Digby was dumbfounded by her online success and her starring role in the online revolution. "I'm still stunned," she conceded.

If you squinted and tried really hard you could sort of see how Black's path from economics professor to blog player made a certain amount of sense: a policy wonk starts broadcasting his daily observations online. But nothing in Digby's background logically explains, let alone predicted, her emergence as a clarion voice for the progressive community and her hand in changing, in small but steady ways, the face of Democratic politics in America.

Like Black, she grew up "all over the place," as a navy brat. Her dad moved the family almost every year of her childhood, to Turkey, Thailand, and six different U.S. states. The family never knew how long they were staying in one place, or if the latest move might finally be the last one. But she got used to it and after a while looked forward to the opportunity to reinvent herself in the next town.

Digby's final stop on her childhood tour was Fairbanks, Alaska, which she calls home because that's where she stayed long enough to graduate from high school. Her father had moved on to a new location during her junior year, but Digby stayed behind and lived with a friend's family so she could attend her senior year at Austin E. Lathrop High School, home of the Malemutes.

After the long, dark winters of Fairbanks, Digby headed for the sunshine capital of California and studied theater at San Jose State. She returned home a couple of years later to work full time on the Alaska pipeline, for which she went to radiographer school and learned to read pipe X-rays. She traded in the tundra for backpacking in Europe during the late 1970s, living on her brother's boat (and largesse) and following the canals of England, and from France sailing south to the Mediterranean.

Back in the States she eventually finished film school and moved to Los Angeles with artistic ambitions, but quickly found her niche on the business side, or got "sidetracked," as she put it. She worked for years in the film business at Chris Blackwell's Island Pictures, as well as Polygram and Artisan. The corporate studio consolidations of the late 1990s left fewer places to find work at the same time the work became less satisfying for Digby, who was increasingly self-conscious about being a woman "of a certain age," as she put it, working in an image-obsessed industry. So at the turn of the decade, like a school kid transferring to yet another new town, Digby was looking for a way to reinvent herself one more time. She found it online.

She followed the blogs from their earliest days, and even the precursor bulletin boards that sprouted up online during the CompuServe 1990s, where she watched with stunned amazement as the GOP impeachment crusade unfolded. At the turn of the decade she became a regular at an online liberal forum called Bart Cop, and when fellow Bart Cop commenter Atrios started his own site, Digby migrated over to Eschaton, where she posted here way-too-long comments and was politely told to go start her own blog.

Clicking around the blogosphere, she loved what she saw: the beginnings of a truly independent progressive movement. An emerging apparatus that wasn't attached to the Democratic Party and wasn't built to simply cheerlead pols, it served as a conduit for grassroots interests and concerns. It was a place to give voice to liberals, plain and simple.

She had always been a political junkie, and the chance to host an ongoing, in-depth discussion with curious and articulate readers was pure heaven for her. For years she had observed politics with great interest, devouring books on the subject, and was well prepared to start discussing politics publicly. Thanks to her lucid take-downs and insightful analysis, Digby was instantly admired and toasted as among the best essayists in the entire overeducated liberal blogosphere. "She's the best writer in our little gang," Markos at Daily Kos told me.

And yes, she was surprised by how the cogent, sweeping, and entertaining essays, covering a wide array of current event topics, just began flowing from her keyboard. She wrote about college admissions, antitrust investigations, presidential politics, right-wing talk radio, Saddam Hussein, oil production, and the Florida recount. And that was just during her very first week of blogging. "I had no idea that I had the capacity," she conceded. "I was astounded, number one, that I could do it. And number two, that people liked it and got something out of it."

Her work represented the kind of smart, tough-minded analysis that liberals online craved but searched in vain to find in the mainstream press. ("I honestly don't know how this could have been handled any worse," Digby wrote ominously just days before the invasion of Iraq.) But they couldn't find it among the Beltway pundits, so they flocked to the Internet and the blogosphere flourished. Articulate and wise, funny and fearless, Digby, like Black at Eschaton, personified the new shit-kicking brand that liberals were giving birth to online.

At the time of Digby's rise to prominence, virtually every Hullabaloo reader, and every other blogger, assumed that Digby was a man simply because her elbow-on-the-bar writing style *sounded* so much like a man. In truth, Digby was a nickname her husband had given her years ago, and when she first ventured online to the bulletin boards she used it instinctively. Heather Parton is her actual name. She was very attached to the idea of pseudonyms and anonymity. She assumed people thought Digby was a man because of the name; she had no idea it was because of her

shot-drinking writing style, which embraced Atrios's "WTF?" indignation at Republicans and the press and then ratcheted it up to another
level.

Digby didn't set out to use a male persona to throw people off her scent
so she'd never be discovered. But the reaction she got from readers was
one that she very much appreciated. Like Black's Atrios, the Digby persona in no way reflected the real-life quiet and unassuming person behind
the name. And she liked that contradiction just fine.

IN EARLY 2005 a steady stream of annoying emails from a West Coast
blogger named Jane Hamsher began filling up Digby's in-box. Hamsher
had just started up a site called Firedoglake, which she named after her
three favorite things: sitting in front of the fire with her dog Kobe, watching Los Angeles Lakers games. The persistent emails represented Hamsher's
effort to meet Digby in person. Digby checked out FDL and thought it
was provocative and that Hamsher was a talented writer with a knack for
the blogging art form. At FDL back then, the snark was unvarnished and
the F-bombs were dropped freely, which Digby could relate to. But for the
most part, Digby wasn't an in-person type of person. It wasn't because she
didn't want anybody to know her identity or gender. The issue wasn't that
big of a deal for her. It was just that one of the things Digby loved about
the blogosphere was that it didn't really require human interaction; that
she almost never had to leave her secure "bunker" in the "People's Republic of Santa Monica," as she lovingly described her home. She had no desire to go out and socialize. "I guess I'm a typical blogger," she said with a
laugh.

Whereas Digby leans toward being reclusive, Hamsher is very much an
in-person type of person. Unlike most bloggers, Hamsher wanted to press
the flesh offline, a very unbloggy approach to networking at the time.
Outgoing, vivacious, and comfortable in the spotlight, Hamsher arrived
relatively late to the netroots game in late 2004, when most of the blogosphere's prime shoreline property had been scooped up. She liked to joke
that she was the girl who discovered punk rock in 1977, when all the cool
kids got turned on in 1976.

She decided early on that she wanted to meet as many blogosphere players as possible face-to-face because she believed that the strength of a community is built around personal relationships. She learned that in her days as a Hollywood movie producer. On the top of her must-meet list sat Digby, who just wasn't interested. But Hamsher was relentless in her pursuit. "I asked her like a million times to meet with me before she finally agreed. I wasn't going to give up," Hamsher recalled. "It became a challenge, sort of like the movie business, where you keep knocking your head against the wall and hopefully it will give through. So Digby finally agreed to meet me, and the night before, she sent me an email that said, 'When you see me I look less like James Bond and more like Judi Dench.' I was shocked." Like everyone else, Hamsher assumed Digby was a man.

Early on, the two friends formed something of a blogosphere good cop–bad cop duo, with Digby playing the role of the slightly more serious writer, while Hamsher, sporting short spiked hair at the time that went every which way, always seemed to be rummaging around online, looking for ways to stir up trouble. She behaved in the blogosphere just as she had in her Hollywood days, when she once climbed onto the roof of the Whisky-a-Go-Go, a legendary Sunset Strip rock club, and promoted a movie by illegally spray-painting its name onto a 40-foot billboard.

During her post-Hollywood blogging career, Hamsher launched a new advertising company to help boost online ad revenue, created a weekly online book salon that became a must stop for lefty authors, helped raise a ton of money for deserving progressive congressional candidates, and reached out to labor unions on behalf of the blogosphere. She also redefined journalism by live-blogging the Scooter Libby trial, helped drive Connecticut's increasingly conservative, pro-war senator, Joe Lieberman, out of the Democratic Party, and turned the vibrant FDL site into one of the most influential stops in the liberal blogosphere.

The to-do lists sprang from Hamsher's days as a Hollywood movie-maker and professional organizer. "It was just her natural inclination to be a producer," Digby observed. "Except now she was producing progressivism. And it was badly needed."

The similarities between Hollywood and Washington were immediately apparent to Hamsher. Both were filled with big egos and drowning in spin, and both company towns celebrated messaging and storytelling. The skills that helped Hamsher in Hollywood also helped her blog about politics: telling a story quickly, and with sharp elbows.

The physical acts of movie producing and Internet blogging were also alike. Both took a chaotic, no-blueprint approach. "Producers have to be very adaptive to what's going on. Every time you produce a movie it's like starting a new business. It's not like IBM, which has been going for centuries," Hamsher told me. "For a movie, you have to hire the entire staff, figure out what the business plan is, and do everything from the start. And you have to be very adaptive because you never know what's going to happen. And that's kind of the fun of the blog world. You never know. You wake up and you never know what's going to happen because it's like the Wild West."

A self-described "slightly rebellious, unrepentant minister's daughter" with "blind burning ambition," Hamsher grew up in Seattle, down the street from the future Microsoft founders Bill Gates and Paul Allen. (She attended Roosevelt High School; they went to Lakeside.) Her dream was to land a job at *Rolling Stone* and become the next Hunter S. Thompson or Cameron Crowe. Unfortunately, the year she began her pursuit of journalism glory was the same year Jann Wenner packed up *Rolling Stone*'s San Francisco office and moved the magazine's headquarters to New York City.

She took an internship at the muckraking *Bay Guardian* newspaper in San Francisco instead, where Abbie Hoffman used to call in to the newsroom to talk to the staff's senior reporter, who was just 24 years old. Journalism was her dream, but in the 1980s she moved to Los Angeles to enroll in film school because she realized she'd be poor forever if she remained a reporter.

After emerging from the University of Southern California, Hamsher started banging on doors as a producer, trying to get projects off the ground. At the time, Hollywood was enjoying a creative burst and embracing some independent filmmaking; it was the *Sex, Lies and Videotape* era. For Hamsher, it felt very similar to San Francisco's punk rock vibe from the late 1970s, which featured a low barrier to entry and free-floating creative anarchy. That vibe traveled to the indie film scene, and Hamsher was able to make a very risky, hot-button film, the ultraviolent *Natural Born Killers*. Directed by Oliver Stone, the film got swept up in the larger cultural wars and was widely condemned by conservatives as a celebration of mindless lawbreaking and glorified violence.

But just like the old punk scene, the risk-taking cycle eventually played out inside Hollywood as corporate studios became hostile to the notion of independence, and Hamsher found it increasingly difficult to make movies that took chances. The struggle just didn't inspire her anymore. The day she spent on a movie set trying to coax an uncooperative actor who wouldn't come out of his trailer until he had an ass wax was one of the days Hamsher realized she needed to begin plotting the next chapter in her life.

In autumn 2004, living in Oregon while the White House election unfolded, Hamsher sat on a beach reading a Sunday *New York Times Magazine* feature about a bunch of bloggers who covered the national conventions that summer. She got home, poked around online, and found a few key haunts: Daily Kos, the Moderate Voice, Eschaton, and Matt Yglesias's site. She wanted in.

After weeks of commenting on other people's blogs, in December she created her own simple blogspot site where she could count her readers on two hands because she was pretty much related to all of them. Months later she was still attracting only 50 or 100 people each day. If five of them posted comments, Hamsher declared the day a success. And the successes would have been even fewer if her blogging friend Tbogg hadn't regularly steered his readers to FDL during the early days.

Despite humble beginnings, at the end of 2005 FDL, "a yeasty mix of commentary, invective and inside jokes," as the *New York Times* later dubbed it, was tapped as one of the blogosphere's best sites thanks largely to its obsessive coverage of the unfolding Lewis "Scooter" Libby perjury case. The saga began with the outing of CIA operative Valerie Plame, whose identity was first revealed by Robert Novak in his syndicated newspaper column. The war in Iraq may have been unstoppable by the nascent netroots, which got steamrolled in its attempts to raise red flags about the invasion in 2003. But the unraveling Plame caper represented the bloggers' revenge; it was a Bush White House calamity they personally helped uncover with some of the most meticulous analysis found anywhere.

More important, the Plame story offered progressives the prospect of a victory during a very dark period when Bush reigned supreme in America. "There didn't seem to be any hope. There was no place you could look that there was any chance of the Bush administration being busted for what they were doing. They had so completely gamed the system," Hamsher recalled. "There was no hope. Democrats were in the minority everywhere. We had no subpoena power. It was the age of despair before we moved into the age of cynicism. It seemed like there was one guy [Special Prosecutor Patrick Fitzgerald] who had the power maybe and the ability to figure out what happened."

When it came time for Libby's 2007 trial, the idea of leaving the coverage in the hands of the mainstream press corps made no sense to Hamsher because reporters and pundits had shown for months that they were not up to the job of covering the unfolding White House saga. Bloggers had owned the Libby story for two years. Why give up ownership at trial?

Back during her very early days online, when she hung around Daily Kos, Hamsher used to chat online with Marcy Wheeler. A business consultant from Ann Arbor with a Ph.D. in comparative literature (her doctoral thesis was "Early 19th-Century Responses to Napoleonic Censorship"), Wheeler, who blogged at the Next Hurrah under the name emptywheel, used her academic training to analyze the Libby story with an astonishing level of detail and insight. Firedoglake readers rewarded Wheeler's hard work by helping raise money to publish her pretrial Libby book, the definitive *Anatomy of Deceit: How the Bush Administration Used the Media to Sell the War and Smear a Critic*. With Libby's court case set to begin in early 2007, it was Wheeler who hatched the idea of live-blogging the entire trial from the courthouse with a rotating roster of FDL contributors. They would be the blogosphere's eyes and ears in the courthouse so readers wouldn't have to wait to read the Beltway media's daily accounts and wonder which key facts had been left out or played down.

Because the court barred audio and video feeds being broadcast from the trial, the FDL blogger on duty that day sat in the court's media room, watched the piped-in proceedings via closed-circuit TV, and then typed up in real-time, nearly verbatim accounts of legal arguments unfolding in court, which were then immediately posted online at the website. By applying their flood-the-zone approach and flexing their encyclopedic knowledge of the case, the FDL team helped rewrite the rules for journalism in the online age.

Hamsher almost didn't make it to the January trial though. In December she was diagnosed with breast cancer for the third time. Determined to be inside the federal courtroom when witnesses were called, the earliest she could schedule her 14-hour surgery was January 18, with the Libby trial slated to begin the following week. She wouldn't let her California doctors operate on her until they promised she could fly east soon after the surgery. After much grumbling, they relented. On the day of the operation Hamsher was talking up the Libby trial as her doctors administered the anesthesia.

"I had to be there and see all those people," Hamsher told me. "It was my dream. There was no way I was missing that. None!"

Online reader donations helped pay for the FDL crew's travel expenses, including $3,500 for the Washington crash pad they rented and stayed at throughout the trial. Dubbed Plame House, the villa provided a home away from home for Hamsher, who, coming directly from surgery, didn't want to spend weeks schlepping to and from some Beltway hotel. (After the trial, Hamsher moved to the Washington area permanently.)

Each morning, her FDL friends put her in a cab in front of Plame House and then wheeled her into the E. Barrett Prettyman Federal Courthouse. If Hamsher needed to sleep during the day she went down to the media room, found a seat in the back against the wall, and took a nap. Her insistence on being in the courthouse wasn't just about the trial; it was also about her health. "I had to start chemotherapy immediately after the trial. If you've never had a serious illness it's hard to explain, but there's really something to not feeling like the illness beat you," she told me. "I actually kind of flew through chemo feeling like this thing hadn't gotten me. And to do that I knew that going to the Libby trial was very important. If I had missed that—if they'd kept me from it—I would have been emotionally devastated. Just completely defeated."

By chance, Hamsher was standing near the elevator banks inside Prettyman on March 6 when word came back that a verdict had been reached. She jumped in the first car, rode to the fourth floor, and grabbed a choice seat in Courtroom 6, right behind Libby's wife, for the final drama. After two years of obsessing over the case, Hamsher could feel her heart pounding when the guilty verdicts were announced, convicting Libby of lying and obstructing the Plame leak investigation.

Said Hamsher of the untold hours spent dissecting the case, "It was worth every minute of it."

HAMSHER'S TEAM MIGHT never have made it to the Libby trial if it weren't for the Internet media mogul Arianna Huffington, who lent her expanding clout to secure FDL its courtroom press pass.

The blogosphere succeeded and rose to prominence despite having very few big-foot sponsors and despite having very few cheerleaders inside the political and media establishment. Right-wing bloggers had allies inside Fox News and the Drudge Report and on AM radio who would routinely trumpet whatever they dubbed the Outrage of the Day.

For years, progressives had looked at the GOP-friendly Drudge Report, with its worldwide reach, and longed for a megaphone that loud and that brash. They desperately wanted to build a must-see media platform that could broadcast their agenda, pick fights, and push back against Republican spin. Some hoped the 2004 launch of Air America, the liberal talk radio network, would serve as that media counterbalance.

Instead, it was the Huffington Post, with its colossal readership, that provided bloggers with a seat at the larger mass media table. It was the Huffington Post that helped bring them into the national conversation. "The Huffington Post is a bookmark for everyone in the business," *Time*'s editor Richard Stengel confirmed to a journalist in 2006. "We have to deal with it all the time."

As the Huffington Post grew over the years and adopted a more tabloid feel it shed some of its early similarities with the liberal blogosphere, which was not in the habit of posting headlines about supermodels, celebrity re-habs, or weekend box-office returns, the way the Huffington Post regu-larly did. But even as the Huffington Post expanded into Entertainment and Living sections, the engine that still drove the site, the signature sound that still boomed from its homepage, was hard-hitting liberal poli-tics, a modern-day voice born in the blogosphere. Huffington embraced and amplified it.

From the time she first started writing about the emerging blogosphere, Arianna Huffington fell in love with the new generation of know-it-alls. She loved their abrasive style and the way bloggers relished skewering sa-cred cows, especially those in the press. She also loved that OCD quality, the idea of hitting one topic over and over and over. For years, while writ-ing her syndicated newspaper column, she had been monumentally frus-trated by her editors telling her she could not return to the same topic again and again, that if she wrote once about the Iraq war she needed to write about something else for the next few weeks, even if dramatic new events were unfolding there. Huffington admired how bloggers often wrote about the war more than once a day, even once an hour.

When Jane Hamsher planned her first Los Angeles meeting of area bloggers in 2005, she emailed Huffington an invitation. She'd never met or even spoken to Huffington before, but she sent a note saying she should show up at the blogger party. And Huffington did. "In the early days she would show up anywhere," Hamsher recalled. "Somebody would say, 'Hey let's all have breakfast at the Farmers Market [in Los Angeles] and anybody who wants to show up can.' And the first person there would be Arianna Huffington."

From the beginning Huffington adored the netroots world. "We would go have pizza parties with bloggers and I was in heaven and I would just sit there and talk obsessively about everything," she said. "I remember having a conversation with [the blogger] Mark Kleiman over drug policy. Mark Kleiman knows more about that issue than anybody else I had ever talked to just because he follows it obsessively. So I loved that. I just love learning and being part of that conversation. And to me it didn't matter if that conversation was held over pizza, or great wines over at David Geffen's."

Part of the netroots appeal, as well as its underdog status, stemmed from its cast of unlikely characters. They were, at the outset, basically a bunch of nobodies with almost zero background in politics or journalism who helped spark a political awakening. And they did it for free or by scratching out meager to modest blogger earnings.

None of those traits applied to Arianna Huffington. She had been a permanent political celebrity since the 1990s, when her billionaire husband, Michael Huffington, ran for the U.S. Senate. She was a noted author who hobnobbed with the upper echelons of the Beltway political elite and enjoyed first-name friendships with media big shots in New York City (Jann, Mort, and Rupert). Yet Huffington fit seamlessly into the netroots movement, which, it turned out, did not discriminate against the super-wealthy.

Her relentless dissection of the unfolding Scooter Libby case, her public broadsides aimed at the Beltway press for its shoddy prewar coverage, and her willingness to openly criticize big-foot journalists like the *New York Times'* Judy Miller and NBC's Tim Russert ("journalism's answer to the EZ Pass"), practically made her a blogger by birthright. That, and the fact that her stinging prose jumped off the computer screen, in stark contrast to the mushy, timid language so many Beltway pundits had universally adopted. By posting more than 500 items under her own byline within the first 18 months of the site's launch, Huffington confirmed her blogosphere work ethic.

Still, the rarified environment in which she lived and operated represented a completely different world from that of most blogosphere denizens. Huffington's gated manor sits in the Brentwood section of Los Angeles, the posh neighborhood O. J. Simpson made famous a decade ago and where Porsches and Mercedes are parked quietly in driveways draped carefully in manicured shade. Suffice it to say the Internet connection at Huffington's home was never turned off because of an overdue $145 utility bill, as it was at Chris Bowers's Philadelphia apartment days before the 2004 election.

Unlike the homes of all the other bloggers I visited, when guests are announced at Huffington's home they ring the buzzer at the end of her graceful U-shaped driveway, wait for the metal gates to slowly open, and then are greeted at the expansive front doorway by a young, attractive assistant who offers coffee and croissants and invites you to wait inside Huffington's home library, with its 20-foot ceiling, floor-to-ceiling bookshelves filled with tomes, and a circular staircase in the corner. (Digby's entire apartment could easily fit inside Huffington's Henry Higgins–style library.)

Past the landing at the top of the circular staircase and hidden behind a sliding bookcase is the Huffington Post's West Coast bureau, where young staffers monitor the Web for news and keep tabs on the roiling comments and conversations being posted online by Huffington Post readers. The main editorial offices are in Manhattan's SoHo neighborhood.

When I visited Huffington in Brentwood on the morning of the Puerto Rico primary, one of the last in the Democratic Party's long march to a nominee, CNN broadcast silently on a flat-screen TV on a wall in Huffington's home office. The TV faced a lush, pillow-filled couch, kitty-corner from a massive wooden desk where three computer screens broadcast the latest news. Sweeping into the office looking statuesque, with her signature chestnut hair falling just above her shoulders, Huffington ducked over to her desk before settling in for an interview. She peeked at her Huffington Post homepage and picked up the phone to call the on-duty editor to dictate a headline change. "I should never look at the site because I always want to change something," she said.

It was within the cushy confines of her Brentwood home that the Huffington Post was born. It happened at a meeting of the Hollywood liberal tribe right after Bush's reelection victory in 2004. Even weeks later, stunned West Coast liberals, as well as some Democratic insiders who flew out to attend the day-long bull session at Huffington's house, were still scratching their heads, wondering, How did that guy win again?

Hosted by Huffington with help from her friend Victoria Hopper, the wife of the actor Dennis Hopper, the living-room summit attracted 30 to 40 activists, including MoveOn's cofounder Wes Boyd, the Hollywood mogul David Geffen, the famed TV producer Norman Lear, the environmentalist Laurie David, the Democratic Party activist Simon Rosenberg, and Huffington's confidant Roy Sekoff, who became the site's editor. Looking over the binder full of articles handed to them at the door, attendees resolved that liberals needed a new kind of media operation, a platform beyond the nascent blogosphere to help push stories and opinions forcefully into the mainstream press and shape the national debate. They needed an online anchor to help build a movement around. Names for a possible site were even bandied about that day.

The site would aggregate news headlines as Drudge did, but also feature a stable of (unpaid) bloggers, including Huffington's A-list friends John Cusack, Jamie Lee Curtis, Rosie O'Donnell, and others, who would provide an opinion element, the cocktail party chatter, and a community of readers who could interact with the site. It would be Drudge Plus.

Huffington Post founders thought the celebrities and boldface names from Huffington's gold-plated BlackBerry were going to be The Thing, the big draw that separated theirs from other news sites. That's certainly what the press focused on at the time of the launch. But it quickly became apparent that the celebs were not The Thing, although some, such as Nora Ephron and Alec Baldwin, distinguished themselves as insightful writers. Instead, editors learned that readers cared more about good writing and a passionate point of view than they did the boldface byline.

So previously unknown writers, such as the consultant RJ Eskow, the communications professor Marty Kaplan, and the full-time animator Bob Cesca, along with scores more, emerged as the unlikely breakout star bloggers at the Huffington Post. The site was two-fisted and ballsy from the beginning. Editors didn't want writers trying to create their own serious *New York Times* op-ed for the ages, or, for that matter, to hatch half-baked conspiracy theories, which were strictly forbidden. They wanted contributors to write about the stuff they'd tell their friends or what might piss them off. They wanted them to *blog,* to be impulsive and incisive.

The site was irreverent, but with a purpose, like the old *Esquire* magazine. When Attorney General Alberto Gonzales testified before Congress in 2007 and responded to questions 129 times by saying he could not remember, the Huffington Post plastered Gonzales's photo 129 times across its front page.

Editors knew the site had arrived, that its brand had landed, when Jay Leno made an on-air reference to the Huffington Post in his monologue at the end of 2005. It wasn't just that the late-night host mentioned the site, it was the fact that he mentioned it without bothering to explain what it was.

Still, at the time of its launch, some members of the blogosphere were skeptical. Was Huffington trying to supplant them by co-opting the anti-Bush momentum they had built up? Was it really a good idea to have Left Coast celebrities become the public face of liberal politics in America? And what if the project turned out to be a colossal flop? ("The equivalent of *Gigli, Ishtar* and *Heaven's Gate* rolled into one," was how one critic prematurely panned the site.) Would its demise tarnish the burgeoning blogosphere as well?

To calm fears, Huffington reached out and promoted bloggers and helped them build larger readerships. She celebrated their scoops on her site without ever skimping on doling out credit. She obsessed right alongside them over the Plame case, and she urged A-list bloggers to write whatever they wanted and assured them their work would be featured on the front page. One of the bloggers given the early keys to the Huffington Post was John Amato, the founder of Crooks and Liars. And if ever there was an example of somebody accidentally stumbling into the blogosphere, where he unleashed all kinds of unintended consequences in terms of growing the progressive movement, it was Amato.

IT DIDN'T REALLY make much sense how, or why, a former professional saxophonist who'd performed at rock festivals in front of 50,000 fans ended up becoming an invaluable anchor of the liberal blogosphere. Or how, during the darkest and most physically painful period of his life, he was able to channel his disappointment and frustration into something creative and groundbreaking. The path Amato took nobody would ever have tried to map out as a way for liberals to create their own media platform: a way to create a progressive movement in America. But Amato, it turned out, was the right person at the right time with the right mixture of creativity and passion. His site, Crooks and Liars, revolutionized political blogging when he was the first to bring video to the blogosphere. "I was YouTube before there was YouTube!" he liked to announce.

If the caricature of a liberal blogger brings to mind a young, wonky, overeducated elite college grad who prefers interacting with technology to engaging with actual people, than Amato represents the antiblogger. He turned 50 years old during the 2008 campaign, he is proud of his working-class roots, he embraces commonsense politics, and he is a garrulous talker. Conversations with Amato are often measured in hours, not minutes.

Hamsher called him the Everyman straight out of Central Casting. "He telegraphs who he is in a second," she said. With his eyes often in a permanent squint and a thick head of black hair—he looks a little like an older James Dean, had the rebel actor lived a full life—Amato is friendly and laid back. He tosses out "fucking" a lot in conversation but rarely in anger or spite. It's just a habitual, New York placeholder for "amazing" or "unbelievable."

"I came from what I think people would call the middle class," said Amato, lounging on a couch in front of an old-school, big-screen television. Just feet away the open screen door let in the cool breeze from his Del Rey neighborhood, helping to circulate the smoke that Amato's late afternoon cigar was producing. Thanks to the reach of satellite television, a New York Yankees, Rangers, or Giants game is always on in Amato's Los Angeles bungalow home, which helps him recall his New York City youth.

As a kid, Amato lived for the Yankees, as well as those Sundays when his grandfather would take him to games in the Bronx. He loved sports, but at 5 feet, 6 inches at William Hunter Bryant High School back in the mid-1970s it was tough to compete. Instead, Amato became a musician. First he played the trombone, but he didn't like lugging it on the bus and then having to walk eight blocks to his home. He wanted to switch to the more portable flute, but his music teacher gave him a saxophone, which was an improvement bulkwise over the trombone. The music came easily to him, and by graduation he was playing local clubs as part of Gypsy, a nine-piece disco-rock band he and his buddies assembled.

During the 1980s Amato canvassed the island of Manhattan, hopping from gig to gig: weddings, clubs, bar mitzvahs, catering halls. He picked up $100 here, $125 there. When he got a chance to visit a friend in California, he left and never returned. While still playing music he began to segue into a regular working week. After making cold calls in his bedroom as a computer parts salesman, in 1995 he started his own computer-repair supply firm that sold parts to maintenance companies.

But music remained his life's passion, and like a minor league baseball player or a rookie in the NFL, Amato kept practicing his craft, often three hours a day, to stay sharp so that when opportunity arose he was ready to perform and impress with his grade-A chops. One of the musicians he met in Los Angeles in the late 1990s was John Taylor, former guitarist for Duran Duran, the British teen idol band that rode an MTV wave to '80s rock fame with hits like "Hungry Like the Wolf." Soon Amato was touring with Taylor's solo band while running the computer parts company on the phone from the back of the tour bus. "I was what you would call a fucking entrepreneur," Amato recalled with a grin.

When the dot-com bubble burst in 2000, a lot of the companies Amato sold parts to went out of business. That's when he turned his attention to politics. When he looked at the candidates for the 2000 presidential race, picking between Clinton's number two, who helped steer the country toward unprecedented prosperity, or a guy who'd been governor of Texas for a few years, the choice seemed obvious: Gore. In 2000 Amato switched his voter registration from Independent to Democrat, but it was the Florida recount that radicalized him. He was stunned when the Supreme Court took the case. "When they ordered that Florida stop counting the vote I couldn't believe it," he said. "That was a huge awakening for me, and I realized I needed to start paying attention."

Amato got distracted, though, when John Taylor called in 2003 to tell him Duran Duran was getting back together. Did he want to play the sax solo on the band's signature song, "Rio," in front of 50,000 people? Taylor didn't mention the 50,000 people part, but Amato knew that the band's reunion was going to draw monster crowds, especially in Europe. People could say what they wanted about Duran Duran's brand of music, but he knew "Rio" featured one of pop rock's great sweeping sax solos and offered a rare opportunity for a musician to shine on a stage that large. Literally. The stage for the outdoor shows in Europe was monstrous, featuring a runway-size catwalk that Amato would roam with his wireless mic during his "Rio" solo.

Amato never planned out a career or even his life's trajectory. "I'll walk through a door and then something else will happen," he explained. He lived his life like most musicians do, from project to project. But as 2003 turned into 2004, it seemed his dream was coming true. No longer a computer supply salesman, he was playing in a world-famous rock 'n' roll band whose lucrative reunion tour would likely be good for one or two years of global touring work. Plus, he continued to inch closer toward his own record deal. "The world was opening up huge to me musically," he remembered.

But his stomach hurt.

Actually, it hurt again. The original injury occurred during a show years ago in Chicago at the House of Blues. He jumped up onstage and felt something pop inside, as if he'd stretched or pulled a muscle. Over the years it would occasionally flare up, and Amato couldn't understand what triggered it. In February 2004 the pain came back big time. Two months before he was set to leave for England to tour with Duran Duran, he went to see a neurologist. "I said, 'Dude, look, you can't hurt me. I'm going on tour in eight weeks,'" said Amato, recalling the day the door to his musical career slammed shut and the unlikely door to his blogging life opened.

It was February 6, and the internal exam did not go well. Something was likely torn, or possibly nerve damage had occurred. Amato screamed for his life and practically crawled out of the office, he was in so much pain. He was supposed to go the Grammy Awards ceremony two days later; he had a friend who worked on the show and whenever the Grammys were in L.A. Amato got to go for free. He got dressed up and drove to the Staples Center, but had to leave before Coldplay's "Clocks" won Record of the Year because the pain in his stomach was excruciating and would not go away.

He made it home, but then he couldn't get out of bed for days. Instead of preparing to ship out for Europe with Duran Duran, Amato spent weeks at home just praying that the pain would go away. But it just got worse, paralyzing at times, and the doctor couldn't help. Amato paraded in and out of offices to see more doctors than he could remember, who adminis-

trated tests, offered consultations, and even performed a few hernia operations. Nothing much helped the pain, which was constant and at times
debilitating, like a hot poker in his stomach. And there was no relief.

Finally he called John Taylor and told him he couldn't play with the
band; they'd have to get a replacement.

Amato doesn't like to talk about his medical saga and rarely makes reference to it on Crooks and Liars. He doesn't want the setback to define
him. But "the injury," as he calls it, changed his life to the point where he
was at times handicapped, unable to leave his home for long periods of
time. When he did venture out, it often took him days to recover physically. "I lost my job. It was very depressing," Amato told me. "But I'm always a guy who has a smile on his face when stuff goes bad. Everybody
has their ups and downs. But what happened was, I decided I'm not going
to roll up in a ball. And that's one of the reasons I decided to go online
and start blogging. Because I said I'm going to do something, regardless
of this injury.

"Even though I was hurting, I did not like what was happening to my
country. Since I wasn't on tour I could actually take some time and start
trying to do something about it. That's what the injury sort of did. But I
wasn't happy, trust me. Let me put it this way: I couldn't even listen to
music for a year I was so distraught about the injury."

During the spring and summer of 2004 Amato tried to recuperate.
As he watched the new Duran Duran album debut at No. 17 on the *Billboard* charts, Crooks and Liars remained only a vague idea, driven by his
desperate need for an outlet for the simmering anger that continued to
build up inside him. The anger wasn't about his injury or his sad physical
state. It revolved around what was happening to the country. First, the
war with Iraq, and now Bush's pending reelection.

His musician friend Mike Finnigan, who toured for years with Crosby,
Stills and Nash playing keyboards, was a longtime political junkie. When
he went on the road he'd send emails to friends with interesting news articles and blog posts. He's the one who turned Amato on to Eschaton and
Daily Kos, which opened up a whole new media world made up of people
who felt the same way Amato did. They believed that Bush didn't really

win the 2000 election, that the war in Iraq was going to bankrupt America, and that the Beltway press had abdicated its responsibility as a watchdog for Americans.

Amato read a lot of books, too, including David Brock's *Blinded by the Right*, which opened his eyes to the conservative infrastructure that had been created to influence the media in America. Injured and unable to play music, Amato spent a lot of time at home with the cable television turned on, getting pissed off about the war and about the campaign.

That July Amato decided he wanted to make his voice heard. He posted items on his new site and was happy to have an outlet. But it was just another blog; something was missing. He didn't like how blog readers were restricted to simply reading the words on the screen. He wanted the netroots community to *see* what he was seeing, especially when he was writing about some atrocious bout of misinformation broadcast on Fox News. He knew if people could see the clips rather than just read his descriptions, it would be a hundred times more powerful.

But how to cut and paste snippets of TV shows and put them online? In the summer of 2004 that remained uncharted territory. The user-generated video phenomenon, YouTube, wouldn't officially launch until December 2005. It was a puzzle Amato was determined to solve. "I remember a friend of mine then said, 'Don't waste your time on a blog.' I said, 'Dude, what I'm doing is going to be important.' And I said, 'I've got to do this.' So I started just fucking around with the software and I called a friend from my computer business days."

Eventually he and his friend were able to figure out a way to create edited, two-to-three-minute clips from television programs and store them online. Back then it took Amato hours just to produce one clip. By the time he was done he was sometimes in so much pain he'd have to lie down because it hurt to stand up or walk. But then he'd see Bill O'Reilly say something really stupid on TV and he'd crawl across the floor, back to his computer, and start making another video clip for the site.

With his fledgling video capability Amato wanted to shine a massive spotlight on the crooks and liars in the Republican Party and the Beltway press corps. But in September 2004 the Crooks and Liars spotlight barely shone beyond his Del Rey neighborhood. When the site started Amato had virtually no traffic, no readers. He'd put up a clip and tell friends about it and maybe land 50 hits that day. To spread the word he emailed Democratic Underground, Talking Points Memo, Suburban Guerilla, Talk Left, and other sites. If he had a good clip of John Edwards on TV, for instance, he'd go into the comment section at those sites, find where people were discussing Edwards, mention that he had a real-time video up at his site, and leave behind a link.

Soon his clips were getting 300, 500, even 1,000 hits.

At the time, Amato paid a company called Streamload $25 each month for 100 GB of bandwidth, which was enough to support Crooks and Liars' modest online traffic. Then in October, a few hours after he posted a video clip of Bush's foreign policy advisor Danielle Pletka on CNN accusing the liberal gadfly Michael Moore of "giving aid and comfort" to Osama bin Laden, Amato received an urgent email from Streamload. He had surpassed his monthly bandwidth limit and needed to immediately buy another 100 GB for an additional $25 or his account would be blocked. Confused by the request, Amato looked at his site meter and saw that Eschaton had linked to his Pletka video, which had created an additional 10,000 hits for Crooks and Liars. He quickly paid the charge so Crooks and Liars could handle all of the Eschaton-related traffic. An hour later he got another email demanding another $25, and then another and another. Within 24 hours the Eschaton link had generated 20,000 hits for Amato, which cost him a couple hundred dollars in additional bandwidth.

"The price of success," he said with a grin.

In the months that followed Amato had to spend a lot more than $100 on bandwidth as Crooks and Liars became the go-to site for news-making clips from cable, like when Jon Stewart appeared on CNN's *Crossfire* and lamented the "partisan hackery" the pseudo-debate program produced, and when Keith Olbermann's then-fledgling program on MSNBC, *Countdown,* was alone in doing postelection reports on possible voter fraud in Ohio. Almost overnight Crooks and Liars became a cornerstone of the burgeoning liberal blogosphere. Traffic really jumped in early 2005, when he found clips of the fake right-wing reporter Jeff Gannon asking Bush spokesman Scott McClellan a question during a White House briefing. The Gannon saga blossomed into a blogosphere media scandal.

That summer Crooks and Liars averaged 60,000 hits a day, and Amato was dumbfounded by the site's popularity. When Katrina swallowed up New Orleans, traffic at Crooks and Liars soared to 275,000 hits day after day. Then, during the televised celebrity fund-raising for the victims of Katrina, when the rapper Kanye West abandoned his script to announce "George Bush doesn't care about black people," Crooks and Liars posted that clip and 800,000 people clicked on it. For context, that represented more viewers than CNN and MSNBC usually got for an evening of prime-time programming back in 2005.

In 2005 netroots readers tapped Crooks and Liars as Best Blog. At the end of 2006 Nielsen Media released its list of the most linked-to blog posts on the Internet for the year; 4 of the top 10 came from Crooks and Liars. No other site had more than one item on the list. *New York* magazine tapped Crooks and Liars as the tenth most-linked site, out of a universe of 27 million blogs. When YouTube launched and became a video-sharing sensation in 2006, Amato worried that his audience would drop off; it doubled instead. By the 2008 general election, Crooks and Liars, which by then was produced by a roster of writers Amato used, landed 300,000 to 400,000 hits each day.

"I'm a fixture, so to speak," Amato said with a laugh.

And so was the blogosphere, the accidental empire.

five

DIY POLITICS

"Do you like to walk?" asked Howie Klein with the hopeful antici-
pation of a golden retriever suddenly blessed with the gift of speech.
Sporting jeans, two-day stubble, and a sweatshirt, Klein had just greeted
me on a carbon-copy gorgeous spring Los Angeles day in the foyer of his
spacious, two-story home high up in the hills north of Hollywood. Klein,
who logged more hours behind his computer than most humans would
think possible, didn't want to be inside anymore. It was time for his daily
walk along the narrow, twisting roads in the mountainous, celebrity-
saturated section of Los Angeles known as Los Feliz. So Klein, liberal
blogger, activist, and campaign guru, grabbed a fistful of doggy treats
for Murphy and Sergeant, who lived up the street, and the mile-plus hike
was on.

Klein bought his Los Feliz home sometime around 1997. (He's awful
with dates.) He liked the location not for the star power but mostly because by commuting to work against traffic on the Ventura Highway, he
could be at his reserved parking spot at the Warner Bros. Records lot in
nearby Burbank in 10 minutes flat. In his previous, 1990s life, Klein was
among the most successful record executives of his generation, and a passionate defender of free speech and artistic integrity. The all-star label he
presided over, Reprise, was considered a rock 'n' roll jewel in the music
industry, and an artist's label, and Klein did his best to keep it that way.
He also had a hand in the success of Sire Records, and between the two
labels he helped parent Warner Bros. print money during the CD boom
years by minting gold and platinum records for Neil Young, The Smiths,

Green Day, Madonna, The Cure, Depeche Mode, Barenaked Ladies, and Talking Heads.

That was then. These days Klein, who has lived more chapters to his life than most novelists would dream of creating, spends his weeks and months happily hunched over his computer 12 to 14 hours each day in his Spanish-style home at the base of the Santa Monica Mountains, blogging six or seven items per day on his site Down With Tyranny. He tracks campaigns, helps fund-raise for selected candidates, and vets congressional hopefuls.

Life is minimal now. Klein has a Mercedes parked in the driveway, but it looks to be at least 10 years old, a relic from his music industry life. These days he gets up at dawn, logs online to see if there are any campaign emergencies that need to be addressed, swims mandatory laps in his swimming pool, and prepares a milkshake that has to contain at least six different kinds of fruits and vegetables. Then he settles in behind his computer for another day of blogging. Often his only break comes when somebody calls him on the phone.

Klein works harder now, logging longer workdays, than he ever did as president of Reprise Records. It's true the blogging pay is terrible (i.e., he does it for free), but he saved up enough music industry money over the years to afford his new life as a full-time movement volunteer. Without a family to support, this is the next act he's chosen for himself.

Prior to 2005 Klein had never read a blog. Now at the forefront of an activist movement to change the face of Democratic Party politics, he helped to unleash a campaign revolution by trying to take congressional campaigns out of the hands of Beltway professionals and put them back into the hands of voters and small donors.

Klein would never use the term "power broker" to describe himself or his humble netroots activism. He'd stress that he represented just one of many important, dedicated players online who were trying to grow a progressive movement. But the fact remains that for aspiring liberal candidates for Congress, as well as their campaign mangers and especially fund-raisers, Klein has emerged as a key go-to guy for progressives nationwide who want to tap into vibrant liberals online, who want to establish a progressive base, raise money, create an early grassroots buzz, and who maybe want to circumvent the Democratic Party establishment in a way that had been unthinkable just two election cycles earlier.

Bloggers are convinced that America is a left-leaning nation and that the Democratic Party ought to reflect that. If the only way to get that message across to the Party establishment was to field liberal primary challengers for incumbent Democrats, then that's what the netroots had to do to push the Party to the left and away from its safe, centrist tendencies. The ultimate goal was clear: to create a progressive majority in American politics. To that end, some bloggers willingly transformed themselves from writers, critics, and essayists into on-the-ground organizers, fundraisers, and activists dedicated to reshaping Democratic politics. Perhaps nobody personified that push better than Klein, whose obsession with tracking congressional races online was unparalleled.

Klein's newfound fascination with blogging and electoral politics had simply reignited a passion that had burned for years. As a kid growing up in Brooklyn he poured over the *New York Times* for hours at the nearby library on the day after elections to find out who had won obscure Upstate races. He stayed up past midnight listening to Adlai Stevenson on the radio address the Democratic convention. As a kid in Brooklyn in the 1950s and 1960s he was taught that it is a mortal sin not to be a Democrat. (Socialists were actually preferred, although Democrats were acceptable.) As a young boy listening to his relatives, he thought that a Nixon was something that plopped into the toilet bowl when he went to the bathroom. In school he had no idea what an RBI meant or which team Pee Wee Reese played for (the hometown Brooklyn Dodgers!), but he could recite the name of every member of New York's congressional delegation. "That was my life," he recalled.

Today he could pretty much name all 435 members of Congress as well as detail exactly how to turn the 13th District in New York into a permanently safe Democratic seat. (Answer: Extend the district's western border by just a half a mile, so it stretches into the more heavily Jewish and Democratic neighborhood of Brighton Beach in Brooklyn.)

Sporting a closely shaven scalp, Klein, age 59, resembles the cue ball actor Alan Arkin, who, like Klein, speaks with a distinct Brooklyn accent. Arkin, though, delivers his lines through a mouthful of marbles; Klein's delivery is more rapid-fire. And once he builds up some momentum and the stories from his fantastic past start falling out—paragraph after paragraph, page after page—they are often punctuated by loud bursts of laughter as he tosses back his head and recounts his countless adventures.

The first topic for discussion during our neighborhood walk that day in early June wasn't the looming elections or the small-mindedness of Beltway Democrats who drove Klein to distraction. It was The Ramones. Specifically, what happened the first time Klein saw the rat-tat-tat punk rock band down in the Bowery in 1975. The answer: It changed his life. Or more accurately, it renewed his faith.

When the '60s turned into the '70s, Klein, who had submerged his college life in rock 'n' roll and all the revolutionary promise it offered, abruptly tuned out American music. After years of living abroad, he returned to America in the mid-1970s and ran into his old friend Danny Fields, who managed The Ramones, a garage band out of Forest Hills, Queens, who took the stage in torn jeans and leather jackets and armed with a fury of machine-gun guitar riffs. Fields begged Klein to come see the band at a great new dive bar called CBGB. Klein refused, but Fields was unrelenting. When Klein finally went to a show and heard bassist Dee Dee Ramone hollering out the night's first signature song intro, "One! Two! Three! Four!," he was transported.

"Everything had gone back to where it had been when I loved music," he said with a grin, climbing higher and higher into his mountainous neighborhood. "It was like grassroots again. Like I could see Johnny [Ramone] was playing guitar in a way that meant you no longer had to compete with Jeff Beck in order to get up on the stage. Johnny was doing it his own way. It was the people's way. And he made you feel like you could be part of it. There was a give-and-take between the audience and the band, and that's what I had loved in music and that's what I felt was missing in those corporate rock days."

Klein was dissecting rock 'n' roll, but he might as well have been analyzing politics. The same DIY (Do It Yourself) ethos that The Ramones embraced—that immediate connection the band created through its "people's way" approach to bass, drums, and guitar—was exactly what Klein loved about the blogosphere's brand of politics and how the netroots were helping (or at least trying) to take the Democratic Party back to basics. The blogosphere made voters (and blog readers) feel as though they were part of the process again. The netroots was making politics accessible and chaotic and fun again, just as those punk bands had done for music 30 years ago.

A Zelig-like figure, for decades Klein had a knack of being at the right place at the right time to watch history unfold firsthand. Honestly, what other person alive today can say he'd met JFK in person as a kid, did drugs with Jim Morrison of The Doors, ran the elevator in Robert Kennedy's Manhattan office, went to high school with Chuck Schumer, befriended Harvey Milk in San Francisco, was pals with Madonna, and attended a Clinton White House state dinner in the East Room?

Klein's unlikely backstory helps put the burgeoning blogosphere into perspective. His path to online activism, where he was among a handful of key bloggers in 2008 who were completely focused on changing the face of Congress, only highlights the unscripted, accidental, and at times bizarre blueprint of the liberal blogosphere. Klein's improbable rise puts to rest any idea that the birth of the netroots could have been planned or plotted in any logical way. What possible blueprint would have set aside crucial space for a retired hippie radical record executive?

For those who might still wonder how people become prominent liberal bloggers, and what is the surest path to achieve online success, the strange tale of Howie Klein provides the simple answer. Nobody has any idea.

KLEIN GREW UP in Brooklyn and attended prestigious Madison High School in the 1960s, where he counted future U.S. senators Chuck Schumer and Norm Coleman among his classmates. Schumer, who represented Madison on *It's Academic,* a local high school television quiz show, was several years younger than Klein. But Klein remembered Coleman; as young boys they served as cosecretaries for their class at PS 197.

Klein was a clueless kid in high school. "I didn't know shit from shinola," he said. He didn't even know who the Beatles were. His only association with popular music came from his little sisters, and he only noticed the music when they played songs too loud for him to study, at which point he'd fling the records off the family's back deck. Growing up, Klein felt utterly alienated both from his Brooklyn family—"I just figured I was left on the doorstep as a child"—and his country. "For a couple years in high school I literally did not want to live in the United States, and didn't want to be part of our society," he said. His solution to his chronic isolation was to hitchhike to California and become a stowaway to the desolate island of Tonga. He actually got as far as California and onto a South Pacific–bound ship, but the rest didn't quite work out.

On the way back across country, Klein met a group of beatniks (it was 1963, so there weren't any hippies yet) who were living in a VW van and smoked lots of marijuana. Attending Brooklyn's Madison High, Klein had been taught in Mr. Reiger's hygiene class that smoking pot led directly to heroin use, which would instantly kill you, so of course Klein had no interest in smoking pot since he was not interested in killing himself. But hanging around the beatniks for a few days in Colorado he noticed that none of them was dying. In fact, they were among the most free and happy people he'd ever met. So Klein started smoking with them. And he liked it. But when he got back to Brooklyn he couldn't find any marijuana to buy. Certainly none of his friends were using it or had access to it. What Klein could find, at the corner of 16th Street and Kings Highway in Brooklyn, was heroin. And since in school he'd been taught that heroin was just like pot, he started using heroin at the age of 16.

The corner of 16th Street and Kings Highway is the same spot where, years earlier, Klein met John F. Kennedy in person. It happened inside Dubrows cafeteria, known throughout Brooklyn for its kasha varnishkes. Klein got hustled inside the cafeteria through the revolving doors by his frantic mother after he got stepped on by a police horse on a day in October 1960, when half the borough showed up to catch a glimpse of the dashing young Catholic candidate. Kennedy, who ducked inside Dubrows to meet with local Party bosses that day, heard about the injured boy and stopped by to wish Klein a speedy recovery.

Klein experienced an awakening at college, the State University of New York at Stony Brook out on Long Island. There everything changed, as though somebody had flipped a switch. It had a lot to do with music. It had a lot to do with drugs. And it all came at him at the same time, on his first day at college.

At freshman orientation the president of the student body came to talk to the incoming students, and Klein was mesmerized. The student body president was wearing a black leather jacket and John Lennon glasses. Klein thought he was brilliant, and he did something he almost never did: he approached a stranger and introduced himself. The student body president promptly asked Klein to run for freshman class president. The big man on campus (Sandy Pearlman, who later became Blue Öyster Cult's record producer) quickly introduced Klein to the world of radical politics, the Vietnam War, the civil rights movement, and the Rolling Stones.

Obsessed with politics, Klein became president of the Young Democrats on campus. But they were not radical enough for him, so he joined Students for a Democratic Society and attended a draft card burning rally in New York City, where he chained himself to the peace activist Dr. Spock. The two of them spent the day in the same jail cell. Klein was thrilled. (It was during a college summer that Klein worked the elevator in RFK's New York City office, regularly seeing the local senator come and go.)

Politics took up a lot of Klein's time and energy in college. So did drugs. At Stony Brook, Klein became one of the main drug suppliers for Long Island's Suffolk County. "Nowadays a drug dealer's a scumbag. Back then I was doing it for the Revolution," Klein laughed. He wasn't getting rich or anything; in fact, he lowered his prices for students. When he first started, pot sold on campus for $35 an ounce, but Klein sold it for $12 an ounce and soon had put lots of other dealers out of business. Truth was, the drug distributor had started off as a cooperative campus effort; friends would take turns going into the city, buying the drugs, and hauling them back 50 miles east to Stony Brook. But in the end, nobody else was willing to take the risks, so the job fell to Klein exclusively. He was selling mostly pot, then also some hash and acid. There were only two days of his college career when he did not get stoned, and on both days he got in car accidents, which he took as some sort of sign.

It helped that Klein was in New York City almost every night working at the legendary Greenwich Village hot spot on Bleecker Street, the Cafe au Go Go. He also ran all over Manhattan seeing as many new bands as he could. As president of Stony Brook's student activities board, he was charged with booking the on-campus concerts, and in the late 1960s no campus in America got the kinds of concerts that Stony Brook landed: Pink Floyd, the Grateful Dead, the Temptations, Otis Redding, Jefferson Airplane, The Who, the Byrds, Janis Joplin, Smokey Robinson, Sam and Dave, Traffic, The Band, and Cream.

Thanks to Klein, Stony Brook landed The Doors for just $400. He saw the band before they had even signed a record deal. It happened in November 1966, when Jim Morrison's band took up a residency tour at the Ondine, a tiny basement club and hangout for the Andy Warhol crowd, in the shadow of the 59th Street Bridge in New York City. Klein was enthralled by the L.A. band and its groundbreaking sound: lots of drugs and lots of keyboards. He went every night The Doors played, and he also helped the band's lead singer score drugs. Klein immediately booked the still unknown band for his college gymnasium. Between the time they were booked and the time they performed, The Doors released their first album, which created a rock 'n' roll sensation. But a deal was a deal; The Doors played Stony Brook for $400.

Klein's obsession with music was matched only by his fixation on the Vietnam War. He secured a high draft number and was in no danger of being sent into combat when his undergraduate days were up. Nonetheless he'd become consumed by the war, to the point where, if he bought a piece of candy, he obsessed over how the tax on that purchase went to buy a plane or a gun to kill children. He realized he couldn't stay in America anymore. Plus, the police were on his trail for his drug-dealing ways.

So he went to Europe and ended up on the last two days of August 1969 at the Isle of Wight Festival in England, where he saw Bob Dylan as well as The Who, fresh off the band's 25-song set at Woodstock two weeks earlier. The next day Klein decided to drive east. He bought a Volkswagen van, threw in an eight-track tape of Blind Faith, the first rock supergroup, featuring Eric Clapton, Ginger Baker, Steve Winwood, and Ric Grech, and started driving toward the sunrises. His three-year odyssey took him through Turkey, Iran, Afghanistan, Pakistan, India, Sri Lanka, and Nepal. On December 1, 1969, while waiting to be waved across the border into India, Klein stopped using drugs forever.

He lived in Amsterdam for four years, during two of which he called his van home. When he started dreaming in Dutch he decided to return to America. By then the Vietnam War was essentially over and Richard Nixon had been driven from office. Klein landed in New York City, and that's when he had his Ramones epiphany at CBGB. He was in love with rock 'n' roll again.

After New York he settled in San Francisco, basically penniless. A friend owned a music store on Castro Street called Aquarius Records, and right next door to that was a small shop, Castro Camera, run by a neighborhood activist and aspiring politician named Harvey Milk. Milk, who lived above his camera store, bankrolled Klein by letting him use the darkroom to make money as a photographer. Milk told Klein he could pay him back when he had the money. Klein served as Milk's photographer when the small businessman ran for citywide office, trying to become one of San Francisco's city supervisors. In 1977, on his third attempt to get elected, Milk succeeded, becoming, as *Time* magazine put it, "the first openly gay man elected to any substantial political office in the history of the planet."

That November 27, former city supervisor and policeman Dan White walked into George Moscone's City Hall office and shot the progressive mayor twice in the head. Minutes later White tracked down Milk inside City Hall and killed him too. ("Oh boy," said Klein, catching his breath as he started to recall Milk's murder 30 years later. When Gus Van Sant's bio film, *Milk*, was released in late 2008, Klein cried whenever he saw the trailer online.) During the trial White's attorney employed the so-called Twinkie Defense, claiming that too much sugar and junk food had impaired the defendant's judgment. After White got off with a lenient manslaughter conviction instead of murder the White Night Riots erupted in San Francisco and Klein spent the night trying to overturn police cars in front of City Hall.

The political juices were pumping again, but rock 'n' roll soon took precedence for Klein, who hosted one of the first punk rock shows on FM radio, *The Outcastes,* on San Francisco's flagship station, KSAN. Together with his friend at Aquarius Records, the Castro Street mecca where new acts like Blondie, Talking Heads, and Elvis Costello performed in-store during concert swings through the Bay Area, Klein helped start up a local label, 415 Records, and quickly scored a hit with the band Romeo Void.

Klein soon made a deal with Columbia Records and went to work for the staid corporate outlet. It was a disaster, as Klein watched and learned everything he needed to know about what *not* to do to a band. After he couldn't stand it anymore he quit and started looking around for his next chapter. He thought about heading to Thailand.

That's when his music industry mentor, Seymour Stein, called and asked him to come aboard Sire Records and be his general manager. It was 1987, and Sire, a piece of the Warner Bros. Music empire, played home to Madonna, Depeche Mode, Lou Reed, Morrissey, and Talking Heads. Eight years later Klein was tapped to be president of Reprise Records, which was first founded by Frank Sinatra in 1960. At Reprise, Klein helped sell hits by Green Day, Fleetwood Mac, and Eric Clapton.

When conservative culture czars like Bill Bennett took aim at gangster rap and applied all kinds of political pressure on record companies to drop key acts during the 1990s, Klein stepped forward as one of the music industry's most outspoken free speech advocates. At the time he also wrote lots of big checks to Democratic politicians who came through the entertainment corridors in search of campaign cash. Repulsed by Republicans and their alliance with the religious right, Klein felt the Democratic Party itself was too centrist.

He wasn't a particular fan of Bill Clinton or Al Gore either. The censorious streak exhibited by Gore's wife, Tipper, as well as Gore's 2000 running mate, Joe Lieberman, both of whom had waged war on the music industry, made Klein question Gore's judgment. Still, in September 1998, just days after Ken Starr's final report on President Clinton's sex life was released and sent Washington into a tizzy, Klein found himself being ushered into a White House state dinner honoring Czech Republic president Vaclav Havel. There, Klein mingled with the guests, including Henry Kissinger, Mia Farrow, Kurt Vonnegut, and his longtime musician friend Lou Reed, who performed for the presidents that night.

Then, in 2001, Klein got squeezed out. Reprise's parent company, Time Warner, had just entered into a disastrous $156 billion merger with America Online, and Time Warner's music properties were told to cut 600 jobs. At the same time, consumers were embracing an all-music-should-be-free vibe thanks to Napster, which crippled CD sales. When Klein got offered a buyout in June, he took it. Between Sire and Reprise, he'd had a great run.

On the bright side, Klein had always wanted a swimming pool, so as a farewell-to-the-music-industry gift to himself, he had one built. Indoors. It's right off the back study, where 6,000 CDs line the mahogany walls. (Thousands more discs were packed away in storage, along with countless gold and platinum albums awarded to Klein over the years.) And it's where he swims laps every morning.

Klein did some charity work and served on the board of People for the American Way, which the television producer Norman Lear established in the 1980s to counter the rise of the religious right. That political itch was coming back again, but Klein still needed a next chapter in his life to really express it. That chapter arrived on May 9, 2005, the day the Huffington Post launched.

A CHRONIC EARLY riser, Klein turned on CNN that May morning and heard reports about Arianna Huffington's new political website. He went downstairs, turned on his computer, went to the Huffington Post, and saw that his old music industry friend, Hilary Rosen, had written one of the first featured blog posts there. It criticized Apple's iTunes for proprietary technology. Klein strongly disagreed with Rosen's point, so he posted a comment saying so. In fact, Klein claims to be the first person to comment on Rosen's piece and may have been one of the first people ever to post at the Huffington Post. Not bad for somebody in 2005 who had no idea what a blog was.

A couple of things happened after Klein posted his comment. First, he started hearing from people who hadn't contacted him in years after they read his comment and emailed him. Second, Arianna herself asked Klein if he wanted to blog at the site. Sure he did. Huffington asked if he would write about music, given his obvious expertise. But Klein had no interest. He inquired about politics, but Huffington already had enough political bloggers. So Klein decided he'd start his own site, Down With Tyranny. And he started blogging. At least, he thought he was blogging, but he really wasn't. He had no readers, really, which meant there was no interaction (the notion never occurred to Klein), and his posts weren't embedded with live links, which is a signature of blogging. Also, he never read any other blogs. He simply posted his screeds online and then turned off his computer.

That summer a friend asked Klein if he wanted to go to a party where lots of Los Angeles bloggers were getting together. There are other bloggers in L.A.? Klein thought to himself. Sounded like fun. There he ran into Jane Hamsher, who had started Firedoglake in late 2004. Klein knew Hamsher from his San Francisco days decades earlier, when she was a young reporter for the *Bay Guardian*.

After catching up, Klein asked Hamsher if she could help him with a blogging question. He knew how to underline something when he typed it, but he couldn't make his words connect to something else. What he meant was that he couldn't make a link; he didn't even know to call it a link. "Jane started laughing her ass off and she said, 'You don't know anything about HTML [coding], do you?' I said, 'No, I don't know anything like that.' She could have asked me if I knew nuclear physics," Klein recalled.

Hamsher handed Klein the leash to her beloved poodle, Kobe, and started teaching him how to make links, how to do italics, and other simple procedures. Then she asked him if he'd ever read Daily Kos or Crooks and Liars or Atrios. Klein had never heard of any of them. She wrote down a list of websites for him to read. He was stunned by what he saw: the energy, the passion, the smarts on display.

Hamsher also told the would-be blogger that not only did he have to read Daily Kos, but he had to become a Daily Kos diarist and cross-post some of his Down With Tyranny items over there to help build traffic for his site. "So he goes over to Daily Kos and he put up a post calling Chuck Schumer a motherfucker and he got like fourteen hundred comments," Hamsher recalled. "And then people were coming over to Down With

Tyranny and calling Howie an asshole. And then he got attacked by Wesley Clarke supporters, although I can't even remember why. And I said, 'Howie, now you're blogging!'"

Klein was astonished: "I was so excited when I saw my blog jump from ten people to twenty-five people a day. I was thrilled. I couldn't believe it. And then to fifty and a hundred people!"

Because of his obsession with congressional races, Klein started up a fund-raising page on ActBlue that featured his favorite liberal candidates. After he endorsed them on his blog, small donors he didn't even know gave money to the candidates based solely on his recommendation. That amazed him. At that point, he was not in contact with any of the candidates personally. In fact, it never occurred to him to reach out to them. Why would they care about his blog?

Then Hamsher asked him to write a regular weekend feature for her popular site. Like Huffington, Hamsher suggested that Klein mine his love of music and his unique industry knowledge to write a weekend column. It might draw some good traffic, she thought. But Klein wanted to write about his true passion: congressional candidates. Eventually he started vetting candidates for the Blue America Political Action Committee, which was overseen by Hamsher and John Amato at Crooks and Liars and by Digby at Hullabaloo. Klein interviewed potential candidates to determine if they were true ambassadors from the grassroots movement, if they would be progressive legislators, and if they deserved the financial support of the blogs' readers.

"We're not really trying to find [people] who are going to fill potholes for their district the best," said Klein, now perched behind his computer after our mountain hike. He scrolled up and down the Blue America site and highlighted the anointed candidates. "We're interested in building a progressive coalition based on principle and values. And we're looking for leaders who are going to be strong on that."

If the candidates passed Klein's test, which consisted of lengthy phone interviews, they landed the Blue America seal of approval; then the big blogs would encourage readers to donate to the candidate via the Blue America page. Readers could also contribute directly to the Blue America PAC, which wrote big checks for a handful of key races.

Additionally, bloggers like Klein were trying to drain away financial contributions that usually flowed into the Democratic Congressional Campaign Committee, or DCCC, which oversees congressional races from Washington. Traditionally, DCCC bigwigs control the purse strings and decide down the campaign homestretch which congressional candidates are worthy of additional, last-minute funding. For bloggers, those DCCC-approved candidates are inevitably safe centrists who have nothing to do with the progressive movement. Bloggers also didn't like how the pro-incumbent DCCC tried to bump off progressive candidates during the early primary stages. To change that equation, the netroots actively discouraged readers from sending checks to the DCCC, and instead urged everyone to contribute directly to specific progressive candidates or to PACs, thereby bypassing the DCCC, which could not be trusted to back progressives and at times put hurdles up to prevent the success of liberal grassroots candidates.

That's why, for Klein and lots of other netroots activists, the DCCC was often seen as part of the problem. Sure, its leaders, such as Rep. Rahm Emanuel (D-IL), who oversaw the DCCC in 2006, and Rep. Chris Van Hollen (D-MD), who took over for the 2008 campaign cycle, wanted more Democrats elected to office. But according to Klein, they didn't want liberals, and they didn't even want natural leaders. They just wanted warm bodies with D-for-Democrat on their office doors, regardless of whether or not they ran for office vowing to end the war in Iraq. For the blogosphere, grabbing control of the House and Senate in 2006 wasn't enough. They wanted *better* Democrats sworn in, Democrats who would reflect progressive values and start leading the country in that direction.

They wanted more candidates like Donna Edwards, whom the netroots, led by blogger Matt Stoller, strongly supported in 2008. An attorney and community activist, Edwards ran for Congress from the heavily Democratic Fourth District in Maryland and defeated the entrenched, eight-term Democratic incumbent, Al Wynn.

That was the kind of break the bloggers wanted to make with the Democratic establishment. And that's why the tension often ran high between the two camps. That's also why Klein loved to tell the story about the time in the spring of 2008, just months after Edwards defeated Wynn, when he traveled to Washington and had dinner with a couple of guys from the DCCC. Despite his frustration with Emanuel and the Democratic leadership, the truth was that more often than not Klein worked with the DCCC to help elect Democrats, to help flip districts from red to blue, and wasn't always waging war with the Beltway organization. Over the years Klein had developed a friendly working relationship with some DCCC insiders with whom he could share campaign information. So when he came to town they all decided to have dinner together, along with the blogger Jane Hamsher. Klein joked about not forgetting to bring along Emanuel, their famously hot-headed boss. Ha-ha.

But wouldn't you know it, as dinner wound down Hamsher casually announced that Rahm Emanuel had just walked into the restaurant. The DCCC guys turned ashen and practically crawled under the table, freaked out about what would happen if Emanuel saw them fraternizing with Klein, who ridiculed their boss online nearly every chance he got and who was trying to funnel crucial fund-raising dollars away from the DCCC. But Klein told them to relax: Emanuel had no idea what he looked like since there was no headshot of Klein posted at Down With Tyranny. The only way Emanuel would know who Klein was would be if Klein went over and introduced himself.

So that's what he did. As Emanuel was waiting at the bar, Klein went over and extended his hand in greeting, which meant that before he could announce who he was the two men were in mid-handshake. The moment Emanuel heard the words "Howie Klein," his face took on a tense, contorted look, said Klein.

Then Klein told Emanuel that he wanted to help him with more than Al Wynn's seat in the House, at which point the veins in Emanuel's neck started to bulge and Klein thought about the dress shirt he had on. It was one of his nicest. It was from his days as a Warner Bros. big shot, the kind of shirt he didn't purchase anymore. And he was suddenly concerned that if he and Emanuel started rolling around fighting on the restaurant floor, his favorite shirt would get ripped.

"You wanted to talk about Al Wynn?! You want to get Al Wynn?" Emanuel started yelling.

"We already got Al Wynn. I want to talk about the *next* Al Wynn,"

Klein responded. At that point, he said, Emanuel looked like a madman. Thankfully, Hamsher suddenly appeared with her cell phone to snap a commemorative photo of the historic meeting, which both broke the tension and concluded the blogger-DCCC showdown.

Still, Klein marveled at the serendipity of the evening: "How amazing is it that you go to Washington and there is Satan right in front of you?"

six

THE TWEETY EFFECT

Rachel Maddow was jonesing for an Internet connection.

As the crucial New Hampshire primary unfolded on the second Tuesday in January 2008, Maddow, a host on the liberal talk network Air America, as well as an occasional blogger, prepared to pontificate on MSNBC's prime time about the Granite State results coming in. As the day unfolded, the only real questions, following Barack Obama's commanding win in the Iowa caucus five days earlier, seemed to be how large his margin of victory would be, how awkward Sen. Hillary Clinton's concession speech would be, and when Clinton would get out of the race altogether. In other words, the political obituaries had already been written by members of the Beltway press corps, few of whom bothered to hide the glee with which they undertook the assignment.

Sitting in the small sixth-floor studio at NBC's midtown Manhattan headquarters and waiting to go on the air with MSNBC's Keith Olbermann and Chris Matthews, Maddow was desperate to get online for the latest news and information from New Hampshire. One week earlier, she had been a featured analyst on MSNBC for the Iowa caucus returns. But she found herself without Internet access for five hours straight that night, an unspeakable restriction on her usual diet of constant online updates.

So when MSNBC invited back the on-the-rise pundit for the New Hampshire primary coverage, Maddow, known for her rapid-fire delivery and razor-sharp debating style, polished during her years as a Rhodes scholar, insisted she be able to hook up her laptop at the television studio and have Web access. Some prime-time pundits would have made sure a black Town Car was ready to drive them home from the TV studio. But the only perk requested by the sneaker-wearing Maddow, who took the subway home to her 275-square-foot Greenwich Village apartment—"It's the size of a van," she joked—was free-flowing Internet access.

As she settled into her satellite studio and took note of Clinton's surprisingly strong early showing in New Hampshire, Maddow quickly discovered that the NBC Internet connection she was using, like many corporate office accounts, contained a firewall that blocked her from visiting some of the websites she most wanted to read that night, such as the Associated Press, the *New York Times,* New Hampshire Public Radio, and Josh Marshall's Talking Points Memo, a favorite destination for online progressives, featuring breaking political news as well as thoughtful commentary.

It's true that in early 2008 Maddow earned her living as a radio pro as well as an occasional television pundit, but she, like all political junkies of her generation, had become a creature of the Internet. (She almost never watched television.) The Internet was where she went first for news, and as an analyst, that's where she went to take the temperature of voters, as well as to see what ideas and arguments were being posted, tossed around, refined, and articulated. It's where Maddow went in search of a fresh angle to bring to her television commentary. Later in 2008, when she landed her own show on MSNBC, Maddow described herself as a "blogger on TV."

Now, sitting in her closet-size MSNBC studio on primary night and not being able to point and click to crucial websites, Maddow quietly fumed. So naturally she blogged about it. Over at the Air America website, fans gathered for a night of live-blogging the New Hampshire results, where they posted their opinions and reactions. Maddow joined the crowd around 8:30 p.m. Emailing from MSNBC (the firewall allowed her to send and receive emails), she bemoaned the fact that NBC was denying her access to some of her favorite websites.

Within minutes a reader emailed a response, suggesting that she get around the NBC firewall by going to a website called hidemyass.com, which would essentially disguise her laptop computer's address, thereby fooling the firewall and allowing her to access any website she wanted.

It worked, and soon Maddow could read the front page of Talking Points Memo, the muckraking site run out of a three-story walkup office in New York City's Flower District, where computers rested on card tables.

The New Hampshire primary night was still early, not yet 9 o'clock, and no winner had been declared in the Democratic race. But the evening's headline had already been written. By defying the pollsters and the pundits, simply by staying so close to Obama in the vote tally, Clinton had scored an upset and had rescued, at least temporarily, her faltering campaign. It was a campaign that just hours earlier had been hurtling toward its certain, shocking demise. How had Clinton engineered such a miraculous showing? What did that mean for the unfolding Democratic race?

At Talking Points Memo, the editor and founder, Josh Marshall, a 39-year-old with a Ph.D. from Brown University in colonial American history, was wrestling with those questions. He was also receiving emails from readers offering their interpretations of the night's unexpected results. One popular theory held that it was the media's fault. Marshall decided that the emails, from self-identified Obama supporters, merited wider attention. So at 8:45 he posted excerpts of one on the TPM homepage under the headline "Late Shift?":

I almost wonder if more Dems didn't vote for Hillary to counter the BS media narrative about rejecting the Clintons once and for all. I say this as someone who has given 1500 bucks to Obama, gone to several of his events out here in CA, met him, and plan to vote for him. Part of me, however, was so pissed about this media narrative about Hillary and the Clintons in general that I had in the back of my mind that I would consider voting for her just to piss the media off. . . . I mean this whole weekend we see people like Andrea Mitchell and Chris Matthews salivating over how the Democrats "rejected the Clintons" and want to puke. This whole media narrative sickened me.

The Beltway media's almost gleeful narrative about Clinton's impending demise had been unmistakable in the days and weeks leading up to

New Hampshire. "These exit polls just destroy her argument for going forward," gushed NBC's Andrea Mitchell on the night of the Iowa vote, suggesting that Clinton not even bother with the first-in-the-nation primary in New Hampshire. Four days before that showdown, Jonathan Chait announced in the *New Republic* that Clinton's campaign was "toast" and that she would lose the first primary "by double-digits."

Watching the coverage unfold for days, Maddow was struck by the media's flipped-out, blood-dripping-from-the-fangs glee at the prospect of Clinton being out of the race. "The filter that the mainstream media was trying to put on the candidates did not comport with how we felt about them," she told me. "And so it chafed, and people were mad and felt like Hillary Clinton was being beat up unfairly. You didn't have to like Hillary Clinton to feel that way. I do think it looks different when a female candidate gets piled on by a mostly male media."

The sexist language that seeped into the media's coverage was also impossible to miss. And driving the media's crowded and crude gender-resentment bus was MSNBC's Chris Matthews. While hosting a talk show during the primary season, he had posted an on-screen graphic that depicted Clinton as a "She devil" and featured a photoshopped image of her sporting devil's horns. He repeatedly likened Clinton to Nurse Ratched, the scheming, heartless character in Ken Kesey's novel *One Flew Over the Cuckoo's Nest,* set in a mental hospital. He referred to Clinton as "Madame Defarge," one of the villains in Dickens's *A Tale of Two Cities,* and described male politicians who endorsed her as "castratos in the eunuch chorus."

Matthews compared Clinton to a "strip-teaser" and wondered whether she was "a convincing mom." He described her "cold eyes" and the "cold look" she gave and how her voice sounded like "fingernails on a blackboard." To Matthews, Clinton was "witchy," "uppity," "antimale," and "a fraud." He wondered if she was unable "to admit a mistake" because doing so would lead people to call her a "fickle woman." He claimed that Clinton was on a "short . . . leash" as a presidential candidate, lacking "latitude in her husband's absence" to answer a question.

Even for bloggers who didn't support Clinton's candidacy, the media's hit parade of female stereotypes—Clinton as a ruthless, humorless, ambi-tious crybaby—was too much. "The misogynistic crap cannot be allowed to pass without pushback," wrote Christy Hardin Smith at Firedoglake one day before the New Hampshire primary. "What is being done in the press is akin to a pack of rabid 7th graders trying to haze the nerdy girl in school simply because they can. It has nothing to do with her qualifica-tions—it has to do with gender, and these lemming pundits think that it's perfectly acceptable because everyone is doing it."

JUST AFTER 9 P.M., having been granted full Internet access courtesy of hidemyass.com, Maddow logged on to Talking Points Memo and read the highlighted reader email suggesting that voters had pushed back against the press for its contemptuous Clinton coverage. "It was like, 'Bingo,'" she recalled. "My job as an analyst in a situation like that is to help explain and distill what's going on. And I felt like that was a really clear distillation. And it was a real punchy, specific thing to get Chris Matthews's attention."

Minutes later Maddow's on-air tag-team partner that night, the right-wing pundit Pat Buchanan, announced that Clinton's strong showing in New Hampshire, despite the torrent of predictions about her demise, meant that voters had "body-slammed" the press corps. Maddow saw her opening:

> Do you want to know who they're blaming for women voters break-ing for Hillary Clinton over Barack Obama? They're blaming Chris Matthews. People are citing particularly Chris not only for his own views but also as a symbol of what the mainstream media has done to Hillary Clinton.

Never at a loss for words, Matthews immediately asked for the name of the website where Maddow found the reference to him. "His reaction was hilarious," Maddow later recalled, as she slipped into a robotic voice and captured the host's somewhat confounded response: "What is this Internet of which you speak? This is some sort of site of webs? What is this machine? I have never heard of this. They have crowned me king? I must find this kingdom."

In general, though, Matthews, an old-school Beltway pol and journalist, seemed mostly amused by the online attention being paid to him that night. He brushed off the suggestion that he had affected the New Hampshire vote or that he had, in the days and weeks leading up to the primary, been unfair to Clinton.

Matthews didn't know it at the time, but his exchange with Maddow marked the beginning of a blogswarm, a guttural, viral roar from the netroots, that raged throughout the night and detonated again the next morning, when Matthews returned to the MSNBC studios to make one of the most blatantly sexist comments ever aired about Clinton's political career. And he did it just hours after announcing on live television, "I will never underestimate Hillary Clinton again."

One week later, as the Matthews controversy continued to rage, women's group activists gathered in the snow outside the NBC News Washington studio with picket signs that spelled out MSNBC as "Misogyny, Sexist, Narrow-minded, Boys Club." Matthews, never known for self-reflection, was forced to air a lengthy monologue to open his January 17, 2008, program, which eventually touched down with an indirect apology to Clinton.

None of it would have happened without the power and the passion of liberal bloggers, many of whom, despite their ambivalence toward Clinton and her centrist candidacy, led the charge on her behalf. In fact, the blogswarm that soon engulfed Matthews was sparked independently of the Clinton campaign, which, according to bloggers, did nothing to try to fuel the online firestorm. The blogswarm was sparked, and spread for days, because progressive bloggers got fed up with the way the press was treating a Democratic front-runner. Just as they had become fed up twelve months earlier when Fox News tried to smear Barack Obama as a madrassa-going youth and decided to torpedo the Fox News Democratic debates. In both cases, the blogosphere flexed its media muscle and altered the political landscape.

"None of this would have happened without the blogosphere," said the blogger Taylor Marsh in the wake of the Matthews swarm. "It was an historic event."

Watching MSNBC on the night of the New Hampshire primary just outside of Washington was Jane Hamsher, who had founded her influential blog, Firedoglake, in 2004 as a way to express her frustration after John Kerry's defeat that November. When Hamsher heard Maddow's comments about Matthews she knew they were a big deal, and she quickly posted an item on FDL headlined "New Hampshire: Tweety Did It." "Tweety" is the netroots' dismissive shorthand for Matthews, in reference to the Looney Tunes bird, because of the distinctive, bright yellow hair color that the 63-year-old Matthews favors.

The netroots saw Matthews as more than an old-fashioned goof, remnant of an era when middle-aged white men gathered around tables to lecture Americans about how politics really work. As Media Matters for America routinely chronicled, Matthews was often patently unfair to Democrats. He portrayed them as phonies and cowards out of touch with "regular voters," at the same time flashing signs of his man-crush on the prominent Republican politicians George Bush, John McCain, and Rudy Giuliani, Aqua Velva men with broad shoulders who could lead the country to greatness. For years Matthews had relentlessly perpetuated negative stereotypes about Democrats. So when Maddow had the nerve to point out to Matthews, on the air, that his conduct had been cited as the reason for a voter backlash in New Hampshire, the storyline was immediately embraced by bloggers who were tired of pundits dumping all over Democratic leaders.

"The importance of tonight's win can not be understated," announced TalkLeft, an influential Democratic blog out of Denver published by the defense attorney Jeralyn Merritt. "It was a revolt of women sick and tired of the likes of Chris Tweety Matthews and the Media Misogynists. Their hatred of Hillary Clinton was soundly rejected by the voters." TalkLeft's declaration went up just minutes after the Associated Press declared Clinton the night's Democratic winner.

Sixteen hundred miles away that night, in Durham, North Carolina,

Pam Spaulding blogged the Granite State results from home. The 44-year-old blogger was still recuperating from gall bladder surgery just days earlier. (This being the Internet, Spaulding posted photos of the procedure on her website.) She had been simmering for days about the sexist coverage Clinton was forced to endure, so when she spotted the TalkLeft post about "Media Misogynists" she immediately copied and pasted it into the comment section at Pandagon, a prominent feminist blog that buzzed on primary night with lots of New Hampshire coverage and commentary.

A feminist African American blogger whose widely read political site often focuses on gay and lesbian issues, Spaulding was no fan of Clinton. She admitted that she'd written "horrid" things about Clinton's candidacy prior to New Hampshire. Nonetheless, she felt compelled to come to the former first lady's defense. "It really comes down to gender bias," Spaulding told me just days after the New Hampshire vote. "The press does not know how to deal with a female candidate."

Right after she highlighted the TalkLeft post at Pandagon, Spaulding, who works as an IT manager for Duke University Press and who counts Elizabeth Edwards as a loyal Pam's House Blend reader, saw NBC's Brian Williams discussing the New Hampshire vote on MSNBC and wondering out loud if there had been a Bradley Effect. When Tom Bradley, African American mayor of Los Angeles, ran for governor of California in 1982 he led in most of the polls right up until Election Day, when he lost to the white candidate. The Bradley Effect suggested that white voters told pollsters they were going to vote for a black candidate, but then, in the privacy of the voting booth, they did not.

Spaulding, too, was wondering about the Bradley Effect that night. The granddaughter of Asa T. Spaulding Sr., president of Durham's North Carolina Mutual Life Insurance Co. and Durham County's first black commissioner as well as a civil rights adviser to several U.S. presidents, Pam Spaulding was sensitive to the role race might play in the 2008 campaign. But she quickly rejected the premise that the Bradley Effect explained Obama's surprise New Hampshire defeat. Instead, at 11:50 p.m., she suggested on her blog that a brand-new phenomenon had been introduced in New Hampshire, "The Tweety Effect," "where the misogyny of a talking head in the MSM [mainstream media] so enrages a demographic that they go out and vote in a manner that will put egg on the face of the talking head."

To help spread the word, Spaulding went back to the Pandagon site and posted another election-night comment, this time including her post on "The Tweety Effect." Just moments before she typed up the post, and all the way across the country, out in her Santa Monica home, the stalwart liberal blogger and sharp-eyed media watcher known simply as Digby had already lowered her boom on the press that night: "All the sickening media sexism we saw over the past couple of days didn't work and all liberals of good conscience should be relieved by that."

After publishing her post and still thirsty for more information and more opinions, Digby clicked over to Pandagon to see what the site's bloggers and readers were saying about New Hampshire. Wading deep down into the comments section, she came across Spaulding's "Tweety Effect" reference and knew it was too good not to pass along. "It just spoke to me," said Digby. "It had a nice ring to it, and it really seemed to explain what we had all been feeling over the last few days." So she updated the post on her Hullabaloo blog to include a link to Spaulding's take on the evening's events.

That's when "The Tweety Effect" really began to pinball around the liberal blogosphere. "The hits were out of control. People who have never linked to my blog picked up on it," said Spaulding, who first joined the blogosphere as a diarist at Daily Kos in 2004, before starting up her own blog.

At 3:25 in the morning, Mark Watson at MyDD, another liberal destination online, officially logged the new term into the progressive glossary:

"Tweety Effect" *noun* 1. where the misogyny of a talking head in the MSM so enrages a demographic that they go out and vote in a manner that will put egg on the face of the talking head.

Even though few of the "Tweety Effect" bloggers had been openly rooting for a Clinton victory, by the time they went to bed that night they were basking in the media's loss in New Hampshire. They were thrilled at the notion that the heavy-handed attacks by the press on a prominent Democratic candidate may have so infuriated voters that they took action into their own hands. The best part was that by night's end, Matthews himself seemed chastened and even acknowledged, however indirectly, that for weeks and months he had been spectacularly wrong about the campaign. Interviewing Clinton's campaign spokesman Howard Wolfson just before midnight, MSNBC's nonstop talker pledged that he would "never underestimate Hillary Clinton again," which perked up a lot of ears.

"When I saw him solemnly intone that he would never underestimate Hillary Clinton again, I was like, 'I must remember this moment. This could be interpreted in an important way that could change the media,'" recalled Maddow. "And then the next morning I saw Matthews's comment and thought, 'God, I'm such a dope! I'm so gullible, I believe people when they talk.'"

What Matthews claimed the next morning, less than nine hours after proclaiming he would never again underestimate Clinton, was that Clinton's entire political career had been based on her previous marital difficulties: "The reason she may be a front-runner is her husband messed around." Matthews suggested that millions of New York voters had simply felt sorry for Clinton, and that's why they elected her to be the junior senator from the Empire State.

"She didn't win there on her merit," Matthews announced.

The Firedoglake blogger Christy Hardin Smith nearly spilled her coffee on the white carpet of her living room in her Clarksburg, West Virginia, home, just as Matthews unfurled his "messed around" whopper. Moments earlier, after putting her young daughter on the school bus, Smith had been reading Spaulding's take on "The Tweety Effect" from the night before. Here was Matthews taking the phenomenon to another level.

As soon as she could, Smith, a former prosecutor who set aside her law work to blog full-time with Hamsher at FDL, reran the MSNBC tape on her TiVo just to make sure she'd heard Matthews correctly. Appalled that anybody would be so crass about a sitting U.S. senator who had worked on children's issues her entire adult life, Smith couldn't believe

Matthews was stupid enough to say what he said out loud and on national television.

There was no spilled coffee at the Manhattan offices of Talking Points Memo that morning, but the look on everyone's face asked, Did Matthews just say what I think he said? Ben Craw, the TPM video editor, happened to be watching MSNBC the morning after New Hampshire when he saw Matthews make his "messed around" comment. He yelled out to the other staffers to give them a heads-up. Greg Sargent, who wrote TPM's Horse's Mouth media column, immediately recalled Matthews's pledge from the night before about never again underestimating Clinton. Sargent grabbed the new quote for a TPM item highlighting Matthews's obvious hypocrisy.

Less than 45 minutes after Matthews made his infamous remark, TPM became the first to post the MSNBC "messed around" video online. Having that visual, and letting readers simply click and watch Matthews's jaw-dropping commentary just hours after Clinton's victory, gave the story a whole other dimension and gave bloggers another way to propagate the firestorm. The TPM video quickly got picked up at the Huffington Post's front page, which fueled the exposure, as well as the immediate and expanding outrage, and turned TPM's Matthews item into a breakout post.

The traditional press soon took notice of the Matthews controversy, with columns and news articles published by the Associated Press, the *Denver Post, New York* magazine, the *San Francisco Chronicle,* as well as on National Public Radio, CNN, and even Fox News, among others. The night after the New Hampshire vote, Fox News host Bill O'Reilly called Matthews out for stepping over the line of good taste. (Imagine being lectured to by Bill O'Reilly about on-air etiquette!)

The next morning the women hosts on ABC's morning talk show *The View* picked up the story and carried it into the mainstream, while expressing dismay over Matthews's classless remarks. Still oblivious to the firestorm he had ignited, Matthews told the Associated Press his "messed around" comment about Clinton represented "an unexceptional statement."

Then the blogswarm picked up institutional support from Media Matters for America, which hammered the Matthews issue for days and also launched an action alert urging bloggers and readers to contact MSNBC and voice their concern about Matthews's ongoing and problematic comments about women. (He tended to focus on their physical attributes.) The cause was quickly embraced by the National Organization for Women, EMILY's List, the Feminist Majority Foundation, the Women's Media Center, and the National Women's Political Caucus.

One year earlier, the same MSNBC leadership team had found itself at the center of a similar firestorm after its morning show host Don Imus inexplicably referred to African American members of the Rutgers University women's basketball team as "nappy-headed hos." Media Matters was the first to flag the comment and post it online. Soon an angry coalition of civil rights and journalism groups joined in and demanded a swift rebuke of Imus, who had a long history of making insulting remarks. One week later, as the drumbeat against the shock jock grew louder and louder, Imus was fired by MSNBC.

With Matthews, a similar, albeit slightly softer, drumbeat continued to grow day after day. As in the case of Imus during his man-made firestorm, virtually nobody came forward to defend Matthews or his laundry list of often leering, misogynistic on-air comments. Instead, protesters were marching and chanting outside NBC's studios in Washington.

One week later, under growing external pressure from people who, as the host put it, "normally like what I say, in fact, normally like me" (i.e., the Beltway chattering class), Matthews publicly walked back his "messed around" comment. In nearly five minutes of opening remarks on *Hardball* on January 17, he still appeared bewildered about the uproar that his behavior had sparked and confused that people couldn't see that his "good heart" was in the right place.

Matthews still didn't know what hit him.

For Maddow, the Tweety Effect, and the grassroots effort that spawned it, captured the netroots' maturation as an entirely new place for liberals to create their own narratives and then make real change by pushing them out into the mainstream. "Being able to come up with an analysis of what's going on, toss it around, see if it works, and then pass it on, that's

really important. It's the power of explanation," she said. "If you can explain what's going on in politics and in the media, you get to define what's
happening in politics and in the media. Explaining is defining, and if you
do it effectively it can be very powerful. And with the blogs, we've got a
place to do that now."

seven

GOD SENT HITLER

For John McCain, the staged event at a San Antonio hotel in late February 2008 represented a nifty campaign coup.

As the Republican primary season wound down, that day's endorsement from Pastor John Hagee, the high-profile and politically wired leader of the 18,000-member Cornerstone megachurch in Texas, signaled to the press and to politicos that McCain could shore up his habitually leaky relationship with evangelical Republicans, who for years had remained cool to the Arizona senator. Just days away from finishing off his Republican primary challenger Mike Huckabee, a minister himself, McCain received a prized endorsement from the ball-shaped Hagee in San Antonio. The move confirmed that the candidate had emerged as a viable campaign option among evangelical heavy-hitters, who wielded extraordinary get-out-the-vote power within the Republican Party.

That winter conservative talk show hosts had staged a mini-mutiny by arguing that McCain shouldn't carry the Republican Party mantle into electoral battle because he wasn't conservative enough. Now McCain was standing beside a nondenominational pastor so far to the political Right that he made Rush Limbaugh look like a Rockefeller Republican.

While Jerry Farwell and Pat Robertson remained household names and the religious right's long-toothed ambassadors to the mainstream, Hagee, a televangelist with an international reach, represented the new guard of evangelicals who had an almost obsessive interest in U.S. foreign policy, embracing an Armageddon-driven Middle East war advocacy. And McCain expressed gratitude for his support. "I am very proud of Pastor

John Hagee's spiritual leadership," the appreciative candidate announced as he toasted the pastor from the cream-colored Texas megachurch, which boasts a 5,400-seat sanctuary, classrooms, a gymnasium, racquetball courts, and acres of parking.

On the surface, the staged handshake appeared to be like any other he's-my-guy event that filled up every successful candidate's campaign calendar. It's true some observers might have questioned why a White House hopeful would so aggressively mix religion and politics, especially somebody like McCain, who rarely discussed his faith in public. But Republican candidates long ago stopped pretending that the separation between church and state applied to their campaigns, especially if they were running for president. For years they had walked onto stages to receive endorsements from preachers who seemed allergic to tolerance. McCain's summit with Hagee appeared to be just the latest example of that.

Even so, for the presumptive Republican nominee to so publicly bask in the glow of Hagee's endorsement, a backing McCain had pursued personally for more than a year, was a bit daring simply because Hagee was no ordinary pastor. He was, by some standards, a loon. And Bruce Wilson knew that better than most.

A former car mechanic from Baltimore who gave up restoring autos to become a blogger, Wilson was part of a small online community of liberal activists and writers focused on the religious right. He had been writing about Hagee for years and sounding alarms within the netroots about the radical ministry he led.

When Wilson saw the McCain-Hagee headlines on the penultimate day of February he wasn't surprised, but he was shocked. He wasn't surprised because he knew Hagee represented a plum Republican endorsement, thanks to the political empire the pastor had amassed, and it was inevitable that the presumptive nominee would try to line up his support. But taking a few steps back to survey the scene, Wilson was shocked that mainstream White House politics in America now included prominent platforms for the likes of radical pastors like Hagee. Wilson desperately wanted to educate the masses about Hagee and highlight how ill-advised it was for McCain, or for anybody, to try to be elected president while brandishing the pastor's support.

Although it took 10 weeks from the time McCain unveiled his Hagee endorsement in February, Wilson, through tireless research and ingenious use of the Web, captured Hagee's looniness in full bloom, spread word of it through the netroots, and forced the mainstream media to cover the story, which then prompted McCain to sheepishly, and publicly, renounce his prized Hagee endorsement. Just like that, McCain's carefully orchestrated outreach to the religious right unraveled thanks entirely to a volunteer blogger working from his apartment south of Worcester in the small town of Millbury, Massachusetts.

McCain was forced onto the defensive not by the Obama campaign or the Clinton campaign or the Democratic National Committee or *Newsweek* or CNN. McCain had to backpedal because a 44-year-old blogger had created a no-budget, four-minute YouTube video using his three-year-old Mac and the free movie editing software that came with it. "My resources were a connection to the Internet, electricity, and food," joked Wilson, who never thought he'd be able to alter the campaign, if even for one or two news cycles in May.

Did the embarrassing episode do lasting damage to McCain's White House chances? Perhaps. At the very least, the affair forced McCain to play defense for much of that campaign week. And at a time in mid-May when his Democratic rivals were pummeling each other during the final stages of their bruising race, McCain, rather than taking advantage of the Democratic civil war, had to explain to the press, and to voters, why he had sought the endorsement of a man who claimed that God had sent Hurricane Katrina to punish the city of New Orleans for hosting a Gay Pride parade.

A man who preached that God had sent Hitler to hunt the Jews.

AS THE MOST influential leader of the right-wing Christian Zionist movement in America, John Hagee embraced dispensationalism and preached a literal interpretation of the Bible that mandated support for Israel and the Jewish people because the Second Coming of Jesus Christ would not occur unless the Israelites were in control of all the land of Judea and Samaria (aka the West Bank), fulfilling God's covenant.

For Hagee and the strident masses of the Christian Zionist movement, the State of Israel and its well-being were paramount. Followers expressed their support for Israel not just through prayer or by raising millions of dollars each year, but by sending parishioners there, singing the Jewish national anthem in their churches, and celebrating Jewish festivals. As the evangelical governor of Alaska Sarah Palin once bragged, "The only flag at my office is an Israeli flag."

Hagee's movement sought to channel biblically inspired devotion to Israel into organized efforts to affect U.S. politics and public policy. He and his followers did that by pressing right-wing foreign policy initiatives inside the Beltway and by using their power base within the Republican Party, which meant unleashing a torrent of emails and phone calls to politicians' offices, courtesy of Hagee's Christians United for Israel, to urge the support of pro-Israel policies. Often over objections of the Israeli government itself, Christian Zionists pushed relentlessly in support of controversial Israeli settlements in the West Bank and even bankrolled some of the renegade communes. Christian Zionists also outflanked the neoconservative Bush administration by strenuously opposing a two-state solution to the Israeli-Palestinian conflict because a military withdrawal from the West Bank would break God's covenant and ruin the chances of Christ's return.

Domestically, Christian Zionists emerged as unbending friends to Israel in Washington and began helping to peel away some Jewish votes from the Democratic Party. Of course, some Jews remained suspicious of Hagee's helping hand. They feared that evangelicals visiting the Holy Land were more interested in converting the faithful than sustaining Israel. They were also weary of the Christian Zionist End Times scenario, which always ended badly for Jews: after a biblically foretold world war was fought in the Middle East, a war that would signal the Messiah's return, most remaining unconverted Jews would be cast into a "lake of fire burning with brimstone" as the Rapture unfolded, while true believers would enjoy a thousand years of unending peace on earth.

But Hagee's obsession with Israel and the End Times wasn't the only reason the pastor found himself perched outside of the mainstream. His virulent hatred of Catholicism—he called it a cult and tagged the pope as the Antichrist—also helped push Hagee into the realm of the radical. That, and a series of jaw-dropping comments he made on a variety of social issues.

Thanks to that rhetorical rap sheet, Hagee's initial McCain endorsement did create a minor controversy as the mainstream press leisurely pointed out the millionaire pastor's contentious past. Reporters highlighted the fact that Catholic advocacy groups were upset and asked McCain to reconsider the preacher's support. But after McCain noted that he didn't have to agree with every little thing each supporter of his said, and that he remained proud of Hagee's support, the press pretty much walked away from the story.

Then, during the second week of May, Bruce Wilson found Hagee's "Battle for Jerusalem" sermon online. Even for a Hagee-ologist like Wilson, the contents of the sermon stunned him. Armed with the homily, Wilson hatched a plan to do what nobody else had been able to: turn McCain's coveted Hagee endorsement into a source of embarrassment and create some political daylight between the GOP and the evangelical wing of its party.

LIKE ALMOST EVERYONE else from the netroots who enjoyed a cameo role during the 2008 campaign, Bruce Wilson represented an unlikely actor in the election season drama. For starters, he had been oblivious to electoral politics for most of his adult life. Whether restoring antique cars in Baltimore or running an art gallery there, he simply did not care about Democrats or Republicans at the time. He'd taken some interesting political science courses as an undergrad at UMass and then Northeastern University, but modern-day elections and politics didn't interest him. He also didn't follow the news much. He didn't even own a television and hadn't watched television regularly since he went off to Phillips Academy prep school on a scholarship back in the early 1980s.

In the 1990s, though, Wilson became active in environmental issues and increasingly concerned about global warming. A researcher by nature, he visited his local library (pre-Internet for him) and did as much reading as he could on the topic. He came to the conclusion that a large impedi-

ment stood in the way of fundamental change in America, not only regarding global warming, but for lots of other crucial issues facing the
nation, and that roadblock was the religious right. The impulse of the
Christian right was nothing less than rolling back the Enlightenment,
thought Wilson, spooked by the movement's antiscience leanings and
radical antidemocratic and antipluralist nature.

Wilson wasn't some kind of religion hater. He grew up the son of a
Methodist minister in Connecticut. His father was gently, but firmly,
asked to leave the church in the late 1960s after opposing the Vietnam
War too vigorously and too publicly in town. His parents eventually
found a welcome in the local Unitarian Church, and at the age of eight
Wilson had the option of attending Sunday services. He mostly passed.
Studying the religious right, though, Wilson was actually sympathetic to
the leaders he tracked. He admired how evangelical churches were so
much more innovative than the mainline denominations in the way they
reached out to find new parishioners.

Still, the election results of 2000 and 2004 spooked Wilson even more
about the religious right and its enormous political influence. When bore-
dom finally drove him out of the car restoration business (he was a bit too
cerebral for that line of work), he decided to retrain himself as a writer and
an expert on the religious right. In November 2005, with the help of the
journalist and Christian right expert Frederick Clarkson, Wilson launched
Talk to Action, a community blog where a rotating group of writers
chronicled and analyzed the dangers of the religious right and where readers discussed the political ramifications.

The site didn't make much money, and Wilson's annual income remained "minimal." After moving to central Massachusetts, his wife supported the two of them with her job teaching art. But Talk to Action
allowed Wilson to immerse himself in his research on the Christian right
and position himself as an expert who could get paid to write books on
the topic. In 2006 he began researching Hagee extensively and writing
about his radical brand of Christian Zionism. It was a thankless task, but
Wilson was convinced that a vigilant spotlight, however dim, needed to
be constantly shone on Hagee's ministry and its inroads into mainstream
Republicanism.

Over time Wilson waded through 40 hours' worth of Hagee sermons. They often hit the same thematic points, but because the pastor sometimes went off on digressions and aired his cultural complaints, Wilson listened to the sermons from beginning to end in order and educated himself about the pastor's ways. The sermons were certainly easy enough to find as legions of Hagee's fans recorded them off any of the 160 TV stations and 50 radio stations in the United States that broadcast the pastor. Then followers uploaded them onto the Internet. Some were even sold on eBay. One website in particular, called Manna Reserve, represented a treasure trove of free Hagee sermons.

Wilson's breakthrough discovery came in mid-May. Two-thirds of the way through a recording of a 2006 sermon titled "The Battle for Jerusalem," Wilson heard Hagee's raspy, excited voice describe to his followers how, according to Hagee's interpretation of biblical prophecies, God had sent Hitler to "hunt" the Jews in order to spur the creation of Israel, "the only home God ever intended for the Jews to have," as Hagee put it. It was all part of the pastor's Israelcentric reading of the Second Coming.

Interspersing his own analysis while he quoted specific Bible passages, Hagee forcefully preached, "'And they the hunters should hunt them,' that will be the Jews. 'From every mountain and from every hill and from out of the holes of the rocks.' If that doesn't describe what Hitler did in the Holocaust you can't see that." He went on:

Theodor Herzl is the father of Zionism. He was a Jew who at the turn of the nineteenth century said, "This land [Palestine] is our land, God wants us to live there." So he went to the Jews of Europe and said, "I want you to come and join me in the land of Israel." So few went that Herzl went into depression. Those who came founded Israel; those who did not went through the hell of the Holocaust.

Then god sent a hunter. A hunter is someone with a gun and he forces you. Hitler was a hunter. And the Bible says—Jeremiah writing—"They shall hunt them from every mountain and from every hill and from the holes of the rocks," meaning there's no place to hide. And that might be offensive to some people but don't let your heart be offended. I didn't write it, Jeremiah wrote it. It was the truth and it is the truth. How did it happen? Because God allowed it to happen. Why did it happen? Because God said, "My top priority for the Jewish people is to get them to come back to the land of Israel."

According to John McCain's coveted endorser, God's will dictated that Hitler exterminate millions of Jews because it was the horrors of the Holocaust that prompted Jewish survivors to flee Europe for Palestine, where they belonged. The way Hagee described it, Nazi soldiers were divine agents who put God's master plan into motion and spurred the creation of the all-important State of Israel, which is necessary, according to Christian Zionists, for the Second Coming. In other words, the Holocaust was God's idea.

It was this sermon, and actually hearing the inflection of Hagee's honey-dipped, Southern-accented voice in his emphatic God-sent-Hitler tale, that conveyed just how nuts the preacher was and how inappropriate it was for any presidential candidate, let alone the GOP's presumptive nominee, to be associated with somebody who peddled those kinds of history lessons. That's what Wilson's audio captured. Finding the Hagee tape had been the easy part. Launching Hagee's Hitler clip onto the Internet and making sure the press paid attention would be more difficult.

The key to creating the "God Sent Hitler" clip at YouTube, he thought, was to simplify the narrative, to distill and clarify Hagee's comments and to let them speak for themselves. In some of his early Hagee-related YouTube clips, Wilson added in his own commentary. But for this one he wanted the clip to be as uncluttered as possible, so he created a video featuring just the audio of Hagee's sermon and on-screen text, sort of closed-caption hearing, to walk viewers through the occasionally garbled sermons. It was set against a black backdrop.

Wilson first posted the clip on YouTube on May 15. He wrote an item for his own blog, Talk to Action, and cross-posted it at Daily Kos in hopes of reaching a larger audience. He then sent around a few links to try to gin up interest online. He sent a note to Townhouse, too, the popular listserv for top bloggers and netroots activists, notifying them about his Hagee audio discovery. He thought the item and the video could really be a blockbuster.

But he also knew not to get his hopes up. He'd written extensively about Hagee's church in the past, including its radical political bent and Hagee's altar full of hateful remarks, and he didn't feel he'd accomplished that much. Progressives who monitored the religious right were used to riding that frustrating treadmill. For years they had been trying to shame Republican politicians for their right-wing religious alliances and trying to convince the press to cover the revelations about radical Christian right rhetoric as news. Activists' foreheads were becoming numb from banging them so hard, and so often, against the proverbial wall.

Within the netroots itself, the topic of Hagee and Christian Zionism remained a tough sell. The problem with launching the Hagee clip and getting it to go viral was that there seemed to already be a netroots consensus that Hagee was nuts, that McCain was crazy to welcome the endorsement, and, even worse, that the press more or less let McCain walk away without paying any kind of political price for his association with the radical preacher. The netroots already knew that, and it quietly drove people online to distraction. That's why Wilson wasn't really expecting much as he readied his online offensive against Hagee.

Sure enough, Wilson's sermon detective work produced an underwhelming reaction within the netroots. Just 83 comments were posted below his Daily Kos diary about Hagee's "hunter" sermon. For nearly a week his tape sat on YouTube mostly unviewed, generating very little buzz. It looked as though his effort wasn't going any further and that he should simply return to the Hagee sermon archives in search of more incendiary quotes in hopes that some recorded utterance would, someday, spark an outrage.

Besides, Wilson was in it for the long haul. Obviously he had no guarantees that he'd be able to uncover a sermon as blatantly offensive as Hagee's "God sent Hitler" stunner, but he figured he'd keep trying and that with the right combination of luck and perhaps a slightly different presentation, something would catch the media's imagination. Still, as his "hunter" tape sat unwatched, Wilson thought the clip should have generated more attention.

One week later it did.

SAM STEIN, A staff political reporter at the Huffington Post, received an email from a friend who passed along a link to the Hagee video Wilson had posted at YouTube. Stein, who had previously written about Hagee, was immediately intrigued by the video and thought it was newsworthy. But he remained skeptical. Unfamiliar with Wilson's work, he wasn't sure if the blogger was a trustworthy source. Plus, Hagee had been in the news for weeks since he had endorsed McCain, and Stein assumed that his sermons had been combed by mainstream journalists looking for potentially controversial statements that might prove newsworthy.

There was also the question of context. Having seen the Jeremiah Wright story unfold during the previous weeks and watched as the same 5- or 10-second clip of Obama's former pastor got looped over and over on cable television, Stein didn't want to grab a snippet of Pastor Hagee's sermon and then claim it captured the pastor's whole message. So he set out to verify the Hagee tapes. He found the same online Hagee database that Wilson used and quickly searched out the Hitler sermon.

"Voilà, there it was," recalled Stein.

He listened to the 90-minute sermon in its entirety. Then he filled out the story by getting Hagee's church to confirm the authenticity of the remarks. Stein's report ran on May 21. It included embedded audio that readers could click on to hear the controversial portions of the sermon. Editors gave Stein's story big play on the Huffington Post front page, which represented one of the largest and loudest platforms on the Internet. Relaunched on the Huffington Post, Wilson's scoop became a breakout hit and was embraced by Washington Monthly, Crooks and Liars, Donklephant, the Carpetbagger Report, the Smirking Chimp, Shakesville, the Brave New Films blog, the Seminal, and Oliver Willis, among others.

In his Huffington Post report, Stein did something a little unusual: he mentioned Wilson's name and his blog report very high up in the article and included a prominent link to his site, which drove traffic to Talk to Action. In fact, that's how Wilson found out about Stein's report. On May 21 he noticed a huge spike in readers coming over from the Huffington Post.

Sensing that the new attention could help break the Hagee Hitler story into the mainstream, Wilson knew the key was to keep ginning up readership for the larger Hagee story so it could climb way up the news ladders, such as Digg. Online news ladders establish a running online scorecard for which blog posts and news reports are the most popular at any given hour, based on online votes from readers.

Wilson quickly blogged about Stein's report over at Daily Kos, and his item got voted up to the top of the website's own ladder, its recommended list. In his post Wilson urged readers to vote Stein's article up the Digg ladder, which they did, as well as to the top of other news ladders. By that Wednesday afternoon, as the Hagee Hitler story ignited online, both Stein's article about Wilson's blog and Wilson's diary about Stein's article were generating A-list links, with readers sending both posts up various online news ladders. That proved crucial because mainstream journalists often use the ladders to gauge the buzz factor on stories breaking online, to see which ones have legs throughout the day and which ones are simply one- or two-hour stories not worth chasing.

Meanwhile, over at YouTube on May 21, Wilson's "God sent Hitler" clip catapulted in total views. By dinnertime Wilson's story was officially, albeit belatedly, a campaign hit on the Internet and had crashed the mainstream media gates.

That night Keith Olbermann featured the Hagee story on MSNBC's *Countdown*, which aired Wilson's viral video. Soon *Newsweek*, the *Wall Street Journal*, AP, the *New York Times*, the *Dallas Morning News*, Yahoo News, ABC News, and the *Washington Post*, among others, all cited Wilson's "God sent Hitler" video and detailed the McCain controversy.

Once Wilson's YouTube clip went viral, once it clicked online and then bulleted into the mainstream media, it took less than 24 hours before a chastened John McCain issued a formal statement denouncing Hagee and his God-sent-Hitler history lesson. "I find these remarks and others deeply offensive and indefensible," the Republican announced. And not a moment too soon. Within a matter of minutes, Hagee issued his own angry you-can't-fire-me-I-quit! directive at McCain.

After years of trial and error, the public rupture between McCain and Hagee represented a rare collective triumph for the online activists and writers who had been touting the dangerous intersection between Republican politics and right-wing pastors. "We don't get many victories," conceded Wilson, who received a call from a fellow researcher who cried when she heard the news about McCain and Hagee's messy public divorce. She cried because she never thought any high-profile Republican would ever be forced to answer uncomfortable questions about a preacher like Hagee. But in May 2008 the blogosphere—not a campaign or a news organization—did just that.

Throughout the controversy, Hagee and his defenders claimed that the Hitler comments, when posted online, had been taken out of context. Wilson didn't see how that could be the case since he posted several unedited minutes of Hagee's sermon. If anything, Hagee's comments were drowning in context. Months later any doubts about missing context were removed when Wilson finally got his hands on a DVD of the "Battle for Jerusalem" sermon, which captured video as well as audio of Hagee addressing his Cornerstone Church faithful. He talked excitedly about how God had used the Holocaust as a way to shepherd Jews toward Palestine in preparation of Christ's return.

Curious about what Hagee's now infamous "hunter" passage looked like, not just what it sounded like, Wilson popped in the DVD and was stunned all over again by the performance the pastor delivered. When the Christian Zionist leader got to the part where he claimed that "God sent a hunter," Wilson said he pantomimed holding a rifle and taking aim at the audience, as if he were a Nazi aiming his rifle at Jews.

eight

THE BLOG WAR OF 2008

Every night the routine was the same for the longtime Daily Kos diarist known to readers simply as Alegre. She would put her young children to bed by eight o'clock and then log on to her computer from her suburban Maryland home, turn her attention to the unfolding presidential primary, and look for ways to promote her favorite candidate, Sen. Hillary Clinton. On the second Saturday in March 2008, the mother of two with an insatiable desire to support the junior senator from New York decided to weigh in on the fact that it was International Women's Day by highlighting all the great things she felt Clinton had done over her career on behalf of women.

With a child of her own who battled developmental delays, Alegre appreciated the nonprofit work Clinton did in the early 1970s as a Yale Law School grad who passed up lucrative corporate jobs and advised the Children's Defense Fund instead. And Alegre was grateful for the way Clinton helped get laws passed to require public schools to accommodate students with special needs. "That's been a huge reason I've been in her corner for the last year," Alegre told me during the Democratic primary season.

So, nearly every night, while her kids were asleep, she posted diary entries on the landmark liberal website, Daily Kos. She posted chunks from recent Clinton speeches and linked to articles online that she liked. She got into debates with hothouse Daily Kos readers who posted comments about her work. She defended her candidate when she came under attack and she raised doubts about Clinton's opponents. Sometimes she stayed up until 1 a.m., and the next morning she'd be back online at 6 before the kids woke up.

Politics have been running through Alegre's veins since childhood, and her chronic blogging represents a natural outlet for her activist streak. (Her screen name came from a cat she once owned; she prefers to remain anonymous.) As a little kid in Michigan she went to antiwar rallies with her Democratic parents, then to McGovern campaign events in 1972, when she was 10 years old. Jane Fonda slept in her house when the young actress with a radical streak came to town to attend a protest event.

As a teenager, Alegre attended environment rallies in Lansing, the state capital. She studied international relations and third world development at Michigan State University during the Reagan years. Her first taste of the Beltway came in 1984, when she served as an intern on the Hill. She stayed in the area after graduating college and remained active in retail politics. During the final eight Sundays of the doomed 1988 Michael Dukakis campaign, she boarded buses bound for battleground states, where she'd hit the streets during the day and then sleep on the floor of the local campaign office.

She eventually moved out to Maryland to start a family. Now she works as a paralegal. "Nothing too exciting," she remarked to me. "It pays the bills and provides health care." She loves a good argument and began posting at online forums in the 1990s, when shouting matches over the Clinton impeachment dominated the nascent community. But it was at Daily Kos in 2004, after the birth of her second child, that Alegre, like so many others in the progressive movement, really found her voice.

Alegre's diary represented just one of thousands that filled up Daily Kos on a weekly basis. In October 2003 Daily Kos switched over to the open-source, easy-to-use Scoop software platform, which turned over the site's content to readers, who created their own diaries, which in turn augmented the writing done by Daily Kos's hand-picked front-page writers.

Over four years of posting there, Alegre established herself as a meaningful writer, and her diaries were taken seriously within the community, in part because her smart, analytical posts covered a wide array of progressive issues, including the genocide in Darfur, benefits for U.S.

troops, education, strengthening the economy, health care, and alleviating poverty.

In the spring of 2007 Alegre began attending nearby volunteer meetings for the Clinton campaign. In June she decided to make her pro-Clinton feelings known on Daily Kos, where Clinton was routinely ridiculed as a cautious, triangulating centrist. For most of Alegre's fellow denizens, known as the Kossacks, Clinton certainly did not represent the blogosphere's model of a fighting Democrat ready to wage partisan war with George Bush's Republican Party, or someone embracing a new brand of grassroots-powered activism and campaigning. Clinton routinely got trounced in the presidential straw poll votes conducted by Daily Kos, where readers were much more drawn to the more hands-on candidacies of John Edwards and Barack Obama.

Yet much to Alegre's surprise, her coming out as a full-throated Clinton supporter was met with an unexpectedly warm, or at least civil reaction from the community's readers, who posted more than 300 comments in response to her declaration. And so for the next eight months, both enthusiastic and prolific, Alegre became one of Clinton's most energetic supporters online, posting nearly every night at Daily Kos and almost always to extol Clinton's virtues as a candidate.

By early 2008, though, as the race tightened between Clinton and Obama and as the contest became more personal, she sensed an unmistakable shift online toward more abusive commentary about Clinton and in the online responses to her posts. The same collection of Clinton haters, she complained, were posting nasty messages, spamming the comment section of her posts, and not even debating the issues Alegre addressed in her messages. Worse, Alegre complained, the Daily Kos administrators who tried to keep some semblance of order and civility within the freewheeling community of hotheads were letting the anti-Clinton bullies get away with it.

When John Edwards dropped out of the race in January and lots of his supporters filed out of Daily Kos, the site, which feeds off conflict, looked around for somebody to be angry at. They found a very large target in Hillary Clinton, who quickly became less a left-leaning centrist Democrat in good standing who needed to be opposed, and more a looming villain who needed to be vanquished. The blogosphere was built on a rowdy kind of us-versus-them mentality, and in early 2008 that "them" became a Dem: Clinton. The site was bursting with new energy and excitement over the historic Democratic primary, but the vibe was less "We love Barack!" than "We hate Hillary!"

"It makes me sick that the Clintons are still in our party," wrote Blue Texas, a prolific diarist at Daily Kos. That sympathy wasn't confined to one site. By late February and early March, the anti-Clinton vitriol found online often surpassed the kind of language once used exclusively for the Bush administration and its rogue criminality. "What a contemptible wretch Sen. Clinton has turned out to be," wrote the pro-Obama blogger John Cole at Balloon Juice. "What an asshole." On the night in May when Clinton won the West Virginia primary, John Aravosis, the prominent online writer who founded AmericaBlog, one of the netroots' most popular sites, posted a Clinton attack under the headline "Go Away You Horrible Human Being." That type of name-calling had become common on the site. "She is a disgusting unvetted untested racist liar," announced one reader in the AmericaBlog comment section the day after Clinton won primaries in Ohio, Rhode Island, and Texas. The next week, when headlines were posted about five U.S. soldiers being killed in a bomb blast in Iraq, a commenter at AmericaBlog complained, "And Hillary is suicide bombing us here." Added another, "Go fuck yourself Hillary—since Bill won't."

A lot of real ugliness online came courtesy of readers. "HILLARY CLINTON IS A TERRORIST!" warned one Huffington Post commenter. Though it is not fair to judge the blogosphere, or individual sites, based on anonymous reader postings—that's like assessing radio talk show hosts based on a few nutty callers—the tone of attacks against Clinton had become so pervasive online, hour after hour, day after day, week after week, that in this instance the comments very clearly reflected a larger prevailing mood often expressed by bloggers themselves.

Some neutral netroots writers became concerned about the anti-Clinton hate speech being promoted online (i.e., "We know that Hillary Clinton will do or say *anything* in her mad pursuit of power," wrote

Markos at Daily Kos) and what the drawbacks were for the progressive movement as a whole. The anger "really is indistinguishable from how the right hates her," noted the influential liberal writer Glenn Greenwald, who blogged at Unclaimed Territory. "If you go over to Daily Kos, you would think you were reading Ann Coulter or Rush Limbaugh. The level of hatred towards Hillary by a lot of pro-Obama bloggers is really extreme and even kind of disturbing and creepy." (During the 1990s, liberals mocked conservatives for suffering from the all-consuming CDS, or Clinton Derangement Syndrome, which now seemed to be spreading within the netroots.)

Others were so turned off by the state of the debate—the "febrile and overwrought" atmosphere among readers, as one prominent online writer put it privately—that even at the height of the battle they shied away from writing about the campaign, a campaign most bloggers had eagerly awaited for months, if not years, as a chance to have a national discussion about the future of the Democratic Party and the role of liberalism in today's politics.

"I thought this would be great if the race went on, and we could talk about Democratic issues and have more debates and put the issues front and center that people really care about," said Jane Hamsher from Firedoglake, which did not endorse either candidate. "But then you see those diaries over at Daily Kos and you see what the conversation has devolved into, and it's not getting any better. It's gotten way more emotional than people ever thought—very personal."

The Clinton hate did not originate from the low-key, No Drama Obama camp. Instead, it represented a grassroots, bottom-up phenomenon from within the liberal community. Clinton foes insisted that they were simply responding to what they saw as Clinton's deeply misguided and divisive campaign and that the tone online didn't turn ugly until the Clinton campaign turned ugly. They claimed that the Clinton campaign tried to argue that certain primary states counted less than others, and that Clinton handlers, at least in the eyes of Obama supporters, tried to change the superdelegate rules in the middle of the game in hopes of landing the nomination. "It's a campaign that's not being waged on the merits, but one that's trying to overturn the will of the voter," Markos complained in March about what he saw as Clinton's dirty push to rejigger rules in the contested primary states of Michigan and Florida. "So yes, people are going to be pissed."

"This notion that, 'Oh, Hillary supporters are just a suppressed minority, and they've been so clean and aboveboard and it's those Obama supporters that are the meanies,' that's absolutely ridiculous," Markos told me. "I spend just as much time deleting Obama-is-a-Manchurian-candidate or closet-Muslim diaries [at Daily Kos] as I do deleting Hillary-is-a-cunt diaries."

THE RESPONSE TO Alegre's March 8 post about International Women's Day finally convinced her to stage a walkout at Daily Kos. Her post got trashed in the comment section. Not in a substantive way, but in a juvenile, name-calling way and by the same Obama supporters who swarmed and descended on any Daily Kos diary that expressed even faint support of Clinton.

Six days later Alegre had had enough. Life is too short, she thought. She was concerned about how the anger and insults hurled her way from the Daily Kos community often lingered long after she stepped away from her computer; after all, she had a young family to raise with a husband who worked six days a week in construction. So Alegre posted a notice, "an open letter to the liberal blogosphere," announcing that she was going on strike until the working conditions improved, until the Clinton hate got dialed back at Daily Kos. ("Boycott" probably would have been a better description than "strike," since Daily Kos diarists don't get paid for their contributions.) Alegre declared her stand against "the double standards, the distortions, the hateful, irrational, personal attacks, and the lies about Hillary."

That strident tone at Daily Kos had already driven some Clinton supporters from the site weeks before Alegre's strike announcement. Back on February 14, a Daily Kos diarist from Montana known as jarhead5536 packed up his things and bid a not-so-fond farewell to the community with what's known online as a GBCW (Good-bye Cruel World) diary. "I fold. You win, Obama wins, my candidate has not, cannot, and will not get a fair hearing here, and I'm done," he wrote. The diarist was particularly taken aback by the belligerent Clinton bashing: "For you people, it is not enough that Barack wins, Hillary must lose, and lose completely, crushingly, and humiliatingly badly. You obviously want her face down on the ground, destroyed, ruined, run out of town on a rail. I cannot describe what I read on these posts as anything other than pure hatred."

Alegre's declaration of independence at Daily Kos wasn't the first during the primary season. But coming in March, at a time when the widening gulf between Obama and Clinton supporters online was being punctuated by increasingly shrill attacks on each other, her declaration generated the most immediate buzz and was also widely picked up by the mainstream media, including ABC News, the *Atlantic,* and the *New York Times,* and was hyped on the Drudge Report. Alegre was stunned by the attention: "I'm just a working mom."

At first, Markos responded to Alegre's claims with surprising reserve, informing the *New York Times* that he hoped unhappy pro-Clinton diarists and readers at Daily Kos would find what they were looking for elsewhere on the Web. The next day, after stewing on the subject a bit, he delivered a more scathing, and more characteristic, take-down on his site. No olive branch was extended to Clinton supporters in the name of Democratic unity, or in the hopes of creating a more harmonious Daily Kos. The only branch wielded was the rhetorical reed Markos cracked as he doubled down with more attacks on Clinton, who, he claimed, was running a hopeless, vengeful campaign, "eager to split the party apart in her mad pursuit of power."

His bottom line: a "civil war" had been declared within the Democratic Party and Clinton was to blame. She and her "shrinking band of paranoid holdouts" online, as well as those "low information" voters who supported her, needed to deal with the fact that she had lost to Obama and to get out of the way for the good of the Party.

It was classic Markos. "My site is for fighters. It's designed to gin up passions. I'm not about to tone it down because someone might be offended somewhere," he told me at the time. "The reason Daily Kos has been as successful as it has been is because it's a place for passionate activists, not conflict-averse weenies."

The next day, posting at Jerome Armstrong's MyDD, one of Clinton's few online bastions of support, Alegre shot back at the description of Clinton's supporters as "low information." She thought that jab went way over the line. Since when did liberal bloggers portray Clinton's base of blue-collar, Latino, and elderly voters as nothing more than poorly educated rubes? And since when did liberal bloggers talk about *any* Democratic voting bloc in such a condescending manner?

THE WALKOUT AT Daily Kos, however symbolic in nature, highlighted a very real, deep, and bitter split within the blogosphere.

The unprecedented rift fractured friendships within the normally close-knit blogging community, where most of the top bloggers knew each other and considered themselves allies. Over the years, policy and even personality squabbles had certainly flared up online, but for most of the blogosphere's existence there had been a uniform respect among the most-read bloggers, an assumption that they were working toward the same larger goals and that the netroots community was being intellectually honest and factually accurate in making its arguments online. As the brutal Democratic primary season progressed, though, that assumed good-will evaporated, and bloggers on both sides called out what they saw as increasingly transparent, partisan, and low-quality arguments being made on behalf of candidates.

Naturally, the primary season was bound to create divisions. For various reasons, based largely on demographics, it was natural for Obama mania to sweep over the blogosphere, where overeducated progressives, "the creative class," as one blogger dubbed them, liked to congregate. Surprising was the intramural name-calling and finger-pointing among liberal bloggers, who accused each other of distorting the facts and playing unfair, the regular allegations of sexism and racism hurled online, and the sheer inability to discuss the campaign rationally and with an open mind. The ensuing free-for-all, driven by "irrational loyalties," as one A-list blogger put it privately, represented an unprecedented fracture for the burgeoning netroots. The inevitable growing pains quickly morphed into an uncontrollable, name-calling spasm.

The liberal blogosphere had always represented a bustling open market where all sorts of ideas were exchanged, discussed, and even shouted down. The community had no controlling authority, although the running joke claimed that Markos sent out the netroots' daily marching orders from his hugely popular site. That's how the press often depicted the blogosphere, with Markos in charge and everyone else blindly following behind. The truth is, nobody supervises the blogosphere. There is no top-down management, and bloggers have loyalty to no person or institution. Part of the power and the allure of the blogosphere is that it becomes whatever its passionate, opinionated, hard-charging inhabitants make of it.

But the 2008 campaign created the kind of deep, sustained divide that the young online community had never faced before. And most members never saw it coming. For years the blogosphere had been conveniently unified in its opposition to the Bush administration, whose incompetence represents the central reason the blogosphere swelled both in size and influence. But with the Democratic primary season lasting longer, and getting far nastier, than any of the bloggers ever imagined, the strains burst into open view.

The divide became so wide that even the blogosphere's two biggest names, and its most unified strategists, "Blogfather" Jerome Armstrong and Markos, couldn't agree about Obama and Clinton. The two men had ignited the netroots movement in 2002 with their groundbreaking sites, MyDD and Daily Kos. In 2006 the cornerstone bloggers joined to write *Crashing the Gate,* a sort of people-powered blueprint for how progressives could retake the Democratic Party from within and, more important, how they could win elections.

The dynamic duo barnstormed the country following the book's release, urging insurgent Democrats to seize control of their Party from triangulating professionals and grab control of their country from criminal Republicans. But during the 2008 Democratic primaries, the two couldn't agree on much of anything. By March, Markos had become Obama's head cheerleader online, while Armstrong drifted into Clinton's camp.

Incredibly, the two men who shared royalty checks for writing *Crashing the Gate* in 2006, which detailed how Democrats should run for office, completely disagreed in 2008 about which Democratic candidate had embraced the election advice they detailed in their book.

"TO BE A Clinton blogger in the progressive blogosphere is to be hated, shunned, passed without notice in the street," wrote the blogger Tom Watson during one particularly lonely stretch of the campaign. "We're not welcome at all the best dKos parties—if we show up, we're cursed with the universal epithet of those who challenge the Obama hegemony: 'troll,' they call us. Sometimes 'f'ing troll.' We're Rovian in our embrace of the monster, closet Bush backers and much worse—Lieberman types! Oh, the pain. The pure pain. I can't stand it."

Watson's lament was somewhat tongue in cheek, but the truth is that with equal parts dismay and disgust, the Clinton bloggers looked around the blogosphere and wondered what had happened to the political community they joined, and in some cases, the community they helped lead.

It was an eclectic group of outcasts: a Maryland mom (Alegre), a corporate attorney (Armando Llorens-Sar), an executive at a Silicon Valley high-tech company (eriposte), a Las Vegas–based Internet radio talk show host (Taylor Marsh), and an aspiring TV screenwriter (Todd Beeton).

There were scores more, to be sure. There was Riverdaughter, a former Kossack like Alegre, who found friendlier confines setting up her own shop, the Confluence. There was Jeralyn Merritt, Lane Hudson, Tennessee Guerilla Women, Blue Girl, Anglachel, Jeff Jarvis, as well as most of the blogging crew at Corrente, which was formed by Eschaton readers years earlier.

While the rest of the netroots community swelled its collective chest with pride and expanded its influence as Obama marched to the nomination, the Clinton bloggers raised a cautionary flag. They were the naysayers suggesting that something (principle? integrity?) had been lost online in the rush to crown Obama and demonize Clinton.

"Part of my problem with what's happening at Daily Kos in the diaries is that the reality-based approach has really gone out the window when it comes to Obama and Clinton," said Todd Beeton, a blogger at MyDD. A liberal blogger who admitted to "a ridiculous admiration" for the senator from New York, Beeton at the outset of the primary season worked as an aspiring television screenplay writer with a day job at a Hollywood studio, where his lenient, left-leaning boss often let him blog and work simultaneously.

"Being reality-based was one of the things that I thought we prided ourselves on, that we were the rational ones," Beeton told me as the primaries raged. "We had the facts and therefore we should win. And now we're finding out what the Republican Party has found out, which is the power of emotion. And that when you have a candidate who does appeal to your emotions, people can get crazy."

After weeks and then months of watching the pile on, many Clinton bloggers came to the uncomfortable conclusion that the primary season was not being used simply to pick the Party's next nominee or to celebrate Obama's remarkable political ascension. It was being embraced by legions within the netroots as a chance to drive the Clintons, both Bill and Hillary, from power within the Democratic Party.

"This election is a debacle for the net roots," claimed Armando Llorens-Sar at the height of the springtime showdown. A former Daily Kos front-page blogger, known then to readers simply as "Armando," Llorens-Sar spent the 2008 campaign writing under the name Big Tent Democrat at Jeralyn Merritt's site, TalkLeft, which represented another online oasis for Clinton supporters. "I don't think there's anything nefarious in what the liberal bloggers are doing, but I think there's something very wrong about what they're doing. They have lost their way," he said during the primaries. "They have become an echo chamber. The left blogs have basically become what they have despised about the right-wing blogs: cheerleaders for candidates and parties and not for issues."

A self-described "corporate shill," whose day job was as an antitrust and intellectual property attorney out of San Juan, Puerto Rico, Llorens-Sar actually believed that Obama represented the best candidate for the Democrats to win the general election in November, mostly because of how the press would treat Obama as opposed to how it would treat Clinton. Yet he was relentless in his criticism of the blogosphere during the primary season for what he saw as its mindless harassment of Clinton.

Llorens-Sar didn't think Clinton was above reproach. He belittled her

2002 vote to authorize the Bush administration to wage war with Iraq, which he saw as inexcusable. He disliked her political timidity and her decision to pick the entrenched corporate Beltway insider Mark Penn to help run her campaign. But that was on substance. The rest of the blogosphere, he believed, seemed fixated on Clinton's tactics, personality, and alleged motivations.

In other words, the blogosphere became fixated on precisely the distractions it used to criticize the mainstream media for fixating on. From Llorens-Sars's perspective, progressive bloggers who once saw their mission as countering the Beltway media's bias against prominent Democrats were now cheering on the Clinton attackers and even amplifying the mainstream media jabs. "The progressive blogosphere is dead," he taunted during the primaries. "Long live the 'progressive' blogosphere!"

The Clinton blogger known as eriposte wrestled with the same realization during the spring of 2008 and began to wonder whether he wanted to continue as an active member of the liberal blogosphere, the online community to which he had devoted untold volunteer hours in recent years. Of course, eriposte wanted a Democrat to win in November. He had no interest in the splintered PUMA movement, Party Unity My Ass, made up of Clinton online supporters who vowed to not support Obama in the general election. His bigger concern was being part of a movement that had behaved the way it had against a leading Democratic nominee. From eriposte's perspective, the netroots had smeared the Clintons with casual character assassination. "What I am very concerned about is the movement and the people. Can I respect and work with the people who are part of this movement?" he asked during the primaries. "The question is, are there enough people who will step in to rescue the movement from itself?"

He knew that Clinton was never going to be warmly embraced online, but eriposte was shocked by the netroots' treatment of her in early 2008. Blogging during the campaign at Steve Soto's site, the LeftCoaster, eriposte eventually resorted to sarcastic headlines to mock what he saw as the all-consuming anti-Clinton blogosphere: "Hillary Destroys All That Is Decent and Pure, Yet Again!"

The larger blogosphere's turning on Clinton didn't occur in a vacuum. It simply mirrored the wider collective rejection that took place among many progressives and Democrats nationwide as they embraced Obama. That phenomenon was reflected in the liberal alternative media as well, which became at times ferociously anti-Clinton. Off-air, the Air America host Randi Rhodes labeled Clinton a "big fucking whore," and the liberal fighter and media activist filmmaker Michael Moore condemned Clinton as "disgusting" and a "bigot" during the primaries.

The Huffington Post, the must-read liberal bulletin board, transformed itself into an "Obama jubilee," as one blogger privately put it. Each Obama primary season win was celebrated "as a celestial happening" at the Huffington Post, wrote Howard Kurtz in the *Washington Post*. Asked whether the Clinton Derangement Syndrome tag ever applied to her site, Arianna Huffington dismissed the claim: "That is really stunning to me." She noted that the Huffington Post routinely featured blog posts from prominent Clinton supporters, such as Lanny Davis and Joe Wilson. "I'm very proud of our primary coverage," she told me.

And then there was Keith Olbermann's *Countdown* on MSNBC, which had been must-see TV for liberals throughout Bush's second term, as Olbermann eloquently eviscerated White House mendacity with his periodic "Special Comment" essays. But on March 12, 2008, for the first time, one of Olbermann's "Special Comment" segments unloaded on a Democrat. Making dark allusions to the KKK and David Duke, Olbermann excoriated the Clinton team for waging a racist campaign, insisting that the candidate was, among other sins, "awash" in "filth."

For some longtime Democratic viewers, it was depressing to watch Olbermann, seen as one of their few true allies within the mainstream media, publicly turn on a Democrat like that. It wasn't that they thought Clinton was above reproach. No candidate was. But *David Duke*? "I thought that Special Comment about Hillary was not appropriate," said John Amato, founder of one of the blogosphere's most-linked sites, Crooks and Liars, and a longtime supporter of Olbermann's MSNBC program. (Crooks and Liars remained neutral throughout the Democratic race.) In late May, when Olbermann launched another anti-Clinton "Special Comment," it became the first *Countdown* editorial not featured with a video clip on Crooks and Liars.

CLINTON BLOGGERS WERE not naïve. They understood that their candidate was never going to win favor among the liberal writers and their activist readers. Bloggers were about ousting the Beltway establishment, about surging up from the grassroots and taking the reins of power from Party insiders who had become complacent under layers of consultants and corporate lobbyists. Bloggers were about embracing the new generation of Democratic leaders and shoving aside, if necessary, the old entrenched K Street players who had lost touch with the progressive base. The blogosphere represented crashing the gates, not queuing up behind a safe Beltway insider like Clinton.

So yes, Clinton bloggers knew that their candidate was probably going to get roughed up online. Yet, much to everyone's surprise, for most of the 2007 campaign season the junior senator from New York maintained a respectable amount of support, even some begrudging admiration, online.

Clinton and her campaign also appeared to be more actively engaged with the blogosphere and the online movement. In 2006 the campaign flew in more than a dozen bloggers to New York City for a private two-hour lunch with Bill Clinton. The following year it was candidate Clinton's spokesman, Howard Wolfson, who battled on-air with Bill O'Reilly, defending the netroots when O'Reilly compared bloggers to Nazis and hate merchants. And it was Hillary Clinton who voted against a Republican-backed amendment to publicly condemn the netroots cornerstone organization MoveOn.org in September 2007. On the eve of Gen. David Petraeus's Senate testimony on the U.S. military's surge strategy in Iraq the liberal grassroots group made headlines by buying a full-page ad in the *New York Times* asking, "General Petraeus or General Betray Us?" By contrast, Obama skipped the vote on the blogosphere-bashing amendment.

Bloggers were still angry that Obama had endorsed Sen. Joe Lieberman for reelection in 2006 in the face of a massive progressive movement to elect a far more liberal candidate from Connecticut, Ned Lamont. Obama praised Lieberman at the time as "a man with a good heart, with a keen intellect, who cares about the working families of America." Lieberman would repay the Obama favor in 2008 by campaigning at John McCain's side during the general election. Bloggers were appalled in October 2007, when Obama invited a gay-bashing preacher to join his campaign on the road.

Bloggers were frustrated that Obama refused to embrace mandates to ensure universal health care for all, which had long been a progressive policy touchstone. They were bewildered when the Obama campaign released opposition research attacking the progressive stalwart Paul Krugman, the *New York Times* columnist who had been critical of Obama's health care plan. The maneuver was "off the rails," complained the blogger Ezra Klein. They were irked when Obama borrowed GOP talking points and belittled trial lawyers on the primary campaign trail. And they couldn't understand why Obama blamed Democrats for creating an overly partisan atmosphere in Washington during Bush's tenure, or suggested that as president he'd be able to create a new postpartisan era inside the Beltway. That rhetoric represented "the single biggest turnoff of his entire campaign," lamented the OpenLeft blogger Chris Bowers in late 2007.

In early 2008 bloggers still maintained a very public laundry list of their grievances against the cautious candidate from Illinois, whose middle-of-the-road approach Markos at Daily Kos denounced as "the return of Bill Clinton–style triangulating personified." As late as February 2008 the *New Republic* published "Why Liberal Bloggers Don't Love Obama," noting that "many are strikingly ambivalent about his candidacy." But after John Edwards, who had captured lots of online support in 2007 with his populist push, dropped out of the race, the progressive floodgates opened and Clinton got washed away by Obama mania. Following Edwards's withdrawal, Obama's lead over Clinton at the influential Daily Kos straw poll immediately ballooned to 76 percent, 11 percent among Kossacks.

Suddenly all Obama's previous policy sins—attacking Social Security, endorsing Lieberman, praising bipartisanship, and more—were absolved. That left Clinton supporters online confused and befuddled. "The netroots used to be about framing issues and it used to matter how people used words," Todd Beeton complained at the time. "That used to matter to the netroots and I'm really puzzled how he's gotten a pass on that."

It wasn't just the language that bothered Clinton supporters, but the way the Obama campaign seemed to brush off the blogosphere, how outreach to the netroots had been minimal at best—"It sucked," Markos complained—as the campaign embraced a take-it-or-leave-it pitch to bloggers. And how Obama himself had more than once stressed to reporters that he didn't even read the blogs, and that the blogosphere sometimes "misreads the American people." That coolness toward the blogs drove Clinton's online supporters to distraction, not because Obama dissed the netroots or because he refused to kiss the ring, but because he ignored the netroots and was *rewarded* with its loving, enthusiastic embrace. "To his credit, Obama has basically told the netroots, 'I don't care what you say.' He has utterly ignored them," said Llorens-Sar during the bruising primary brawl. "In essence, Obama slaps the netroots in the face and the netroots say, 'Thank you sir, may [we] have another.' That's what's happened."

What also happened, though, was that lots of netroots members began to embrace the idea of Obama as a generational and electoral map game-changer who wouldn't be another twenty-first-century Democrat who scrambled to eke out a win in November, the way John Kerry could have if he had captured Ohio, and Al Gore if all the votes had been counted in Florida. Instead, by expanding the Democratic voting base by bringing in millions more mostly younger voters, as well as attracting independents, Obama would win going away and generate enormous coattails that would create a nearly veto-proof Senate. He would fundamentally change the political landscape and represent the key building block to a permanent Democratic majority.

The allure of Obama's powerful grassroots coalition became impossible for liberals to ignore. They had dreamed for years about swelling Democratic voter ranks and finally pushing past the tight-as-a-tick struggle between red and blue states. Suddenly Obama, especially when he won 12 contests in a row in February, seemed to put that coalition within reach.

•   •   •

PART OF WHAT held the liberal blogosphere together for years was its determination to scold the press when it treated Democrats unfairly. However, throughout the primaries, and specifically surrounding two high-profile February media events, that adhesive came undone. The first event unfolded on the night of February 7, when the MSNBC reporter David Shuster led an on-air discussion about Chelsea Clinton's role in the campaign, criticizing her for contacting some superdelegates in hopes of convincing them to support her mother's candidacy. To Shuster's eye, Chelsea's lobbying efforts meant that she had been "pimped out in some weird way" by her parents.

The vulgar analogy was immediately condemned as offensive, misogynistic, and in bad taste for a news program anchor. That was Progressive Activism 101: loudly complain when media outlets treat Democrats unfairly. But the conversation took a curious turn when the liberal Huffington Post hosted five prominently featured blog posts in which writers, all of them male, either defended the "pimp" quote ("What exactly was Shuster's offense?") or attacked Clinton for criticizing Shuster. To them, Clinton could not "take a joke," she was being "politically correct," "prissy," and "censorious," and the whole controversy was built around "bullshit outrage" because Shuster was "not attacking Chelsea" with the "pimped out" comment. Besides, the MSNBC episode simply confirmed that the "ruthless" Clintons were "little more than political profiteers who will say or do anything to make points at the polls."

Their defense placed the writers in heated agreement with conservative commentators on Fox News, such as Cal Thomas and the *National Review* editor Rich Lowry, who also claimed that Shuster had been "totally innocent" of any offense and that "of course" the episode was blown out of proportion.

Two weeks later, on February 25, the blogosphere glue came completely undone when the notoriously conservative Drudge Report posted the screaming headline "CLINTON STAFFERS CIRCULATE 'DRESSED' OBAMA." The item, reported by Matt Drudge, read:

With a week to go until the Texas and Ohio primaries, stressed Clinton staffers circulated a photo over the weekend of a "dressed" Barack Obama.

The photo, taken in 2006, shows the Democrat frontrunner fitted as a Somali Elder, during his visit to Wajir, a rural area in northeastern Kenya.

The senator was on a five-country tour of Africa.

"Wouldn't we be seeing this on the cover of every magazine if it were HRC?" questioned one campaign staffer, in an email obtained by the DRUDGE REPORT.

In December, the campaign asked one of its volunteer county coordinators in Iowa to step down after the person forwarded an e-mail falsely stating that Barack Obama is a Muslim.

The Drudge item became the most discussed news story of the campaign that week, with the press devouring the whodunit aspect in search of evidence that Clinton had launched a smear. The Clinton campaign denied it had anything to do with the photo or any anti-Obama email, and no evidence ever surfaced to back up Drudge's claim that the Clinton camp had "circulated" the photo.

Clinton bloggers noted that in the past the netroots used to shrug off Drudge's famously unreliable exclusives, especially when the Republican-friendly writer relied on anonymous insiders who always managed to provide him with too-good-to-be-true quotes that implicated Democrats. Liberal bloggers used to stand back and laugh at the mainstream media and how producers and editors from respected news organizations allowed themselves to be led around by the nose by Drudge, how they allowed Drudge to artificially drive the news cycle with his often unreliable scoops.

Yet in late February 2008 lots of liberal blogs spent most of the day right alongside the Beltway press corps, poring over the photograph and trying to decipher the political significance as well as combing the Clinton campaign's statement in search of possible fingerprints. Rather than asking why anyone would believe Drudge and his flimsy attribution in a gotcha story featuring Democratic candidates, lots of liberal bloggers condemned Clinton, denouncing her "dirty campaign" tactics and chalking up the "atrocity" to "an offense against decency."

On its website, the liberal *Mother Jones* magazine, claiming that the Clinton campaign "went nuclear" by distributing the photo, not only took the Drudge Report at face value, but warned that circulating the Obama photo provided "fodder for the wing-nuts" in the Republican Party. That ignored the fact that conservative wing-nuts had been posting the photo online and discussing it days *before* Drudge ever brought it to most people's attention, as the blogger Dave Johnson pointed out. And at that time, there was no mention of any Clinton operative "leaking" the photograph.

The snapshot was actually first published online in September 2006 by a news site called Geeska Afrika, which reported on the new Illinois senator's trip to the continent. The Obama image then resurfaced during the 2008 campaign season in the February 4 issue of the supermarket tabloid *National Examiner,* which used the photo as part of a scurrilous story headlined "Obama's Shocking Al Qaeda Link." The story contained no reference to the Clinton campaign. The *National Examiner* docs not publish its stories online, but the photo itself got uploaded to the Internet on February 23, to the rabid, Democrat-hating site, FreeRepublic.com, whose "Freeper" members first gained notoriety by spinning all sorts of wild Clinton conspiracies during the 1990s.

Freepers were obsessed with the Obama-in-Africa photo and desperately wanted it to reach a wider audience. Wrote one eager Freeper after seeing the photo, "It needs to get to Drudge." Less than 24 hours later, it did.

For Clinton bloggers, that same depressing Drudge drill got played out in late May, when the site hyped a misleading report from Rupert Murdoch's *New York Post.* The paper mischievously, and incorrectly, reported that Clinton had raised the specter of Obama's assassination as a reason why she remained in the race until the end of the primary season. In truth, Clinton had responded to a question during a meeting with a newspaper editorial board about why she was still in the race by explaining that Democratic primary campaigns running into June were not unusual. She pointed out that her husband's campaign in 1992 went into

June, and she made a passing reference to Robert Kennedy's 1968 White House run, noting that it was in June when he was assassinated while campaigning during the Democratic primary season. Clinton made no reference to Obama. Nonetheless, as hyped by the *Post* and Drudge, the story suggested that Clinton made some sort of link to Obama's possible assassination. This set off a wave of name-calling from corners of the netroots, which decried Clinton's 1968 reference as "disgusting" and "ghoulish" and revealing "an extreme lack of character."

After the hype died down, even some corporate media observers who had been relentlessly critical of Clinton's campaign, including some at the *Washington Post* and *Politico,* concluded that there was no way anyone could have construed her passing RFK comment as suggesting that she was awaiting Obama's assassination. Yet lots of bloggers made that leap. Wrote one online writer for the liberal *American Prospect,* "Hillary Clinton suggests, elliptically at the very least, that she's staying [in] the presidential race in case Barack Obama is assassinated."

"I thought it was character assassination," Digby told me a couple weeks after the RFK controversy had passed. She was exhausted by the toll the campaign had already taken on the blogosphere. She was also aware of the kind of pie fights that would erupt on her site if she posted a condemnation of those who unfairly attacked Clinton for her RFK comments. So Digby, who never endorsed either candidate, simply passed on the story. "I'm a chicken shit," she said with a shake of her head.

There were lots of head-shaking online battles for the Clinton faithful, such as when Markos at Daily Kos claimed that a Clinton campaign TV ad in March had "darkened Obama's skin tone" and "give[n] Obama a wider nose" to make him look "blacker," or perhaps "more Muslim." In other words, to turn off white voters. Clinton aides explained that the entire Obama image from the ad in question, including the backdrop and not just Obama's face, was darkened as part of a "saturation-desaturation" process, a common commercial production procedure, and that there was no ulterior motive behind doing so. The nonpartisan experts at the University of Pennsylvania's FactCheck.org found that the very dark image of Obama in the ad that bloggers posted online to make their case did not match the image of Obama in the ad when it ran on television, where Obama's skin tone appeared considerably lighter.

To the blogger eriposte, the episode represented the campaign season low point for the netroots: "That was an out-and-out smear. I could not believe my eyes when Markos kept repeating the charge. It was just very sad to see. There are lots of valid criticisms one could lodge against Clinton. So why go down this path?"

Markos stood by the story: "I have absolutely no regrets or qualms about what I did." Besides, he told me, it took "a blind partisan to refuse to acknowledge the Clinton campaign's pattern of race-baiting" during the winter months.

That certainly captured one of the maxims that emerged online during the primary season: the Clinton campaign was, at best, trying to inject race into the campaign and, at worst, was running a racist operation. As one prominent liberal blogger put it, Bill and Hillary were "vindictive racist losers."

For years, the liberal blogosphere had pretty much avoided discussions about race and politics, and there had actually been little commentary on the blogs about race during all of 2007 as Obama and Clinton battled for the nomination. Instead, Obama's candidacy was viewed through the traditional netroots prism: Was he the best candidate? What were his policies? What were his realistic chances in the general election? Was his campaign receptive to the progressive movement? How would he govern? Those were the same questions bloggers asked about Clinton and the other Democratic candidates throughout 2007 and into January 2008.

Then suddenly—it seemed like overnight to Alegre—Obama's candidacy came to represent much more. And for weeks and months the blogosphere was brimming with emotional claims that racism fueled the Clinton candidacy. The discussions were supplemented by attempts to dig out the code words being used by Clinton's team to smear Obama. Abruptly, the topic of race, which had been dormant within the blogosphere for years, came to define the community during the primary season. The development caught Alegre completely off guard. For years as a netroots denizen she had assumed that everybody online supported civil rights and affirmative action. She certainly did. She didn't think that believing Clinton was the more qualified candidate made her a racist, yet she saw posts online where people speculated that she was a white supremacist. Todd Beeton also became unnerved by how casually the term "racist" got tossed around during the primaries: "Everybody was calling everyone a racist. To me, that term has a much higher bar."

The issue stormed to the forefront following Obama's victory in South Carolina, when Bill Clinton noted that Jesse Jackson had won that primary during the 1988 Democratic primary season. Clinton was condemned for injecting race into the campaign and for trying to marginalize Obama as a minority candidate.

The Clinton campaign came under fire regularly for controversial comments made by surrogates or high-profile supporters, such as the prominent African American businessman Bob Johnson, who made reference to the early drug use that Obama had admitted in his biography, and the New Hampshire Democratic pol Bill Shaheen, who suggested that Republicans in the general election would "jump on" the issue of Obama's early drug use. Clinton apologized to Obama in person for the Shaheen remark, and Shaheen's unpaid ties to her campaign were cut.

In March former New York congresswoman Geraldine Ferraro told a small-town California newspaper that, given the current media and political culture, Obama was lucky to be black; that explained why he was winning the nomination race. The unlikely comments, found at the end of an article that not many people read when it was first published in a small California newspaper, were revived three days later when Markos at Daily Kos highlighted them on his site. He said a reader had flagged the comments and sent a link to the article. Bloggers quickly condemned the remarks and demanded that the candidate distance herself from Ferraro, a "bona fide racist" and "lunatic," wrote Markos, and complained that the Clinton campaign was promoting "unreconstructed, race blind idiocy."

The suspicion online was that the Ferraro comment and others made by Clinton surrogates were part of a coordinated strategy by the Clinton campaign to portray Obama as shady and urban, to "ghettoize" the candidate. "At a certain point you ask, 'Why is this happening over and over again?'" the blogger, Obama booster, and former community organizer

Martin Longman explained to me during the campaign. "The dog whistles never stopped: 'Oh, he's a Jessie Jackson Democrat.' 'Oh, he can't win because he's black.' That's bullshit. And at a certain point you're like, when Jessie Helms did this stuff I flipped out. So why am I not going to flip out now?"

Clinton bloggers conceded that supporters, with varying degrees of affiliation to the campaign, often made clumsy statements that unnecessarily injected race into the campaign, statements that riled up emotions and sparked condemnation within the netroots. But they claimed that when the roles were reversed and Obama surrogates brought up the issue of race, the blogosphere remained mostly quiet. They pointed to a report in *Time* claiming that Obama's national campaign co-chair, Rep. Jesse Jackson Jr., while lobbying African American superdelegates pledged to Clinton, bluntly asked them, "If it comes down to the last day and you're the only super-delegate, do you want to go down in history as the one to prevent a black from winning the White House?"

Sen. John Kerry, an Obama supporter, was soon seen on video telling the editorial board at the *New Bedford Standard Times* in Massachusetts that Obama could bridge divides that no other candidate could. Asked why, Kerry responded, "Because he's African-American. Because he's a black man." The netroots remained mostly mum about whether Kerry had unnecessarily injected race into the campaign. Clinton bloggers noted the same nonreaction when Bill Perkins, an African American state senator from New York and an Obama supporter, likened Bill Clinton to a slave owner when he told the Huffington Post that Harlem was no longer the former president's "plantation."

Did the Clintons play the race card? "It's *conceivable* that the Clintons had hatched such a grand scheme," wrote Greg Sargent at Talking Points Memo in February. "But the evidence, as it stands now, simply doesn't support such an elaborate and conspiratorial reading."

The *New York Times* columnist Paul Krugman agreed that the Clinton race card meme was more fiction than fact: "This really is Al-Gore-says-he-invented-the-Internet stuff," he wrote on his blog, referring to the infamous, media-fueled myth from the 2000 campaign. "And it's deeply depressing to see so many progressives fall for it." To Krugman, the primary season as a whole represented a grave disappointment for the netroots. "It's been disillusioning," he told me just days after Clinton suspended her campaign in June.

A rock star within the blogosphere, Krugman over the years stood nearly alone among high-profile newspaper columnists who not only got what the blogs were about and shared their progressive passion, but was also an enthusiastic supporter. He not only articulated in print the same liberal policy arguments bloggers were making online, but he name-dropped bloggers in his twice-weekly column and attended their conferences. During the Bush years, when lots of Beltway media elites—even the liberals—did their best to ignore the netroots or downplay its significance, Krugman remained an ardent supporter and a champion of the aggressive progressive voice heard online.

In return, the blogs served as an inspiration for Krugman, especially during the time of the Iraq invasion. Back then, Krugman believed that the only sources of information that bore any relationship to reality were the foreign press, Knight Ridder newspapers (whose prewar reporting was far more skeptical than most), and the liberal blogs. Whenever the columnist gave bookstore readings to promote his new titles, fans would inevitably thank him for his work on the *Times* op-ed page, stressing how his tough, skeptical Bush dispatches helped keep liberal readers sane during the politically dark period of 2003 through 2004.

What helped keep Krugman sane back then? The blogs.

But as the primary unfolded in 2008, Krugman, a Clinton supporter, did not like what he saw online. He objected to what he called the creation of a false portrait of Hillary Clinton. To him, the pile on recalled how the traditional media savaged Al Gore during the 2000 campaign, portraying him as borderline delusional. In 2008 Krugman watched Clinton get tagged by the press as borderline delusional, except this time lots of liberal bloggers joined in as well, he said, twisting stories and quotes to make Clinton look as unappealing as possible.

"It was ugly," said Krugman, who was also startled to see portions of the Obama-loving netroots alter their views on cornerstone issues, such as the need for universal health care. Specifically, the netroots had been stalwart in calling for government mandates to insure universal coverage.

Clinton supported mandates and Obama did not, yet progressives online flocked to Obama despite his position. "Suddenly being opposed to mandates, which for me is basically being opposed to universality, becomes a touchstone of being a real progressive?" Krugman asked incredulously. "Wow. There was a definite [Orwellian] 'We-have-always-been-at-war-with-Eastasia' feel to that."

For the columnist, the Democratic race represented a turning point for the blogs, an end to innocence. Said Krugman, "I don't think people like myself are ever going to look at Daily Kos the same way."

nine

"IT WAS LIKE A BIG GIANT ZIT THAT JUST POPPED ALL OVER THE PLACE"

S usie Madrak sat perched on a bar stool at Lucy's Hat Shop, an Old City neighborhood watering hole in downtown Philadelphia. Just four blocks from Independence Hall, where the Continental Congress met to map out the new nation's future centuries ago, Lucy's hosted its own meeting of the minds on the last Friday night in March, except this one had an open bar.

The booze flowed in honor of EschaCon08. Named after the Philadelphia-based blogger Duncan Black's hugely popular site, Eschaton, the semiannual weekend-long event organized by readers featured panel discussions, meals, and schmoozing that allowed some of Black's loyal readers and commenters to fortify friendships beyond pithy online quips and to commiserate in person about the Bush years. In late March 2008, a lot of attention was also turned toward the unfolding presidential campaign and the increasingly bitter battle between Barack Obama and Hillary Clinton.

Madrak, a pioneering lefty Philadelphia blogger who had been helping to steer the online conversation for years, had been invited to moderate an EschaCon08 panel on media bias, a natural forum for a blogosphere preoccupied with policing the mainstream press. But the night before the panel at Lucy's, with the back room filled with mostly middle-aged

Eschaton readers—or DFHs, Dirty Fucking Hippies, as they jokingly referred to themselves, since that's how the press usually portrayed antiwar liberals—Madrak wanted to talk about the bias she saw spreading across the blogosphere: the sexist, condescending attacks against Hillary Clinton. Madrak seethed at how Clinton got portrayed as an egocentric ballbuster, the way she got attacked for not stepping aside quickly enough to make room for Obama's historic run, and how she was under siege not only by mainstream media pundits, but by liberal bloggers as well.

"It's disgusting and repellent," Madrak announced at the outset of a 30-minute internal takedown heard just above the din of the bar's jukebox. "It's a real sustained problem that's out of control. I think there are an awful lot of Democratic women that are very, very angry with the netroots right now."

Madrak didn't consider herself a feminist writer and she certainly hadn't made a habit over the years of playing the victim. She preferred playing offense, not defense. Nor was she accustomed to spraying friendly fire across the blogosphere landscape. She had been a proud community member since 2002, when she launched her blog, Suburban Guerrilla, as a way to voice opposition to the looming war with Iraq. The blogosphere was where she had spent hundreds (thousands?) of hours over the years and where she had found a political home. Atop Suburban Guerrilla's homepage she had posted the motto "Keeping a jaundiced eye on the corporate media." But these days Madrak's jaundiced eye was trained less on the corporate press than on the blogosphere. And she didn't like what she saw. She barely recognized the netroots movement she had proudly championed.

"The one thing I have learned from this is that sexism is so much more socially acceptable than I dreamed it was," Madrak announced at Lucy's. "It's been really vile."

Reading the blogosphere, Madrak was upset by the way Clinton's "manliness" was dissected and mocked by progressives, the way Clinton supporters were dismissed as "Hillary's Harpies" and the candidate was decried in pejorative terms as "slutty," an "ugly witch," a "Cruella de Ville," a "fat ass," a "bitch" with "legs-wide-open amorality," the way Clinton was depicted as "hysterical," a "piranha in a pantsuit," and consumed by "her mad pursuit of power." She was "Edith Bunker on helium," whose facial expression revealed "barely restrained humiliated fury." She was "irrational" and prone to "temper tantrums." She was "childish and destructive" and "the female equivalent of [Jack] Nicholson's Joker in Tim Burton's *Batman*. Minus the make-up job." Hillary Clinton was "the Psycho Ex-Girlfriend of the Democratic Party," and worse, "the Joan of Arc of the dry pussy demographic."

And all of that appeared in the *liberal* blogosphere.

"The sexism is unbelievable," Madrak said. "I knew a lot of the male bloggers and male blog readers had some issues with this stuff. But I never knew that they would let it out with such force and such vehemence. It was like a big giant zit that just popped all over the place. And I don't think that they understand how really fucking personally women are taking this."

Unlike Alegre, the Clinton fanatic who called for the writers' strike at Daily Kos, Madrak hadn't even identified herself as a Clinton partisan. She had backed John Edwards's run through early 2008. She didn't really see that much difference between Obama and Clinton policywise and thought the runaway passion displayed by loyalists for both candidates was a waste. The only goal that mattered to her was keeping John McCain and the Republican Party out of the White House. Whether Obama or Clinton denied McCain the post didn't really matter.

But Madrak became protective of Clinton when she started to see "the massive amounts of bile that was being spewed on her from the blogosphere." She couldn't understand why the campaign of a centrist, slightly left-leaning candidate like Clinton tapped into such raw vitriol among progressives. She'd been watching campaigns all her life and she saw nothing extraordinary in terms of the tone or content of the Clinton candidacy. It certainly wasn't some kind of brawling attack machine. So why the exceptional and deeply angry response to it online?

The argument Madrak and others, including more overtly partisan, pro-Clinton bloggers such as Taylor Marsh, Riverdaughter, and Anglachel, made in the spring of 2008 wasn't that whoever failed to support Clinton was sexist, or that being a woman meant you automatically had to support Clinton so that she could make history in the White House.

Instead, the indictment regarding sexism online was threefold. First, lots of progressives, including leaders in the Democratic Party, turned a blind eye to the misogynistic language commonly used to demean Clinton in the traditional media. Second, that kind of language quickly flooded progressive websites in the comment sections and among the daily diaries and did not get policed by progressive bloggers. Third, that kind of language, albeit somewhat watered down, eventually found its way into front-page netroots posts, signaling that it was okay to frame Clinton in a dehumanizing way.

The first task, calling out the mainstream media's sexist broadsides, should have been like counting sunspots at a Florida retirement home; they were everywhere. The sexism became "self-evident," wrote *Salon*'s editor in chief, Joan Walsh, who was dumbstruck that many of her liberal readers denied that the attacks were taking place, and even more stunned when they defended Air America's Randi Rhodes after she called Clinton "a big fucking whore" during an off-air appearance. It was "self-evident" in the way the columnist Mike Barnicle on MSNBC said Clinton looked like "everyone's first wife waiting outside probate court." The way Fox News's Bill Kristol said that among the only people supporting Hillary Clinton were white women, and "white women are a problem, we all live with that." The way CNN's Jack Cafferty likened Clinton to "a scolding mother talking down to a child." The way NPR's Ken Rudin compared Clinton to the obsessive, psychotic Glenn Close character from the movie *Fatal Attraction.* The way Neil Cavuto of Fox News suggested that Clinton was "trying to run away from this tough, bitchy image" and that she reminded male voters of "their nagging wives." The way MSNBC's Tucker Carlson said, "When [Clinton] comes on television, I involuntarily cross my legs." The way the *New York Times* published a news article dissecting Clinton's "cackle" laugh. The way Christopher Hitchens on CNBC described Clinton as "alternately soppy and bitchy." (Host Tim Russert thanked Hitchens for his "intelligence" during that appearance.)

It's true that the blogosphere rallied to Clinton's side and pushed back with great force with a blogswarm when Chris Matthews, on the day after her New Hampshire win, announced that the only reason she became a senator from New York and a presidential front-runner was that her hus-

band cheated on her and New York voters took collective pity on her marital plight. But that was in January. By March and April, with so many
bloggers backing Obama, there were very few examples of the netroots
collectively calling out sexist attacks, in part because some bloggers were
too busy launching their own. It drove Susie Madrak to distraction.

PHILLY-BORN AND -RAISED, Madrak is proud of her roots and her
thick résumé of life experiences, not to mention the bullshit detector she
refined during her years as a journalist. "I'm working class," she announced. The fourth of five kids in an Irish German Polish Catholic family in southwest Philadelphia, she likes to say that when you're from Philly
and somebody else from Philly asks you where you went to school, you tell
them the name of your elementary school (Most Blessed Sacrament), not
college alma mater, because in Philly it's all about the local tribes. Madrak
understands the Philly tribes, and the tribes of working-class voters who
make up the Democratic base.

For Madrak, a lot of that online snark she saw came from the grad
school crowd. That's how the 53-year-old Madrak referred to the young
crop of mostly white, male, twenty- and thirtysomething netroots players
who seemed to be itching to get Clinton out of the race. She had no pa-
tience for the grad school set; she considered them clever young men with
prodigious debating skills but little life experience and clearly uncomfortable with middle-aged women in positions of power.

"I'm older than they are," said Madrak, peering over the eyeglasses that
slid down her nose. "I've also had a hell of a lot more life experience than
they have. Going and getting a degree in something does not necessarily
translate into judgment. I was a journalist for twenty years. I worked off
and on as a political consultant for the last three years. I worked on a fifteen million dollar Philadelphia mayor's race with the same people who
are doing the Obama campaign. I've been working in campaigns since I
was fifteen years old. I know a little something about practical politics
and feel like I can offer some rather unique insight. And to have these
young kids, who have no real life experience, lecturing people my age . . .
I try to be polite to them, but it's just ludicrous."

Madrak didn't go to college, even though at age 15 she wrote term papers for students at the nearby University of Pennsylvania, earning them A's. When she was 18 she snuck in and took the graduate school admission exam for psychology and history for somebody else. "I'm not stupid," said Madrak. "I just don't have a formal education."

She stumbled into journalism in 1980, back when newsrooms still had a working-class entryway. She covered local politicians from the notoriously corrupt Delaware County. She wanted to stay local and cover county politics rather than graduate to a bigger newspaper in some other city, so she hopped around from paper to paper in the greater Philadelphia area. She got fired from her final newspaper job because, though she had a management position, she supported reporters' efforts to maintain the newspaper's union.

In recent years she had worked on and off as a political consultant. She served as press secretary for one of the Philadelphia mayoral candidates in 2007. In early 2008 she was doing sales work for a management consultant firm; she worked on the phone all day and usually tried to rest her voice at night. But the critique of the blogosphere that she unfurled at Lucy's was just getting started.

She doesn't like bullies, and that's what fueled her support for Clinton. She thought the attacks online against Clinton were cowardly because they were done in packs by male bloggers (and their readers), who formed a reinforcing circle. She thought the venom suggested that more than a few of the netroots members had mother issues, that they looked at Clinton, saw somebody their mother's age, and got very angry at the idea of her running for president. Clinton seemed to tap into something, something that Madrak thought said more about the bloggers than it did about the candidate.

"I really don't know what that is, but there is a depth of anger and hatred that seems really personal and far beyond a political candidate that you don't like," she said, surveying the back bar at Lucy's. "There is a lot of psychodrama being played out online. These are guys who clearly have a problem with women. I don't pretend to know how to identify it, but clearly there's a problem.

"People keep saying to me, 'I've seen just as bad from the Hillary people.' And I keep saying, 'Show me. Show me where there are people saying those sorts of things, where people are demeaning an entire group of people as less than human.' There is some very weird shit going on with this. And frankly I think the whole damn bunch of them ought to be in therapy. But that's just me."

Looking around the room at Lucy's, Madrak said she used to care about what the male bloggers thought; she thought a lot of them were smart people and took things seriously. Not so much anymore. "At this point I see so much of this is driven by psychological compulsion that I can barely be civil with them."

She pushed her glasses back up her nose and let out a sigh. "What can I tell you? It's fucked up."

ACROSS THE ROOM at Lucy's, Jane Hamsher and the blogger known as Digby, two influential netroots commentators, commiserated over the same topic. Like Madrak, Hamsher picked up on a strong anti-Hillary vibe throughout the campaign and attributed it to the dominant demographic of blogosphere readers: white men in their thirties and forties who didn't like Hillary. With so many of them tapping away online, their viewpoint was bound to dominate.

She also noticed the double standard that Clinton had to deal with online, such as the constant criticism of her vote in 2002 to grant President Bush authority to wage war with Iraq and her subsequent refusal to label that vote a mistake. Hamsher thought it odd that four years earlier Sen. John Kerry ran for president as the Democratic nominee after having cast the same vote to authorize the war and it didn't seem to be a major issue online. It certainly was not portrayed as a deal breaker. (Kerry's running mate, John Edwards, also voted for the war. He apologized for it in 2007.) Yet in 2008, Clinton's vote became the central liberal attack against her candidacy. Hamsher suspected that the vote clung to Clinton, in part, because she's a woman.

"John Kerry voted for the war, and so did John Edwards. And so there's this sort of hairsplitting that goes on. 'Well, Edwards apologized for his war vote, and Clinton only regrets the vote, so that makes him a progressive and her not.' The logic behind that never made any sense to me. Why would one provoke irrational hatred of Clinton and the other one was like, 'Well, that's okay'?"

Unlike Madrak, Hamsher didn't blame progressive male bloggers and certainly didn't think they nourished a sexist environment during the campaign. "I'm a big defender of the men in the progressive blogosphere for being big supporters of women," she told me. "There is a lot of good-will, and I don't think calling people out—who really are supportive of women—for being sexist is either fair or a good idea. I think there might be a lack of sensitivity to sexist coverage. I look at those things and [Madrak] looks at those things and we see something really fast because we're women. I think if you're a man you just don't see it that fast. I don't think that's sexism. I just think it's a different perspective."

For Digby, the unfolding primary season had been particularly sobering. The battle of the sexes struck a personal chord for her because for years her pseudonym, her brawling writing style, and the fact that she divulged no personal or biographical information on her blog, led most readers to conclude that there was a man behind that one-word moniker. "When people assumed I was a man they reacted to me a certain way. The minute it became known that I was actually a middle-aged woman—Oh God, the worst of all possibilities!—people reacted to me differently," she explained. "I'm not an idiot. I can tell."

A persuasive media critic, Digby wrote extensively on what she saw as the unfair and at times openly sexist treatment that Clinton received from the press. Lots of readers then assumed she backed Clinton (she did not; she supported both candidates equally in their campaign to replace a Republican in the White House), and they attacked her for it. "I spent years in the blogosphere having most people think of me as a man and I never encountered this before. I'm paying now for being a woman in a way that I never did before. The contrast is startling," she said during the primary season. "It's the way people talk to me online, the assumptions that are being made about me. The response is very different, and it's quite astonishing. There's a lot more rudeness that I'm not used to. I have seen a side of this that was unexpected and kind of sobering. A lot of the stuff that's being said about Clinton, and said about me, in my comment section and elsewhere, is really pretty low and pretty vile."

Like Hamsher, though, Digby didn't see proof of a deliberate attempt within the blogosphere to slight women. Digby chalked up the behavior to Obama's overeager supporters and saw it as an unconscious outpouring rather than a purposeful attempt to snub women.

As for the prominent male bloggers who backed Obama, the accusations of sexism within the blogosphere, or that the netroots looked the other way when the press engaged in it, created all sorts of tension. "I didn't allow anybody on my site to call Clinton a bitch," said Martin Longman, who hosted the pro-Obama site Booman Tribune. "If I saw it—and it was rare—I shut it down immediately. I didn't allow any misogynistic commentary whatsoever." As for calling out sexist attacks lobbed by the mainstream media, Longman conceded that during the campaign he was so "pissed off" at how Clinton ran, and especially the often race-based attacks she and her surrogates made against Obama, that he lowered his outrage threshold in terms of defending Clinton against sexist broadsides.

At Daily Kos, Markos noted that bloggers had jumped on Chris Matthews for his pattern of misogynistic comments, ridiculed the press when it mocked Clinton for tearing up on the campaign trail in New Hampshire, and mostly refused to defend the Obama campaign adviser Samantha Powers, who made headlines when she called Clinton a monster. "So the overt stuff has been dealt with. Beyond that, what exactly is the issue?" he asked in an email response to my query during the primaries. "Commenters calling her a 'bitch' or a 'cunt'? They get troll rated and banned on dKos. Aside from that, what else is there?"

John Aravosis didn't appreciate getting tagged as a misogynist by Clinton supporters for the blog posts at his site, AmericaBlog, which became something of an anti-Clinton hotbed during the primary contests. "The fact is her supporters throw around the misogyny card a lot more than Obama supporters throw out the race card," he told me. "There are a lot of people who don't hate Hillary, who have loved her for 17 years and who have been turned off because they actually see a few things that worry them about her as a candidate. And they're treated as the enemy because obviously they would never have a concern about Hillary unless they were a right-wing woman hater. The best way to turn someone into a Hillary-hater is to treat them as one. You walk around calling people misogynists, and you know what? They end up hating you. They're not hating you because you're a woman. They're hating you because they think you're an idiot."

The OpenLeft blogger Chris Bowers acknowledged that sexist Clinton attacks did appear, but that critics needed to put the outbursts in context. They had to take into account just how vast and unwieldy the blogosphere is, and how relatively few bouts of sexist rhetoric were produced during the extended primary season. "There are millions of words written each day, and that sexist Clinton narrative is out there. You're going to see that language, especially if you're looking for it," he said during the primary season. "Is it somehow pervasive throughout the entire blogosphere? I certainly haven't seen that. Is there some sort of consistent use of sexist language among the A-list bloggers? No. There just isn't."

For some, the extended Democratic primary campaign really did dissolve into a clichéd, men-are-from-Mars-women-are-from-Venus type of chronic miscommunication between the two factions. For years the two camps had been tightly aligned; now they watched the same news events unfold and came away with drastically different impressions. Perhaps nothing captured that phenomenon more clearly than the growing urgency within the blogosphere to get Clinton to quit the Democratic race before the primaries were completed.

For many bloggers, including prominent Obama supporters, the issue revolved around mathematics, plain and simple. Neither Obama nor Clinton could win enough pledged delegates from the primary contests to secure the nomination, but the only way Clinton could win was if the remaining superdelegates chose her over Obama, ignoring the will of the primary voters. The bloggers were simply dealing with the facts on the ground: the math said Clinton could not win.

What was the point of prolonging the potentially damaging nomination campaign if Clinton had no chance? Democrats needed to rally around their nominee and train their collective fire at Republicans. Clinton had lost, and Democrats did not have the luxury of allowing her to continue her campaign just to make herself or her supporters feel better. Sure, bloggers might have teed off on Clinton and tossed in a few insults in the process of making their case for her much needed exit, but they were genuinely pissed at her. Besides, since when did passionate bloggers promise to always play nice?

"It is over," wrote John Sudbay at AmericaBlog in April. "Seriously, enough with the endless Clinton campaign drama." That sentiment was expressed dozens, if not hundreds of times during March, April, and May on many liberal blogs, and certainly within their comment sections. It was equally widespread within the mainstream media. The race was over and Clinton needed to quit. As early as March, Daily Kos urged the remaining superdelegates to crown Obama the winner and end the primary season.

For some women (and men) online, that argument was not so pragmatic. Nor did they view it simply as being a mathematical problem that had already been solved. Instead, they heard, "Get out of the way, lady." They even had a shorthand for the message between the lines that they heard being conveyed week after week as bloggers urged Clinton to go away: WWTSBQ!? Why won't the stupid bitch quit!?

Looking back at recent history they couldn't find much evidence of that sort of deathwatch in response to second-place finishes in the Democratic campaigns of Jerry Brown, Jesse Jackson, Gary Hart, and Ted Kennedy. Those men campaigned through all the primary contests, as Clinton did. All of them, for largely symbolic reasons, then took their futile campaign fights all the way to their party's nominating convention, which Clinton did not. But they never got tagged as power-hungry narcissists, or were told to go home.

In the past there had always been an assumption that candidates had earned the right to decide when they should quit. Prior to 2008 the question of when candidates should drop out had always been dictated by how much money the campaign still had in the bank, how many votes the candidate was still earning, and what very senior members of the candidate's own party were advising. Now the middle-aged woman had to prematurely drop out and make way for the younger, more charismatic man?

That prompted dark memories for some professional working women who recognized uncomfortable similarities between the campaign trail and the real world and the still pervasive model of female self-sacrifice.

"For her core constituency of women—I suppose it's over-forty-five women like me, who came up in the business world at a time when breaking through the glass ceiling was tough—this is a very familiar kind of mantra," said Digby. "We've heard this from others, which is that you work hard and get to a certain point and you consider yourself to be taken seriously on a certain level. And then in comes the new guy and you're asked to step aside for the good of the company. They say, 'We need to groom new people. We'll give you a really nice office and a new title. And it's not that we don't appreciate all your hard work, but this is really for the good of the company. It's best for everybody.' The appeal is made along the lines of 'The family needs you to do this.'"

OUT IN PORTAGE, Indiana, on the south shore of Lake Michigan and in the shadow of the former steel mecca of Gary, Melissa McEwan certainly thought there were ways to argue that Clinton should drop out of the race and not do it in a misogynistic or condescending manner. She just didn't find many examples of that online, which added to her deep sense of frustration and disappointment as she watched the campaign unfold.

For McEwan, age 33, feminism is an integral part of being a progressive. It isn't enough to hate Bush or to oppose the Iraq war or be appalled by the government's torture policy. If you aren't a feminist you aren't a progressive; you are a "fauxgressive," as McEwan calls it. And fauxgressives thought it was okay to portray Clinton in broad stereotypes, as a calculating ballbuster who liked to play the gender card while feigning victimhood.

McEwan expected that kind of stuff from the right wing. Rush Limbaugh and friends had been making those denigrating claims about Democratic women for years. She even expected it from the corporate press, which is why she started her ongoing blog series, Hillary Sexism Watch, which had more than 70 separate entries posted by April 1, 2008. Item

No. 20: The *Washington Post* writer Joel Achenbach, in a January 8, 2008, column predicting Clinton's loss in the New Hampshire primary, wrote that the candidate needed "a radio-controlled shock collar so that aides can zap her when she starts to get screechy," i.e., a *dog collar.*

But when McEwan detected that sexist language within the liberal blogosphere, she felt sick to her stomach. "It's depressing, it really is. It's definitely been the most upsetting trend that I've ever seen online," she said on the eve of the Pennsylvania primary. "And if you complain, the reaction is, 'Oh, you're being hypersensitive and hysterical.'"

The weird part? Like Susie Madrak, Jane Hamsher, and Digby, McEwan wasn't even a Clinton partisan. She'd been a John Edwards booster for most of the campaign. In fact, McEwan worked on the Edwards campaign in 2007 as the netroots coordinator to help with its Internet outreach program. As for Clinton versus Obama, either one was better than McCain. But as Clinton got hit with more and more sexist put-downs, McEwan's guard went up.

Hoosier feminists might be a rare breed, but McEwan became one. Raised in the Indiana blue-collar town of Portage by her stay-at-home mom and history-teaching dad, McEwan from a very early age was the kid asking uncomfortable questions and announcing that the answers were wholly insufficient. For instance, why could women at her Lutheran church teach her Sunday school classes but not become ordained as ministers? That didn't make any sense to her.

She'd been interested in politics from a young age. She remembered sitting in a circle in elementary school at the beginning of the year and kids taking turns telling what their dad did for a living. The most frequent response was "My dad is laid off." McEwan asked her parents what that meant and they gave her an early primer in Reaganomics. With insight into how government and the choices made by politicians can affect everyday people in Portage, McEwan got hooked. "Growing up in Laid Offville was what really got me interested," she told me.

As an impressionable teenager, McEwan fell in love with Al Gore, the dashing young senator from Tennessee who made her wonky heart flutter with his earnest talk (even back then) of preserving the environment. He first caught the junior high schooler's eye during the 1988 campaign. She saw him pontificate on PBS and thought Al Gore was a dreamboat, very eco and very nerdy. Paying especially close attention to the unfolding 1992 race because it was the first in which she'd be able to vote, McEwan remembered pressing her father about whether he thought Bill Clinton would pick Gore as his running mate. Wouldn't those southern Democrats make a great team?

And then the bus tour: Bill, Hillary, Tipper, and Al. It was Democratic Party magic for McEwan, who escaped to Chicago and studied sociology and anthropology at Loyola University, focusing her studies on the political marginalization of gender-based groups: women, women of color, gays, and lesbians. After graduating in 1996, she worked for eight years in marketing and branding for an architectural firm as well as an Internet marketing company.

She paid attention to politics off and on, watching the Clinton impeachment drama unfold. But for McEwan, the Clinton years were all about waiting for the Gore coronation, which would allow Mr. Green to unleash America's true greatness. The 2000 Florida recount took her breath away and she remained inconsolable for weeks. She started blogging in October 2004, for the same reasons every other progressive did: she hated what George Bush was doing to the country and his reelection campaign drove her mad. She didn't plan on creating a feminist blog because there were lots of sites already covering that terrain very well. But she quickly realized she couldn't write about politics and not write about feminism and sexism.

The blog, which grew into a community site featuring more than 20 regular contributors, was dubbed Shakesville, and McEwan adopted the online name Shakespeare's Sister. She borrowed the name from an '80s alt rock song by The Smiths, as well as from Virginia Woolf's classic essay, "A Room of One's Own," in which the writer pondered what life would have been like if William Shakespeare had had a younger, wonderfully gifted wordsmith sister, the closed doors and heartbreak she would have faced at the turn of seventeenth century in England as a woman trying to find an artistic outlet.

McEwan's sharp analysis and her fearless, shit-kicking writing style won her a following online almost immediately. (In person she's quick with a giggle and not as rough-and-tumble as her online persona.) In 2005 her blog was voted one of the best within the liberal blogosphere.

That was the good news in 2005. The bad news was that she got downsized at work, so it was back to Portage. With the support of her progressive husband, who subsidized the blogging effort ("We're constantly broke"), McEwan turned Shakespeare's Sister into her full-time nonpaying job. Following her exit from the Edwards campaign in 2007, she watched the Obama-Clinton battle unfold with equal, albeit guarded, enthusiasm for both candidates. She just wanted a Democrat to win in November.

But as the winter weeks and months passed, McEwan became increasingly unnerved by what she saw of the sexist coverage of Clinton, and how the progressive blogosphere, having embraced Obama, let so much of it pass without comment. She sensed a decision had been made that because Clinton was not perceived as being progressive—in fact, because she had been tagged as the enemy—it was all right for the netroots to look away. Because bloggers didn't want Clinton to win, they'd given the traditional media a green light to demean the candidate.

Worse was the fact that over time, she couldn't help shake the feeling that portions of the netroots were actually pushing the sexist stuff. In April McEwan read a netroots headline that used the word "geld" in describing Clinton's decision to relieve her chief campaign strategist, Mark Penn: "Full Firing? Or Just Gelded?" McEwan was stunned. Making reference to *castration* right in the headline of a Hillary Clinton campaign article? Even more distressing was the fact that the headline appeared on the front page of Talking Points Memo, a longtime must-read blog for McEwan and one of the sites that inspired her to start blogging in 2004.

Didn't progressives realize, McEwan wondered, that by adopting that kind of demeaning language they were helping to perpetrate attacks on all women politicians and future women leaders? One of the contributors at Feministe.com, known as Zuzu, spelled it out in a widely discussed April essay titled "Why Calling Out Misogyny Matters":

This shit hurts women. Women like me. Women like many of you. Women like your daughters, your sisters, your mothers, your friends, your spouses, your SOs. If it's okay to dehumanize a US Senator and presidential candidate as "that thing," then we now have an environment in which it's okay to dehumanize, demean and diminish ordinary women because they're women.

A former newspaper reporter, and now a litigator based in New York City, Zuzu represented yet another dismayed Edwards supporter turned off by the tone and tenor of the Democratic campaign and the nasty online turn it took into sexist territory. "This certainly showed that, despite all the back-patting that everybody had done about how much more sane and rational they were than conservative bloggers, if you give somebody a reason to hate and a way to express their hatred, they're going to go ahead and do it," she told me. "The netroots is obviously not as mature, not as elevated, as people had hoped."

ten

"THE MOST UNLIKELY INSTRUMENT OF CHANGE"

The vast expanse of South Dakota's prairie topography, coupled with the state's thinning population, ordinarily created a driver's paradise for motoring enthusiasts like Mayhill Fowler, for the simple reason that so few cars out on the wide-open South Dakota highways and even fewer patrolmen watching over them meant the speed limit was often whatever drivers wanted it to be.

On this day in early June, as she drove down to the state's capital from the small farming town of Webster, tucked up in the northeast corner of the state where Routes 12 and 25 intersect, Fowler wanted the speed limit to be somewhere around 90 mph. So she couldn't believe her bad luck when she got stuck behind a sheriff's patrol car. Worse, the patrol car was going to the same destination as Fowler: Sioux Falls.

What were the odds?

For more than on hour out on I-29 in a Mazda Six, her rental car of choice because it came equipped with free GPS, a must for a road warrior like herself, Fowler held steady at the posted speed limit of 75. But she wasn't the only one who wished she could hit the gas. Her editors at the Huffington Post were frantically emailing her and calling her cell phone, beseeching her to upload the audiotape that she had captured just hours earlier of Bill Clinton at a South Dakota campaign event, where he uncorked a name-calling critique of a *Vanity Fair* reporter who had just written a lengthy hit piece on the former president.

The Huffington Post had already posted an article based on Fowler's rope line encounter with Clinton, where he called *Vanity Fair*'s Todd Purdum "sleazy," "dishonest," "slimy," and a "scumbag." Now editors wanted the audio. So did producers for Anderson Cooper and Keith Olbermann, who were clamoring for a piece of the breaking story.

For months the press had been devouring Clinton-blows-his-top stories from the campaign trail, ridiculing the former president for his short temper and lack of self-control. Now, on essentially Clinton's final day of campaigning for his wife, he had ended his tour with an invective-laced exclamation point.

Jackpot.

The story was Fowler's second big scoop of the campaign, which put her two ahead of virtually every other professional reporter on the presidential beat, where campaign events were so tightly stage-managed that breaking news was almost impossible to uncover.

Just eight weeks earlier though, in April, Fowler had fundamentally changed the tilt of the Democratic campaign when she reported that Barack Obama, while addressing supporters at a private donor event in San Francisco, claimed that bitter small-town voters often clung to guns and religion to cope with economic disappointment and xenophobic fears.

Fowler's scoop set off political shock waves and unleashed raw emotions in a race already drowning in invective. Fowler herself became a target. Angry Daily Kos readers branded her a saboteur and a few death threats landed in her email in-box. Her scoop was so big, it so defined the 2008 election season, that the Newseum, the sprawling journalism museum in Washington, asked her to donate the $30 tape recorder she used to log Obama's bitter comments. "I think they're hard up for stuff," she laughed.

All from an amateur citizen journalist with no reporting background.

Technically, Fowler did not blog. She was much more like a campaign correspondent whose work was showcased regularly at the Huffington Post. But if it hadn't been for the Internet, and if it hadn't been for the netroots and all the doors that were being thrown open online, Fowler would still be home trying to get one of her novels published. Instead, she had a front-row seat to the presidential campaign and was making the pros look bad with her string of big stories.

Her ticket got punched by Off the Bus, a citizen journalism initiative launched by the journalism professor Jay Rosen and the progressive media mogul Arianna Huffington. It was designed to unleash everyday Americans as reporters on the campaign trail and forbid them from wallowing in yet more media-saturated horse race coverage.

When Rosen and Huffington conceived their plan in March 2007, they envisioned perhaps a young, industrious grad student breaking out as Off the Bus's star reporter and helping to rewrite campaign journalism rules for the Internet age, somebody who would tap into the potential of the netroots and embrace all the new technological tools, who would harness the viral power of YouTube videos and the instant messaging of Twitter and turn social network sites like Facebook and MySpace into new media platforms.

Instead, Off the Bus's breakout star was Fowler, an overeducated 61-year-old mother of two with frosted gray hair from the suburbs of Oakland, who preferred not to drive at night (too stressful) and who, prior to 2007, didn't even read blogs.

Nobody could have predicted it, but it was Fowler who scrambled all the rules. "I'm the least likely instrument of change you could ever want to meet," she told me while unfurling an ear-to-ear grin.

THREE WEEKS AFTER Fowler's rope-line encounter with Bill Clinton we were sitting on a sun-drenched terrace high above Manhattan at the Yale Club. Overlooking Vanderbilt Avenue and across the street from Grand Central Station, Cornelius Vanderbilt's glorious monument to consolidation, transportation, and capitalism, the private Yale Club provided a hushed oasis for New Haven alumni in town for business or to meet old friends.

Sitting in the shade provided by the striped awning, Fowler, in town to take part in a panel discussion about technology and politics, appeared utterly at ease within the elite circles of the Yale Club. Bookish by nature,

Fowler is earnest and intellectual and speaks in fully formed paragraphs, page after page of them. She's also folksy and good-natured. "Oh gosh, yes" was how she phrased responses that required emphasis. Modest about her unlikely campaign notoriety, Fowler nonetheless was clearly delighted by the development. As she told me her campaign trail adventures, she was not always able to hide the twinkle in her eye behind large brown sunglasses that covered half her face.

Born with the southern gift of gab, Fowler loves to engage people, particularly strangers, which made her a natural on the campaign trail. Ostensibly covering the campaign and the candidates, what Fowler really did was cover the people: the locals, the voters, the citizens who turned out for the hundreds of events that she attended as a citizen journalist.

After all, that's what it meant to get off the bus, to break free from the mainstream media bubble that had been created for the traveling campaign press corps. It was a bubble that created a nearly permanent barrier between the press and the voters. And it was a barrier that many campaign journalists seemed to appreciate and even encourage. "I'll watch reporters sort of sigh and pick up a pencil and tablet and go out into the crowd to talk to one or two people," Fowler recalled. "And they're not comfortable out there. I don't know why."

Covering the 2008 campaign, where the media's all-consuming narrative revolved around tactics and process, Fowler's mandate was a radical one. The experience turned ironic when she became famous for a couple of "gotcha" stories from the road: Bittergate and the Clinton eruption. Ironic because Fowler's body of work stood as the antithesis of that kind of quick-strike encounter.

Instead, Fowler brought more of a writer's touch and a novelist's eye to the campaign trail, where most reporters were pressed to produce hourly updates. Even the entrenched Beltway pundits who had more time to write about the campaign seemed determined to drain all the humor and emotion out of the process. Not Fowler: "Pennsylvanians are as friendly as Iowans—and that's a huge compliment. (I love you Texas, but you get up on the wrong side of the bed a lot, or at least you did during the weeks before the primaries.)" During another era her lengthy, impressionistic, and unrushed dispatches from the campaign trail would have been at home in the *New Yorker*.

With her deep southern roots and even deeper affection for conversation, it made sense that Fowler especially enjoyed shadowing Bill Clinton, the gregarious Arkansas native, as he embarked on his tireless stump speech tour of B-list, small-town America in key primary states. Between January and June she attended 24 different Bill Clinton events. She loved the genuine small-town feel of the appearances. She also loved the fact that Clinton was always, always behind schedule, which gave her more time to talk to her fellow Americans, generations of whom showed up to hear him speak.

That kind of gathering of the clans for political events struck a chord with Fowler, whose childhood in Memphis was marked by just such public events. Her grandfather, Watkins Overton, served more years as mayor of Memphis than anyone in that city's history. But her immediate family—she is the oldest of five girls—was not well off. Her father worked as a bookkeeper at a Memphis furniture store and money was often tight. She grew up "poor in a wealthy family," which is a southern thing, she assured me. Yet because of her family's famous heritage and upper-class pedigree, everybody assumed that Fowler lived a charmed life.

That deceiving family history, with its house-of-mirrors optics, helped Fowler on the campaign trail. It taught her to always be attuned to the differences between appearances and what the underlying reality might be.

Fowler came of age in Memphis in the 1950s, a captivating time when she could tune in to blues great B.B. King on the pioneering all-black radio station, WDIA, and see young Elvis Presley driving around town in one of his many freshly minted Cadillac convertibles. Five decades later she still regretted the fact that as a teen she never got up the nerve to hang out at the Malco movie house on South Cooper Street. That's the one Elvis used to rent out at night to entertain his buddies with private parties. Lots of the older girls would try to sneak in, but not Fowler. "I was just too timid," she recalled.

In 1964 she headed east to the prestigious all-girls Vassar College, the year students broke into "unreasoned frenzy" on the night the Beatles debuted on *The Ed Sullivan Show,* according to the campus newspaper's account. Just prior to graduation in 1968, she returned home to Memphis for spring break during the first week in April. She still remembers that Thursday, April 4, when local television bulletins began to flash frantically right around dinner time with the news that Martin Luther King Jr., in town to help rally the city's striking garbage men, had been shot and killed at the Lorraine Motel on Mulberry Street. "It was one of the few times in my life that I saw my mother cry," Fowler recalled. "My mother was not a crier. And she was crying for the city. She knew it was going to be a huge blot on the city."

The city of Memphis, and its state of mind, remained prominent for Fowler's family while she was growing up. Not only was she the granddaughter of Memphis's Mayor Overton, but her great-great-great-great-grandfather, John Overton, had founded the muddy river town at the turn of the nineteenth century. He purchased the land for less than 15 cents an acre, but only after a treaty had been signed with the nearby Chickasaw Indians.

Yet it was precisely because of that heritage that Fowler's mother detested politics and refused to allow any discussion of the topic in her home. She believed that politics had destroyed her family. Fowler, who has done extensive research on her family's Tennessee history, tells the dark Overton tale of how a Memphis political rivalry split up her grandparents and caused her mother to swear off politics forever.

The real political power in Memphis during much of the first half of the twentieth century did not rest in the office of Mayor Overton or any other mayor. It rested in the hands of E. H. Crump, the Memphis boss who for decades ran the city's political machine and wielded power statewide. Mayor Watkins Overton was sometimes ridiculed as being Crump's lackey. Over time, however, Overton began to branch out beyond the confines of the Crump machinery. Crump and Overton had a falling out in 1938 over who would get credit for the deal that brought Memphis Power and Light Company, which had been privately owned since the nineteenth century, under Memphis city governance.

As Fowler told me, "In order to bring my grandfather to heel, Crump hired a man to woo my grandmother and get compromising letters from her. Which he did, and Crump's theory was, 'Well, I can blackmail Mayor Overton with these letters [and quietly end the political feud].'

"Even though they'd known each other for years, Crump did not understand my grandfather at all. The fact was my grandfather did not have that southern sense of honor, because he actually grew up in Wisconsin, which should have been a clue. And number two, my grandfather had a terrible temper. He went home that very day—and my mother and her two brothers and sister talked about it a lot when I was growing up—and he threw my grandmother out of the house. It was a terrible, traumatic scene. And he got custody of the children."

The trauma of the breakup caused Fowler's mother to swear off politics. The topic was not allowed to be discussed as Fowler grew up.

After Vassar, she headed west and earned a master's degree in English literature at the University of California's Berkeley campus. She then spent most of her time raising two daughters with her real estate attorney husband.

During the 1990s Fowler began writing assiduously, honing her craft and trying to get published. She wrote a thriller called *Russia House* that featured Vice President Al Gore as a character.

In 2005 Fowler traveled with her daughter to Turkey. In preparation, she read about Islam. Back home she started a blog and posted her essays about the Middle East and the future of Islam. In one she asked, "Would it be good for Islam to have a realignment like the Protestant Reformation sparked by Martin Luther? Or is that a neo-colonialist imperative?" Her insightful and intelligent writings were of thesis caliber, but hardly anybody read her blog.

Around the same time, Fowler's mother died, and soon Fowler began scratching the long-dormant itch of that previously forbidden topic, politics. Only when she looked back years later did she see the obvious connection between her mother's passing and her own political awakening, her decision to shift her writing passion to the political arena. "I think I never would have done that if she were still alive," said Fowler. "Because to have done it and then to have to deal with her on that subject would have been just too much of a hassle. She would have been ragging on me. Not worth it.

"I'm always telling my sisters that my mother is up in heaven, metaphorically, of course, going 'I told you!' She had a very mordant sensibility. She would be saying, 'Politics is dirty and nasty. What did you think was going to happen? You got yourself in the middle of it, of course people are threatening to kill you. Of course you're getting hate mail. That is what happens.'"

I asked Fowler if she thought her mother was right and if she had any regrets about her late-in-life campaign career, given the amount of personal animus she'd encountered, especially after launching the Bittergate story. She tossed her head and exclaimed, "It's been a ball!"

IT ALL STARTED in the summer of 2007, when Fowler submitted her 500-word Off the Bus application to be a contributor. Fowler had just recently become an Obama believer after a friend sent her a link to a videotaped speech the candidate had made to an evangelical church. His words had moved Fowler to tears. At the time, she had no interest in reading blogs and remained only marginally aware of what the Huffington Post was. But she wanted to write, she wanted to get published, and Off the Bus seemed like an excellent opportunity.

Impressed by Fowler's passion for writing and her enthusiasm for the opportunity, the Off the Bus project director, Amanda Michel, invited Fowler to join the volunteer team. Fowler began her career as an amateur reporter by posting dispatches about the Obama grassroots movement and fund-raising as it evolved around her home, in and around the Oakland and San Francisco area. As she became increasingly intrigued, both with Obama and with journalism, she decided to expand her territory and travel down to southern California and then out to Fresno for day trips to report on the unfolding Obama campaign. By the end of 2007 Fowler was fully committed and spent three weeks camped out in Iowa covering the state's caucus, darting around in her rented car and becoming addicted to the campaign trail.

"It was more fun than my honeymoon!" she announced. Then it was off to Nevada and Texas and Pennsylvania and North Carolina and South Dakota. She handled all the logistics herself—the events, the plane tickets, the car rentals—and she paid for it all out of her own pocket: $50,000 just to cover the primaries. In July she followed Obama all the way to Germany during his overseas trip. She loved being on the road. She loved covering the campaigns and talking to voters. And she got hooked on the adrenaline rush it all created for her.

Then in early April Fowler fundamentally changed the presidential campaign when she attended an Obama fund-raiser in San Francisco. Closed to the press, the meet-and-greet events were a chance for check-writing donors to see the candidate up close and maybe get in a question during the Q&A session.

As a maxed-out donor who had given $2,300 to Obama, Fowler had attended scores of fund-raisers and recorded the candidate's remarks in hopes they might produce an amusing anecdote or add just a dash of human interest to a future piece of writing. Obama's fund-raising remarks had never produced actual news before. And no, in Fowler's understanding the donor events were not off the record. The events were simply closed to the press; being off the record would have meant there was a formal agreement among all the attendees that Obama's comments were not to be repeated to the press or reported outside that room. Fowler was there as a donor and as a citizen journalist and she never for a moment thought she was breaking any ground rules by recording or writing about his comments.

So when Obama began to speak to the assembled guests that Sunday night inside the library of a tony Pacific Heights mansion in San Francisco, Fowler hit the record button. Right away she was glad she did; she knew that what Obama was saying was new and that the language he was using was completely different from his previous rhetoric.

Obama made news, at least in Fowler's eyes, when he explained to the donors the criteria he'd use for picking a running mate. He announced that contrary to conventional wisdom he didn't need a VP steeped in military or foreign policy experience. "[I am] probably most confident that I know more and understand the world better than Senator Clinton or Senator McCain," he said.

He then mocked the fact that Clinton had made official visits to 80 countries, suggesting that they were mostly photo-ops. In contrast, Obama had real-world experience: "When I speak about having lived in Indonesia for four years, having family that is impoverished in small villages in Africa—knowing the leaders is not important—what I know is the people. . . . I traveled to Pakistan when I was in college—I knew what Sunni and Shia was [sic] before I joined the Senate Foreign Relations Committee."

Most of the donors in the room had no idea that Obama had never made those kinds of comments in public before. But Fowler did. An expert in Obama's stump speech, and standing in a room barren of campaign reporters who might also have detected the newsworthiness, Fowler knew the comments were a big deal.

She was definitely perplexed about Obama's passing reference to having traveled to Pakistan while in college. Had she missed something over the previous months, or had that nugget never been reported before?

On Monday morning Fowler's report from the fund-raiser was posted at the Huffington Post. Obama's comments about picking a vice president and traveling to Pakistan created a modest stir among campaign reporters. It represented the biggest mark Fowler had made on the campaign to date. Yet she had additional information from the event that could cause an even bigger newsroom commotion, but she remained conflicted about publishing it. She knew it would harm Obama's campaign, a campaign she greatly admired.

At the same time she was genuinely upset and offended—devastated really—about the condescending remarks Obama had made about Pennsylvanians. His comments, which sounded elitist to Fowler's ears, came in response to a supporter among the San Francisco donors who said he was going to Pennsylvania to knock on doors for the Obama campaign. He asked what he should expect upon arriving in the Keystone State.

Explaining the terrain, Obama told supporters:

You go into these small towns in Pennsylvania and, like a lot of small towns in the Midwest, the jobs have been gone now for 25 years and nothing's replaced them. . . . And they fell through the Clinton administration, and the Bush administration, and each successive administration has said that somehow these communities are gonna regenerate and they have not.

And it's not surprising then they get bitter, they cling to guns or religion or antipathy to people who aren't like them or anti-immigrant sentiment or anti-trade sentiment as a way to explain their frustrations.

Fowler's heart sank. When Obama launched into a clichéd description of Pennsylvanians, echoing the stereotype Californians already held about people who lived in small towns and rural areas and who were religious and liked to hunt, "it definitely struck a chord." She thought about her own religious family and her father, who hunted as a young man.

While editing Fowler's first fund-raising piece, Amanda Michel was impressed by the amount of news Obama had generated with his comments about his upcoming VP pick. Instinctively she asked Fowler what else Obama talked about. What else was on her tape recorder? Fowler said there was more newsworthy information from the Obama event, but that she wouldn't divulge what it was. She would say only that it was damaging, and that she was going to think about what to do about it because she was concerned that if publicized, it would hurt Obama's campaign. Taken aback by Fowler's instinct to protect the candidate, Michel wondered if Fowler had pulled her punches previously while filing Obama-related dispatches. Michel, the 30-year-old editor who served as one of Howard Dean's earliest campaign volunteers back in 2002, thought Fowler was wading into dangerous territory by picking and choosing what to publish based on how it would affect her favorite candidate. Plus, she put her editor in an impossible position. Michel suggested that Fowler ponder her next move; if she decided not to submit a story on the undisclosed comments, they would discuss her future role with the organization at the end of the week.

Fowler quickly decided that of course Michel was right, and that she had to report the "bitter" story. But she still didn't know how to put it in context. That came to her at 32,000 feet, while flying back to Pennsylvania that week to cover the primary vote in April. A perfectionist by nature,

Fowler normally spent four hours writing and rewriting one of her posts. But as she sat on the plane, the "bitter" piece appeared fully formed in her head, and she typed it up in 30 minutes.

As part of the compromise she'd made with herself, Fowler wrote the article and then waited until Friday before filing it in hopes of burying the piece late in the news cycle right before the weekend. She also made her editor agree that the post run in the form of Fowler's choosing, which was impressionistic and with the controversial quotes not appearing until half-way through the piece.

That Friday morning, when Michel opened Fowler's submission and read the Obama quotes for the first time, she knew they were a very big deal. Editors at the Huffington Post read the piece over and gave their okay, including Arianna Huffington, who was vacationing on David Geffen's yacht off Tahiti. She subsequently watched Fowler's Bittergate story explode worldwide and caught updates halfway around the world on CNN International.

"We're a legitimate news organization and we're looking for good stories," another Huffington Post editor, Roy Sekoff, told me, explaining the decision to grant the final green light. "There comes a moment when you have to decide whether you're a partisan or you're a journalist, and this was the story. It seemed worthy of publication, and once we made that determination there wasn't any choice other than to do it." Sekoff later conceded that he had underestimated the story's impact, thinking it would be only a "two-hour" story once it was published.

Minutes after Fowler's piece was posted online, Ben Smith, an influential blogger for *Politico* and widely read by Beltway media elites, linked to it. Then the Drudge Report linked to Smith's account, which immediately launched the story into the media stratosphere. Two hours after being published, Fowler's post had been read nearly 100,000 times and Lou Dobbs's producers were trying to book her on his CNN program. (Despite the countless offers that poured in throughout the campaign season, Fowler refused to do any television appearances; she didn't want the story to be about her.) That night, Michel went home to her New York City apartment and spent four hours in a surreal cable television news haze, just flipping from channel to channel watching the nonstop coverage of the exploding Bittergate story. (Obama later called his clumsy comments the "biggest boneheaded move" of his campaign.)

Right behind the news of Obama's comments was the gathering media storm about Fowler's role and whether she and Off the Bus had acted ethically in publishing Obama's fund-raising remarks.

Some of the loudest complaints came right from the Huffington Post, where Fowler's piece went over like a lead zeppelin among the Obama-loving readers, who quickly logged 55 digital pages of mostly angry comments about the "bitter" story. On the advice of her husband and editors, Fowler never read a single one of them. Still, she could not insulate herself from the venom her story had unleashed. One angry blogger posted Fowler's email address, which set off a torrent of missives. Then some death threats arrived, as did the television news crews, which camped out on her street. Over at Daily Kos, the knives came out. One furious diarist posted an interactive poll asking, "Do you think Mayhill Fowler intended to undermine Sen. Obama's presidential campaign?" More than 90 percent of respondents thought she had. Another attacked "a lying, horrible woman named Mayhill Fowler" and denounced her as a "Clinton operative." The Daily Kos writer known as beebi demanded, "What was her FUCKING motive!!!!!!!!"

Temporarily stunned by the reaction, Fowler, who had no regrets about publishing the story or how she got it in the first place, came to realize that the anger unleashed wasn't really intended for her. Instead, it reflected the fear felt by Obama supporters who had invested so much time and emotion in the candidate, the fear that Bittergate might sink his candidacy.

"The truth is a dangerous thing," said Fowler two months after the hullabaloo and still shaking her head in amazement. "Boy, I sure learned that."

THEN AGAIN, SHE had a lot to learn about journalism in general. Fowler started her campaign experiment with no reporting experience, or even a firm idea of what she should be doing. Truth was, Fowler had never spent much time thinking about journalism, let alone practicing it. Before she joined Off the Bus her editors talked a lot about new media and old media and how the old way of covering a campaign was outdated. As she listened, Fowler, a cautious person by nature, rolled her eyes and thought the whole premise seemed a bit suspect. After all, she liked reading her *New York Times* and *Wall Street Journal* every day; they seemed to do a perfectly fine job of covering the news.

"I was a tabula rasa. I had no preconceptions about the press," she said. Over time, though, her opinion was molded by seeing the sloppy and dishonest journalism on the campaign trail. After spending months on the road she also thought the mainstream press was quite naïve about the changes that technology was bringing to campaign reporting, especially regarding privacy; journalists were slow to understand that an era was quickly drawing to a close. She assumed that the number of citizen journalists like her would multiply in future campaigns, although they might arrive with different standards.

For instance, during a campaign stop in Scranton, Pennsylvania, in the spring, CNN's Candy Crowley appeared at a nearby press table and launched into a lengthy conversation with a handful of cable news assistants. She was oblivious to Fowler and the fact that Fowler's tape recorder was out in plain sight. As Crowley went on in great detail about the election, sharing her analysis of the state of the Obama and Clinton campaigns, Fowler thought about how easy it would be to record those comments—juicy comments the correspondent might not make on the air—and within minutes post them on the Internet and then sit back and watch the controversy take flight. "Exclusive! Candy Crowley Uncensored" would be the screaming Drudge Report headline.

"I'm not going to do it because that's not me," said Fowler. "But right behind me is somebody who will."

However, Fowler's critics within the traditional press corps who felt she played fast and loose with the rules claimed that's precisely what Fowler did when she taped and then published comments made by Bill Clinton on the rope line at a campaign stop in South Dakota. Clinton had no idea Fowler was a citizen journalist or that she was recording his jaw-dropping remarks.

Of course, Fowler never set out to make news when she planned her visit to Milbank, South Dakota. As the primary campaign season came to its conclusion, she was simply searching for closure to her marathon coverage of Clinton and Obama. Sitting in her Sioux Falls hotel room and going over all the itineraries for the first week in June, she decided she would attend Clinton events in South Dakota on June 2, where she could write about Hillary, Bill, and Chelsea. Bill had five events scheduled north of the capital that day and would then join Hillary and Chelsea at a rally in Sioux Falls. The next day, Fowler would drive to St. Paul, Minnesota, for the huge Obama victory rally.

Motoring up to the Visitors Center in Milbank, the small Republican farming town of 3,600 where Bill Clinton held his second event of the day, Fowler's plan of action was to get her business card to him while he worked the rope line. She wanted him to pass it along to Hillary in hopes of landing a postcampaign interview with the New York senator.

During Clinton's hour-long appeal on behalf of his wife that day in Milbank, the former president displayed an unusually elegiac and contemplative mood. Completely absent, Fowler noted to herself, were any of the predictable jabs Clinton took at the press for being unfair to Hillary, for trying to write her off too soon. Such criticisms had become a staple of Clinton's small-town appearances, yet none were lobbed in Milbank.

Not yet anyway.

Fowler also noticed that as Clinton waded into the rope line to shake hands with locals—who were actually kept behind a metal barricade, not a rope—the former president was very gracious with his time. In the past aides had tried to whisk him along in a vain attempt to keep him on schedule; now they were nowhere to be seen. As Clinton made his way toward Fowler, she helped a woman next to her by taking a picture of the woman and her son with the former president. That's probably when Fowler dropped her business card, just when Clinton extended his hand in greeting.

Momentarily stumped, not knowing what to say or what to ask, Fowler just smiled. Clinton moved on to the next person and Fowler backed away from the rope line disappointed. Then, for some reason, Clinton doubled back and extended his long arm to Fowler again. That's when she quizzed him about the *Vanity Fair* "hatchet job."

Titled "The Comeback Id," the 8,000-word article essentially claimed that since leaving office, Bill Clinton had been hanging around people who were too rich and who had sex too often. As journalism, it was an atrocious piece of work. At least that's what Fowler thought after she read page after page after page of *Vanity Fair*'s anonymous quotes trashing Clinton through innuendo and guilt by association. In total, the article featured 39 anonymous quotes. Anonymous quotes had become a pet peeve of Fowler, who, after spending months on the road, had a new appreciation for the way journalists could, if they wanted, easily manipulate stories based on nameless quotes.

So as she watched Clinton extend his hand to her a second time, she was thinking about the new *Vanity Fair* hit piece and how he hadn't said a single disparaging word about the press that day.

As Clinton tightly held Fowler's hand during their entire three-minute exchange, the former president unveiled by far the most startling, unvarnished quote unearthed by any reporter on the campaign trail during the entire primary season. Of course, Clinton had no idea he was speaking to a citizen journalist. Foul-mouthed and expansive, but not nearly as angry as depicted in the press when the Fowler story first broke, Clinton was caught on tape denouncing the *Vanity Fair* reporter Todd Purdum as being a "sleazy," "dishonest reporter" who published "blatant lies."

Fowler immediately knew that Clinton's comments were unusual because of the detail of his three-minute critique and the undisguised contempt he conveyed toward the press. When she got back to her car in the Milbank parking lot, Fowler plugged in her headphones to listen to the audiotape. She started transcribing the exchange on her BlackBerry to send to her editors and then realized she'd forgotten to identify herself to Clinton as a writer for Huffington Post's Off the Bus.

"Oh shit," she thought, slumping into her seat.

But hadn't Clinton seen the tape recorder that Fowler was holding? She doubted he had, because rope lines were so chaotic, with lots of people jostling for position and multiple conversations being carried on at once. Fowler could have waved the recorder right in Clinton's face and it would not have registered with him.

She sent the transcription and a quick early draft of her item off to her editor, and the two of them came up with a Plan A and a Plan B to try to get around the fact that Fowler forgot to tell Clinton that she was a citizen journalist either before or after querying him about the *Vanity Fair* hit piece. Plan A was to drive to a later Clinton event that day, catch him again on the rope line, explain what had happened in Milbank, and ask the former president's permission to use his quotes. It sounded like a long shot, but Fowler had a funny feeling that because it was the final day of the campaign and because the *Vanity Fair* article had so clearly irked him, Clinton might actually agree to her request if she could track him down. Plan B called for Fowler to write a longer piece about how, on his last day of campaigning, Clinton had not taken any jabs at the press during his stump speech, yet when approached during the rope line, he displayed real anger about the *Vanity Fair* article. In that scenario Fowler would not quote him directly.

With those two battle plans in place, Fowler switched off her Black-Berry and drove an hour west on Route 12 to the shrinking town of Webster, South Dakota, population 1,700, the birthplace of the legendary NBC newsman Tom Brokaw. It was in Webster that Fowler and her editors began to test the boundaries of journalism in a brand-new way.

Arriving in town, Fowler powered up her BlackBerry and found two urgent emails from two different Huffington Post editors, instructing her, in capital letters, no less, that under no circumstances was she to approach Clinton and ask his permission to use the quotes she'd gotten in Milbank. The Huffington Post was going to run an item without his okay because they didn't feel that it was ultimately Clinton's decision to make whether those quotes could be published.

"Our belief was that the event was on the record. And that Mayhill did not overhear him talking in confidence to a friend and she did not sneak up behind him," Amanda Michel later explained to me. "Whether he was on a stage or on the rope line, it was a public event. I think we made the right decision."

Michel told Fowler she would be back in touch soon and would read to Fowler the edited version of the dispatch from the Milbank encounter. Entering the historic Webster fairgrounds square dance pavilion where Clinton was scheduled to speak, Fowler started to get stressed about the whole situation. She had never intended to publish Clinton's quotes without getting his permission.

A third of the way into the event, as often happened at crowded campaign events, a senior citizen was overtaken by the heat and had to be removed from the crowd. Fowler helped the local men who carried the small, elderly woman over the barricade and took her outside. As she followed behind with the woman's purse, she was surprised to find no EMT crew present at the event to assist attendees. Soon the elderly husband arrived and Fowler handed over the purse and walked back to the pavilion, where she could hear Bill Clinton speaking.

But as soon as she got back inside the pavilion her editor called, so Fowler had to go back outside in order to hear Michel read the story over the phone. She was surprised that there were still no EMTs, and the old woman, still lying on the ground, looked much worse; she was in fact turning a paler shade of gray. So Fowler got distracted by that. Then she noticed that standing right next to her by the Secret Service SUV were the four aides who accompanied Clinton on the campaign trip, which also diverted her attention.

"So I'm actually talking to Amanda about the piece that they're about to run in minutes. The campaign aides are laughing and talking amongst themselves so close I could have reached out and touched one of them. And there's this eighty-year-old woman lying on the ground in extremis," Fowler recalled. "And Amanda is reading back to me the copy and alarm bells are starting to go off in my head and I'm thinking this is moving way too fast for me, just way too fast. And I'm just not sure about this because I hadn't really planned to put up the entire piece. But at that very moment if I had wanted to stop Amanda I should have said something. And I didn't say anything. And because I didn't say anything I'll always have to take responsibility for it going up. At the time I was upset about the whole thing and mostly upset at myself for not saying what I really thought: that we should have waited and thought about it, that we should have asked his permission." Weeks later, Fowler concluded that publishing the piece had been the right call because it allowed people to see how Clinton really felt about the press.

She returned once again to the pavilion to watch Clinton finish up.

By the time the event ended and Fowler was walking back through the fairgrounds parking lot, the new Huffington Post piece, "Bill Clinton: Purdum a 'Sleazy' 'Slimy' 'Scumbag,'" was already up on the site and exploding like a firecracker across the media landscape. The press was soon chortling over the final campaign trail indignity for Clinton, whom pundits and reporters had contemptuously derided for months as being nothing but "baggage" for his wife. Fowler's dispatch provided the final exclamation point on that caricature.

Almost immediately Fowler began fielding calls from an armada of Huffington Post editors wanting to know how soon she could upload the Clinton audio, because Anderson Cooper's and Keith Olbermann's producers were clamoring for it. Fowler explained that her laptop was back at her Sioux Falls hotel; it was supposed to rain that day so she hadn't brought it. The drive would take 90 minutes. That's when she got stuck behind the sheriff's patrol car on I-29 and had to drive south, past the towns of Watertown and Brookings on the way to Sioux Falls at the maddeningly slow pace of 75 mph.

It turns out there were some rules Fowler wasn't willing to bend.

eleven

OBAMA, THE BLOGS, AND IMMUNITY

Five thousand, two hundred ninety miles. That's how far it was from Barack Obama's campaign headquarters in Chicago to downtown Rio de Janeiro.

It takes commercial airliners 10 hours to make the trip; email circles the globe in just seconds. On June 20, 2008, a news release from the Obama campaign landed in the email in-box of Glenn Greenwald, who blogged from his widely read netroots home base, Unclaimed Territory. Although he's an A-list blogger who helps the netroots formulate its agenda each day for the ongoing combat of U.S. politics, Greenwald actually works out of his first-floor home office in Rio de Janeiro. When he clicked on the Obama release after it traveled more than 5,000 miles that June day, the blogger was appalled.

Obama's statement addressing pending legislation regarding government-sponsored wiretapping did not create much interest among the Beltway press corps, but it lit a fuse within the blogosphere. In June 2008 a congressional agreement was being crafted to rewrite the nation's electronic surveillance laws at the request of the Bush White House, which demanded extraordinary executive powers in its pursuit of terrorist suspects, including the right to wiretap some U.S. citizens without the need of a warrant.

Contrary to existing law, the Bush administration had been engaging in wiretapping for years; now it wanted to get the permission in writing.

The White House–friendly legislation being crafted by Congress would also grant retroactive immunity to telecommunications corporations such as AT&T and Verizon, which reportedly helped the Bush White House conduct illegal, warrantless wiretaps by handing over information about their customers to the government. The telecoms wanted to make sure they would not have to answer to private citizens who filed invasion-of-privacy lawsuits in the wake of the wiretapping revelations. The new legislation would grant that blanket immunity, immunity that could not be repealed.

For years, the liberal blogosphere had made warrantless eavesdropping and retroactive immunity two of its primary battle sites. The laws of the land were quite plain: it was a felony to eavesdrop on Americans without a warrant. Bush essentially got caught, admitted he did it, and then said he needed to keep doing it anyway. The bloggers' message to Democrats was equally plain: If you don't stand up to Bush's naked lawbreaking, you're never going to stand up to anything.

No doubt the wiretap issue was wonky, but the netroots was built around an adult appreciation of serious issues. Politics and governance wasn't a game or a sport, though the Beltway media often treated them that way. Elections had consequences, and bloggers were distressed that America had become a country whose government disregarded civil liberties and was allowed to break existing laws to wiretap its citizens, and do it with the help of billion-dollar telecommunication giants.

Since August 2007, when Greenwald began to urgently push the issue online, the netroots had been completely committed to thwarting any congressional effort to further water down electronic surveillance laws; these were already lenient laws that had been spelled out for decades in the Foreign Intelligence Surveillance Act, or FISA. Bloggers formed a potent alliance with presidential campaigns, congressional staffs, and outside advocacy groups and raised hundreds of thousands of dollars among readers to try to block the effort under way to codify Bush's wiretapping, while also pardoning the communication companies that facilitated the lawbreaking. For months, through 2007 and into early 2008, the scrappy, ad hoc, netroots-led coalition posted win after upset win on Capitol Hill

in its wiretapping fight against Republican leaders, large portions of the
Democratic Party, a compliant press, the White House, and the telecom
giants. It wasn't David versus Goliath. It was more like David's little
brother versus Goliath. Yet bloggers kept tallying wins in the FISA fight.

Then, in the spring of 2008, another decisive vote approached, and for
the first time that year Barack Obama, the Democratic Party's presumptive nominee, had to take a definitive stand on the wiretapping issues as
well as the immunity ploy. During the Democratic primaries Obama had
repeatedly, and with his signature rhetorical flair, assured progressives that
he supported their fight to roll back Bush's lawless wiretapping efforts.
Pressuring his rival Hillary Clinton from the left, Obama even announced
he would support the filibuster of any bill that tried to hand the telecoms
a get-out-of-jail pass in the form of retroactive immunity.

By June, though, the netroots' wiretapping winning streak in Congress
looked in doubt. Thanks to Democratic leaders in the House and Senate
who finally capitulated to Bush's demands, bloggers turned to Obama as
their last hope and urged him to use his high-profile platform as the most
powerful Democrat in the country to change the dynamics of the wiretapping debate in Washington. Even if the battle were already lost and
the new FISA legislation would pass, if Obama stepped up and used his
newly minted Party leadership status and talked forcefully and openly
about why warrantless wiretapping was not needed to win the war on terror and why retroactive immunity represented a repugnant notion for any
democracy—if he invoked the same FISA rhetoric he used during the primary season—then maybe he could change the larger debate.

When Greenwald, who had blogged 300 to 400 items about the larger
issue of Bush wiretapping during a 30-month span, opened his email on
June 20 to read Obama's much anticipated statement regarding wiretapping and retroactive immunity, his expectations were low. Yes, Obama
had been a forceful FISA ally during the primaries. But just looking at the
politics in play, Greenwald thought it unlikely that as the Party's nominee
Obama would now break on FISA with Democrats in the House and Senate. Greenwald suspected there had been some sort of behind-the-scenes
signal that Obama would be okay if Democrats gave Bush what he wanted

in terms of wiretapping and retroactive immunity, and that Obama would not bitterly oppose it. In fact, he might even quietly support the policy initiative.

Still, Greenwald, who remained agnostic during the Clinton-Obama primary battle, was startled when he clicked on the email and read Obama's statement. In it, the candidate not only walked away from his previous statements denouncing wiretapping as well as from his commitment to thwart retroactive immunity, but he actually embraced specific Republican talking points when discussing the national security issue of electronic surveillance. "Given the grave threats that we face, our national security agencies must have the capability to gather intelligence and track down terrorists before they strike, while respecting the rule of law and the privacy and civil liberties of the American people," Obama announced.

Furious, Greenwald tore off the gloves and excoriated Obama in a way no neutral, big-name blogger had done during the entire campaign:

> What Barack Obama did here was wrong and destructive. He's supporting a bill that is a full-scale assault on our Constitution. What's more, as a Constitutional Law Professor, he knows full well what a radical perversion of our Constitution this bill is, and yet he's supporting it anyway. Anyone who sugarcoats or justifies that is doing a real disservice to their claimed political values and to the truth.

Greenwald wasn't looking to proclaim Obama unfit to be the Party's nominee. But as he searched around the blogosphere looking for some early signs of life from a community that had just been dissed by the most famous Democrat in America, he found mostly silence. Rather than straight talk in response to Obama's FISA proclamation, Greenwald saw creeping timidity, with portions of the blogosphere expressing concern that openly criticizing Obama's FISA stance might damage the Democrat's chance for a White House win.

For Greenwald, that was too much. Partisan cheerleading was not why the liberal blogosphere was created. There were already plenty of Beltway institutions that would applaud Democratic politicians no matter what they did. The netroots, he thought, ought to oppose Democratic complicity and capitulation just as forcefully as the netroots battled GOP corruption and media malfeasance. All three were of equal importance; none of them should be discarded for the sake of a campaign.

Whether because of Greenwald's scolding or the fact that bloggers just needed time to process Obama's flip-flop, soon the blogosphere condemnations began to pour in as Obama's turn away from FISA and retroactive immunity was presented as a paramount pivot for the netroots. It represented an awkward moment for the burgeoning online movement as it was forced to ask some uncomfortable questions about its heralded candidate.

But the FISA episode was about more than the Democratic candidate. This important chapter in netroots history was about how bloggers, with virtually no allies in the traditional media and without spending a dime on lobbying, harnessed enough grassroots passion to alter the national debate, at times dramatically, about national security during the campaign season.

LEADING THE ONLINE FISA fight from his Rio home in the tropics, 1,000 miles south of the equator, was Greenwald, who nearly single-handedly elevated the wiretapping issue to national importance and forced candidates to take notice. The FISA pushback perfectly captured how the netroots revolution could change U.S. politics. It also spoke to the power and transcontinental credibility Greenwald had built up in less than three years within the netroots movement. "If it weren't for Glenn," said the blogger Jane Hamsher, "nobody would have cared about FISA." That he led the revolt from Brazil simply highlighted the limitless potential of the Internet to connect people.

It's likely very few of Greenwald's readers knew he lived in and wrote from Rio, simply because he didn't mention it on his blog very often. Unlike some bloggers, Greenwald revealed very little personal information in his writing. For instance, he didn't write much about being gay, but that's why he moved to Brazil. His partner is Brazilian, and that government recognized their relationship for immigration purposes, whereas the U.S. government explicitly refused to.

Greenwald started making extended visits to Rio in 2005, and with each passing year he spent more months there. Now he lives in a rented four-story house in the South Zone of the sprawling Brazilian city, in the tranquil neighborhood of Gávea. The house is perched on the side of a mountain, has a pool out back, and is protected by a large wall in front. The city barriers are ubiquitous, due to Rio's high crime rate. Greenwald works out of his first-floor office; from the fourth floor he can see the ocean and the famed Ipanema beaches, which are just a 10-minute walk from home.

He doesn't consider himself an ex-pat (he hates that term) because he still maintains U.S. citizenship and always will. Plus, he owns an apartment in New York City and visits frequently. He spends most of his waking hours engaged in U.S. politics, either reading U.S.–based publications and blogs online or monitoring cable news channels. Most of the people he talks to on the phone are American. To eliminate monster phone bills, Greenwald downloaded the computer program Skype, which allows him to use his computer to place international calls for free. It also allows him to make free video calls via his webcam.

Thanks to new technology, and the ability to connect instantly, it feels very much as if he were in the United States. As far as having a competitive advantage, Greenwald's clock in Rio, depending on the time of year, runs between one and three hours ahead of the U.S. East Coast, which gives him an upper hand when posting items each morning. An early riser by nature, Greenwald often keys his beefy, 2,000-to-3,000-word essays off that morning's news. They are sometimes ready to read by 8 a.m. in New York and Washington, much to the amazement of his fellow bloggers, many of whom are not aware of the head start Greenwald gets each morning from his office in South America.

Of course, being in Brazil means the blogger has to turn down offers to appear on television; producers who make such offers, via email, have no idea the blogger is 5,000 miles away. But popping up on MSNBC for three minutes to bicker about politics never interested Greenwald much to begin with. Not that he doesn't like instigating a good row.

As a kid, Greenwald was destined to become an attorney. Precocious and boasting a healthy argumentative streak, he enjoyed being in the spotlight during his high school debate team matches. Growing up in the south Florida town of Lauderdale Lakes, the grandson of a political junkie, Greenwald ran for city council when he turned 18. He campaigned against the local condominium power structure but couldn't knock off any of the incumbents.

A curious contradiction, Greenwald sports a boyish look and appears ten years younger than his actual age of 41. But in terms of his personality, he is very much all business, and he carries himself like a man 10 years his senior. Whereas lots of bloggers embrace a Peter Pan outlook on life, Greenwald is the opposite. He's the one providing constant adult supervision over the blogosphere. His posts are deadly serious and often much more earnest than those of his colleagues. The illustration of Greenwald that appears on his site shows him sitting ramrod straight with his arms crossed and wearing a dress shirt and tie. Very unbloggy.

After graduating from George Washington University, Greenwald studied law at New York University and became a constitutional attorney in 1994. His work was at times political in the sense that he took on unpopular clients in free speech cases that spotlighted the practical tensions between the rights of individuals and the collective urges of the community. In 2002 he defended a strident anti-immigration group, National Alliance, in a New York civil rights lawsuit after two Mexican day workers were beaten and stabbed on Long Island by two men posing as contractors in search of laborers. The victims claimed that the anti-immigration rhetoric of National Alliance, which urged racist violence against Latino immigrants and other racial minorities, was partly to blame for the beatings. Greenwald argued that the case represented a misguided attempt to impose liability and punishment on groups because of their political and religious views. A federal judge threw out the case.

He started reading the liberal blogs in 2003 and was amazed by the depth of insight and the caliber of writing posted on an almost hourly basis. The discussions unfolding online, the detailed political analysis, were fascinating and far more sophisticated than what he was seeing and reading in the mainstream press, and he wanted to be part of them. Around the same time he decided to ease out of law. He wanted a change, although he wasn't sure what kind. He loved litigation, but he hated practicing law. He grew tired of attorneys and judges and clients (especially the clients). After 9/11 he became much more engaged in domestic politics as the country lurched to the right. The terrorist-related legal saga of Jose Padilla and the claim that the federal government had the authority to imprison a U.S. citizen on American soil without due process were especially alarming to Greenwald. As was the country's creeping reverence for the commander in chief as a legal arbiter.

Then one day in late October 2005, Greenwald woke up and decided he'd launch his own blog, simply because he had a few things to say and thought they were worth saying to others. After christening his site Unclaimed Territory, he wrote a post about the unfolding CIA leak investigation involving a former operative, Valerie Plame, and Vice President Dick Cheney's No. 2, Scooter Libby, who stood accused of outing Plame in retribution for her husband's prominent war criticism. Six days after Greenwald's maiden blog post, Libby was indicted. One of the immediate talking points embraced by Libby defenders in the conservative press was that a trial would simply pit Libby and his word against journalists who became part of the investigation; the whole case would come down to whether jurists believed Libby or journalists.

Greenwald found the Libby indictment online, read it, and thought that the conservative press was completely wrong. Prosecutors had outlined several instances in which non-journalist witnesses would be called upon to contradict Libby's testimony regarding the leak case. Thus the trial wouldn't feature Libby's word versus a journalist's word.

Greenwald blogged it and his Libby item quickly got picked up by a writer at the *New Republic*, who included it in an item he wrote that day. From there, Duncan Black linked to Greenwald's post at Eschaton, and Unclaimed Territory was immediately deluged with new readers. When he posted the link that day, Black had no idea who Greenwald was. How could he? Greenwald hadn't even been blogging for a week. Yet in the space of five days, Greenwald's site went from 30 readers to 30,000.

His meteoric rise continued in December, when the *New York Times* broke its wiretapping exclusive: the National Security Agency had been ordered by Bush to sift through phone calls and emails without first obtaining a warrant, which had been the law of the land for nearly three decades. Greenwald obsessed over the story for months and blogged about it incessantly, carving out a niche for himself as an online go-to guy for sharp legal analysis regarding the rapidly expanding field of Bush wiretapping disclosures.

"Greenwald changed blogging," claimed the netroots pioneer Digby. For years, the blogging formula most people aspired to was posting five or six insightful items a day that gave readers enough to chew on and also kept them coming back often to check the site for fresh content. Kevin Drum and Matthew Yglesias were two early archetypes of that classic approach. But Greenwald eschewed that style and usually wrote about just one topic each day and at great length, although he often added lots of updates throughout the day. "I didn't know that somebody could come along at that late date, do blogging in a completely different way, and become a sensation," said Digby. "Glenn truly was an overnight blogging sensation. People loved his work immediately."

Within six months of his debut, Greenwald had ascended to an unofficial leadership position within the blogosphere. Online he was a relentless writer who just steamrolled his foes through sheer force of facts. "He knows his stuff, hits hard and keeps on hitting," commented one Huffington Post reader. Amassing details, tearing through primary documents, and building his case much like an attorney does, Greenwald had the ability to make complex issues easily understandable. Like a good lawyer presenting a complicated case to a jury, he constructed his narratives from the ground up, adding in doses of appropriate indignation as he proceeded, all wrapped in meticulously researched writing.

Reflecting a new online generation of progressive writers and partisans who did not aspire to go along and get along with Beltway elites, Greenwald did not suffer fools gladly, especially those in the press and especially partisans on the far right. His takedowns, which often unfolded over days via multiple posts, with Greenwald returning to rhetorically pound his foe again and again, were epic. That's why he got dubbed "Glennzilla" online. Greenwald notched more clear knockout wins in his belt than perhaps any other blogger.

. . .

TO UNDERSTAND THE netroots you have to understand FISA. And to understand the netroots' sometimes complicated relationship with Obama over the course of the White House campaign, you have to understand FISA. Over most of the decade, three issues had come to define the liberal blogosphere: ending the war in Iraq, unraveling the CIA's Valerie Plame leak case, and stopping Bush's assault on the Constitution, which included his desire to circumvent FISA.

And to fully understand the origins of the FISA fight you have to go back to 1974 and the banner, page-one headline on December 22 in the *New York Times:* "HUGE C.I.A. OPERATION REPORTED IN U.S. AGAINST ANTIWAR FORCES, OTHER DISSIDENTS IN NIXON YEARS."

For a nation that had hardened itself to the constant revelations of President Richard Nixon's lawlessness, which cost him the presidency just four months earlier, and a nation that was trying to move on from the Watergate stain, the *Times* exclusive, nailed down by Seymour Hersh, contained unpleasant reminders of how the Republican administration had turned the government on its own people. Specifically, the *Times* reported that the Central Intelligence Agency, in direct violation of its charter forbidding domestic spying, had "conducted a massive, illegal domestic intelligence operation during the Nixon Administration against the antiwar movement and other dissident groups in the United States, according to well-placed Government sources."

The *Times* revealed that the CIA had created secret dossiers on nearly 10,000 Americans, including some members of Congress. One month later, on January 21, 1975, Hersh returned to the *Times* front page to report that the U.S. Senate had voted to establish an 11-member body to investigate the coordination of spying, if any, among intelligence agencies, to determine the extent to which any intelligence units had been directed by secret orders from the executive branch, and to document any violations of federal law by any intelligence agency, including illegal wiretapping and surreptitious monitoring of mail.

Known formerly as the U.S. Senate Select Committee to Study Governmental Operations with Respect to Intelligence Activities, the body became known simply as the Church Committee, named after its chairman, Sen. Frank Church (D-ID). Over nine months the bipartisan committee interviewed more than 800 officials and discovered evidence of rampant illegal wiretapping and the undermining of constitutional rights by the CIA, the FBI, and the National Security Agency, the world's largest intelligence agency. Examining the NSA's activity tracking overseas communications involving Americans, the bipartisan group uncovered a massive lawbreaking scheme called Operation Shamrock, perhaps the government's largest ever domestic espionage initiative. As part of Shamrock, the NSA received copies of most international telegrams transmitted by America's largest communications operators, such as Western Union, from the 1940s through the 1970s. At the program's peak, 150,000 telegrams per month were read by NSA analysts in search of foreign intelligence. Americans had no idea their communications were being monitored without warrants.

How did the NSA obtain copies of all those telegrams? The agency simply asked the telegram companies for them.

In an effort to curtail that kind of activity, the Church Committee, as part of its 14 published reports, recommended that the NSA enjoy no greater latitude in monitoring the communications of Americans than any other intelligence agency: "To the extent that other agencies are required to obtain a warrant before monitoring the communications of Americans, NSA should be required to obtain a warrant."

Out of the Church Committee, and through the bipartisan work of Democrats, Republicans, civil rights organizations, and national intelligence agencies, the 1978 Foreign Intelligence Surveillance Act was enacted. It requires a warrant to intercept international communications involving anyone in the United States. For decades, the secret FISA court, staffed by seven judges appointed by the chief justice of the U.S. Supreme Court, granted the warrants quickly and nearly every time the government made a request.

In hopes of avoiding the creation of another Operation Shamrock, the Church Committee specifically recommended that the NSA "not request from any commercial carrier any communication" without first obtaining a warrant. Over the years FISA was updated periodically, and after the terrorist attacks of 9/11 the USA PATRIOT Act made it even easier to conduct surveillance, especially when pursuing terrorists.

But the Bush administration, seeking even more executive power, ignored the FISA law and authorized the NSA to intercept phone calls and emails between people abroad and people in the United States without a FISA warrant, and without any judicial oversight, as long as "the target" of the intercept was not in this country. Bush never announced that decision, and only a handful of lawmakers were briefed about it. Even the special intelligence court that oversaw FISA remained unaware of the initiative until the *New York Times* disclosed the spying in a Pulitzer Prize–winning article on December 16, 2005, by James Risen and Eric Lichtblau. (The *Times,* bowing to White House pressure, had delayed publishing its wiretapping exclusive for more than a year.)

To secretly collect the communications, the administration turned to telecommunication giants such as Verizon and AT&T. Likely eager to improve relations with the federal government, which doled out enormous telecom contracts each year, the companies provided the data to the government, which was clearly illegal. According to the existing FISA law:

> A person is guilty of an offense if he intentionally—(1) engages in electronic surveillance under color of law except as authorized by statute. . . .
>
> An offense described in this section is punishable by a fine of not more than $10,000 or imprisonment for not more than five years, or both.

As Greenwald reminded readers, such spying also violated the Fourth Amendment, which forbids the government from invading private communication without showing probable cause before a court. But even following the *Times*'s wiretapping revelation, Bush claimed that FISA remained too limiting for the Internet-speed war against terror.

On August 5, 2007, just prior to its summer recess, Congress rushed through passage of the Protect America Act (no public hearings were held), which again gave American spy agencies expanded power to eavesdrop on foreign suspects without the need of a court order. The law basically circumvented the FISA court and granted Bush's attorney general and the director of national intelligence the power to order international surveillance, including the authority to eavesdrop on international phone calls and email messages of American citizens. In essence, the bill legalized warrantless eavesdropping.

The best that Democrats who opposed the bill could do was make sure it included a 180-day "sunset provision," which meant the Protect America Act would expire on February 1, 2008, and would need to be revisited by Congress. If Congress did not act, FISA would once again become the law of the land. Almost immediately, congressional leaders began working on new legislation to permanently codify the Protect America Act when it expired in February.

Although the administration got virtually everything it wanted in the draconian Protect America Act, the bill did not include retroactive immunity for the telecoms. Bush demanded that immunity be included when Congress amended the Protect America Act before February 2008. In October 2007 it looked like that demand had been fully met by Democrats when news leaked that Sen. John Rockefeller, the Democratic chairman of the Senate Intelligence Committee, had conducted secret negotiations with the office of Vice President Dick Cheney and agreed to include full-scale retroactive immunity in the pending FISA legislation, along with virtually every other administration request. The proposed legislation shielded conglomerates such as Verizon and AT&T from paying millions of dollars in potential lawsuit damages from invasion-of-privacy claims. The fact that the telecoms so desperately sought retroactive immunity from Congress seemed to suggest that their attorneys understood that privacy laws had been broken.

In essence, if a targeted telecom got a note from the Bush White House saying it asked the company to help spy on Americans without any cause and without a warrant, then courts would be allowed to toss out the lawsuits. For bloggers, the wiretapping and the trampling of basic rights were bad enough. But the Bush administration's insistence that telecom companies that helped with the illegal wiretapping be granted retroactive immunity was too much to take.

Yet, as repugnant as the immunity clause was, it provided the netroots with a crucial hook. It gave bloggers a populist angle to channel their outrage and help create a grassroots coalition to try to raise awareness and kill the legislation.

During most of the Bush administration, Democrats and liberals often struggled with the larger mainstream debate about whether it was necessary to curtail liberties when fighting the war on terrorism. Liberals often felt hemmed in when they argued that habeas corpus did not have to be suspended, that torture should not be employed, and that illegal wiretaps were not a necessity. They felt defensive making those points when Republicans habitually rolled out scare rhetoric about how Democrats were more concerned about protecting the rights of terrorists than protecting America's national security.

But retroactive immunity provided a break from that Groundhog Day debate cycle. A get-out-of-jail-free card for phone companies that made money helping Bush break the law and spy on innocent Americans? That debate bloggers and their readers were eager to have because it had nothing to do with national security. How would letting multibillion-dollar phone companies escape legal retribution for their actions make America safer?

The immunity grab also came despite the fact that dozens of civil violation-of-privacy lawsuits had already been lodged against AT&T, Verizon, and Sprint. The suits were moving through the legal process, and the telecoms, despite their armada of attorneys, were *losing* in court.

On July 20, 2006, U.S. District Court Judge Vaughn Walker denied the telecoms' attempt to have a spying lawsuit dismissed. The judge, appointed by President Bush, noted that it simply was not believable that officials at AT&T did not realize they were breaking the law by honoring the administration's dragnet requests, which arrived without warrants. Yet despite that signal from the court that cooperating telecoms might be in trouble legally, or actually, *because* of that signal, Congress wanted to step in and act as judge and jury by declaring that the telecoms were immune to the legal system.

•   •   •

ON OCTOBER 18, 2007, the *Washington Post* broke the news that Democrats, led by West Virginia's Rockefeller, were ready to sign off on telecom immunity. With that consent, the new FISA legislation would certainly be passed with ease by year's end. That same Friday morning a small group of bloggers were venting, via email, about the *Post* story and searching for a last-minute way to stall immunity. Rising early in Brazil, Greenwald posted a blistering denunciation of the Democratic capitulation at 7:45.

A few minutes later a *Salon* reader and prolific online commenter, Jim White, posted an idea in the comment section below Greenwald's post: Why not find a Democratic member of the Senate who would place a hold on the legislation, which would make passing the bill significantly more difficult? Senate tradition allows any senator to keep a piece of legislation from reaching the Senate floor by placing a hold on the bill, either publicly or in secret.

Days earlier Sen. Christopher Dodd, while campaigning for president, had appeared on Air America radio, where blogger Jane Hamsher had asked him if he would be willing to filibuster the FISA legislation if it made its way to the floor of the Senate and included immunity for the telecoms. The Democratic Connecticut senator, who had made the Bush administration's lawbreaking a cornerstone of his White House run, indicated he would take the task seriously if called upon.

On the morning of October 18 an action plan was hatched. Without the aid of hired publicists or a single lobbyist, bloggers decided to try to derail the FISA bill even though it already enjoyed bipartisan support. Bloggers started by urging readers to convince a single Democrat, Dodd, to take a stand against FISA. If he did, readers were to reward his campaign with donations.

At Dodd's campaign office, the candidate's 25-year-old blogger, Matt Browner Hamlin, along with Dodd's Internet director, Tim Tagaris, could see the blogswarm forming. They read the posts online and saw the Dodd-FISA chatter among bloggers on the Townhouse listserv that morning. They could also see that extra interns were needed to staff the phones, as calls swamped the campaign office and filled up voice mailboxes.

Browner Hamlin and Tagaris agreed that the callers were right: the bill was terrible, and Dodd was in a position to do something about it. Plus, the netroots had put the Dodd campaign on the spot and it needed to act decisively. But the campaign office could not dictate Senate policy, and Dodd's Capitol Hill office was less enthusiastic about taking the radical step of placing a hold on a piece of bipartisan national security legislation.

Traveling in Iowa, Dodd was briefed on the situation by his aides. Already angry at Rockefeller for negotiating in secret with the White House about FISA, Dodd thought back to the fall of 2006, right before the midterm elections, when the administration pushed through the Military Commissions Act, yet another piece of national security legislation that dramatically expanded executive power. The law essentially gave the president absolute power to decide who is an enemy of the United States, to imprison suspects indefinitely without charging them with a crime, and to define what is and is not torture and abuse.

For Dodd, who often carries with him a copy of the U.S. Constitution given to him as a freshman legislator by Senate stalwart Robert Byrd of West Virginia, the Military Commissions Act represented an assault on the rule of law. Back in September 2006, along with liberal Senate colleagues Patrick Leahy and Russ Feingold, Dodd huddled with Senate Majority Leader Harry Reid to voice deep concern that the legislation would damage habeas corpus and codify torture. The three senators told Reid they wanted to try to stop the bill. It was futile, Reid told them. The trio would get rolled in the Senate and be embarrassed by the lack of even symbolic support they'd be able to corral among their Democratic colleagues.

To the surprise of many, though, 34 senators voted against the Military Commissions Act. Dodd couldn't help wondering whether, if he had filibustered the bill, he could have converted a handful more senators, which would have been enough to seriously impair the bill's passage. After it passed, Dodd had deep regrets and felt a sense of shame that he had sat on his hands. He vowed that if another piece of legislation as bad as the Military Commissions Act were presented to the Senate, he would do everything in his power to stop it.

Just after noon on October 18, the white-haired liberal from Connecticut who had never placed a hold on any legislation during his nearly three-decade stay in the Senate, posted a statement online announcing that he would stand in the way of the FISA bill. The next day, after Reid suggested that the hold might not be honored, Dodd, now in New Hampshire, posted a video online announcing that he would filibuster the pro-immunity FISA bill if it came to the floor.

Immediately netroots money began to pour in to Dodd's campaign headquarters. The total didn't reach Obama or Clinton levels—it was only six figures, not seven or eight—but it represented the biggest spike in on-line fund-raising that Dodd had ever enjoyed: more than $200,000 in the 24 hours after the FISA hold was issued. (Between October and January, the Dodd campaign pocketed $1 million online from FISA-related dona-tions.) The following week Daily Kos held its regular straw poll among readers to pick their favorite Democratic candidate; Dodd, who had been at the bottom of the pile, just above the option "No F'ing Clue," leap-frogged over Clinton as well as Obama to land in second place behind John Edwards. Wrote Daily Kos's Markos in late 2007, "Dodd is now the go-to guy. Losing faith in Obama." After months of watching the White House race from outside, the Dodd campaign suddenly found itself in the game, thanks to FISA.

The netroots then turned its sights on the Democratic front-runners and pressed them to join Dodd's fight and to use their media-saturated campaign platforms to denounce the FISA cave-in. Led by Taylor Marsh, Christy Hardin Smith, McJoan, Howie Klein, and Ian Welsh, as well as sites such as Daily Kos, Eschaton, OpenLeft, MyDD, Crooks and Liars, AmericaBlog, and Hullabaloo, bloggers urged readers to call the cam-paigns of Clinton and Obama and demand that they clearly articulate their position on the FISA bill, including their stance on retroactive im-munity.

Bloggers actually caught a break while lobbying Obama on FISA in late October. At that time controversy had erupted when the liberal blog-ger John Aravosis at AmericaBlog unleashed a wave of Obama attacks, widely echoed across the blogosphere, after the candidate scheduled an on-stage appearance at South Carolina "Embrace the Change" rallies with the strident antigay gospel singer Donnie McClurkin, who claimed that homosexuality was a "curse" that could be cured. Obama in October 2007 was far behind Clinton in national polls and was looking to repair his tenuous relationship with the progressive base. It was against that backdrop that Obama's campaign issued the October 24 FISA statement, a statement that would come back to haunt him in June 2008: "To be clear: Barack will support a filibuster of any bill that includes retroactive immunity for telecommunications companies." Obama and his aides would reaffirm that pledge throughout the primary season.

FISA became a campaign issue in the fall of 2007 only because the bloggers, through a viral movement and Dodd's cooperation, made it one. If it hadn't been for bloggers the FISA bill would have effortlessly passed into law without any public debate, without any public accountability, regarding the controversial measures and the constitutional issues in play.

Still tangled up by the looming threat of a filibuster coming from Dodd, who quoted Greenwald by name on the floor of the Senate during his passionate FISA speech, Senator Reid withdrew a scheduled FISA debate on December 17. In February the House voted to pass a three-week extension of the controversial wiretapping law, the Protect America Act, but Congress refused to include retroactive immunity as part of the deal. Angered, the White House threatened to veto the measure. But Democrats still balked and adjourned for recess, allowing the Protect America Act to expire. In March, House Democrats passed a very netroots-friendly version of the FISA bill. Bloggers were stunned by their winning streak. "It didn't seem quite real," recalled Jane Hamsher. "I remember talking to Glenn and saying, 'Is this really happening?'"

Unfortunately for the netroots, the Democratic leadership apparently always intended to capitulate to the White House regarding FISA and telecom immunity. Democratic leaders, headed by House Majority Leader Steny Hoyer, simply wanted to do so on their own timetable, which turned out to be June, just weeks after Obama effectively clinched the Party's nomination. On June 19, just before 6 p.m., a so-called compromise FISA bill, which gave the telecom attorneys what they wanted, was sent to the full House. Again, no hearings were held and no amendments were allowed. The bill was voted on after less than one hour of open floor debate.

Around noon on June 20 an Obama aide was asked by a reporter on a

conference call about the candidate's position on FISA, now that the controversial legislation was clearly moving toward passage. The aide said he
did not know. Hours later the campaign released a statement outlining
Obama's support for the controversial bill.

The blogger Atrios promptly gave Obama the dreaded Wanker of the
Day award. But that seemed polite compared to what Ian Welsh posted at
Firedoglake:

> What Barack Obama has just told us is that he's an essentially con-
> servative democrat who will compromise with reactionaries and to-
> talitarians (the impulse to be free to spy on anyone, with only the
> executive deciding who, is a fundamentally totalitarian one and has
> no place in a republic). Whatever sympathies Obama may have for
> liberalism, or even for the Constitution, he cannot be trusted to
> fight for either if he feels it is not politically in his interest.

AT HOME IN Charlottesville, Virginia, a 39-year-old blogger, Mike Stark,
stewed over Obama's new FISA position. A staunch Obama supporter
during the Democratic primaries, Stark was tapping his activist instincts
to find a way to boldly relay to the candidate that the FISA vote mattered
and that supporters were not going to dismiss it just because the media
didn't much care about the constitutional issue.

Stark thought about using Obama's vaunted online social network system and maybe tweaking it a bit to hold the candidate accountable. Instead of using the campaign's revolutionary MyBarackObama.com site to
organize events, to recruit supporters and raise money, what if Stark used
it to send a signal of discord to the campaign? Why couldn't Obama's
social-networking site become an organizing tool and the home of frank
dissent among his backers?

The next day, a buddy IM'd a link to a FISA group that had been created at Obama's website. Stark clicked on the link and provided his name
and address and 30 seconds later was among the group's first members. In
fact, Stark's friend, who created the group, had already resigned and
tapped Stark as the group's administrator. In other words, Stark was now

in charge of the group, called Senator Obama—Please Vote NO on Telecom Immunity—Get FISA Right. It had eight members.

Stark quickly posted items at Daily Kos and the Huffington Post announcing the creation of the group and emphasizing that it was not for
people who were swearing off Obama or who were former Hillary Clinton
supporters looking for a place to say "I told you so." The group was for
those who remained committed to Obama and wanted to try to persuade
the Democrat to do the right thing about FISA. It was for people who
wanted to test the social-networking waters and see what happened when
they turned their attention not to praising the host candidate, but to critiquing him.

Two days after its formation the FISA group had ballooned to 800
members. After one week, the forum tallied 9,000 and became the largest
self-organized group on Obama's website. Days later, Senator Obama—
Please Vote NO on Telecom Immunity—Get FISA Right notched its
24,000th member and became the largest group ever organized on the
site, either by supporters or the campaign itself.

Stark's online FISA organizing effort struck those who knew him as a
bit out of character. A former marine, Stark had carved out an online
niche for himself as a gadfly and professional agitator. Sort of the liberal
blogosphere's unofficial kamikaze pilot, he seemed to thrive on provoking
face-to-face confrontations using tactics that sometimes earned him ridi-
cule within the netroots. By contrast, his thoughtful, calm, and productive response to FISA seemed so *civil*.

After all, it was Stark who made headlines in late October 2006, when
he got manhandled by campaign aides for Sen. George Allen, the Republican running for reelection in Virginia. The takedown took place inside
an Allen campaign event at the Omni Hotel in Charlottesville. When
Allen emerged from a ballroom after addressing supporters, Stark began shouting questions about the senator's sealed divorce records and rumors that swirled about the split. "Did you spit on your first wife?" Stark
shouted, paparazzi-style.

Three men wearing Allen stickers jumped on Stark, put him in a head-
lock, and wrestled him to the Omni carpet. The whole fracas was captured on tape by a local NBC affiliate and the clip soon whipped around

the Internet; it also made national news outlets, including MSNBC, where Stark was featured on Keith Olbermann's program. Days later Allen, who was expected to use his reelection win in Virginia to kick off a White House run in 2008, lost to Democrat Jim Webb. Allen claimed that Stark had worked in tandem with the Webb campaign; Stark strenuously denied the claim.

And it was Stark who raised eyebrows even at the Fox News–hating Daily Kos, when he paid an early morning visit to Bill O'Reilly's home in Manhasset, New York, in July 2007 and distributed to the talk show host's neighbors copies of a three-year-old sexual harassment lawsuit filed against the Fox News star. Stark and his blogger buddy also placed signs saying "Bill O'Reilly: PERVERT" around the tony enclave and greeted O'Reilly with a camera when the host emerged from his home in running shorts, flip-flops, and a New York Knicks T-shirt to retrieve his morning newspaper at the end of the driveway. Stark claimed he was retaliating for all the times O'Reilly sent his producer to ambush people outside their homes to badger them with misleading questions.

When Stark posted details of his ambush online at Daily Kos, some readers were aghast; they condemned Stark's invasion of privacy and feared the maneuver would cement the mainstream perception of bloggers as unhinged and irresponsible. "I've supported Mike in the past," wrote one Daily Kos commenter that morning. "I'm not with him on this one. Period."

Stark's role as one-man political wrecking crew came somewhat late in life. He grew up in Albany, New York, and joined the marines right out of high school in 1985. After he left the military he made $18,000 a year waiting tables and tending bar in upstate New York. He did lots of bong hits and listened to heavy metal music and not much else. He eventually moved to New York City and, like lots of people in the 1990s, taught himself computer programming, which opened the door to a more lucrative life. By the end of the decade he was the director of technology for a start-up company. When the tech bubble burst, it wiped out the consultancy Stark had helped establish. It also wiped out his first marriage. So back to Albany he went.

As a marine who left the service right before the first Gulf war, Stark had all kinds of doubts about the White House's unfolding push to return to Iraq for another war in the fall of 2002. At home cleaning one day that fall, Stark turned on his stereo and mistakenly flipped on the AM switch. On the Dr. Joe Parisi show, on Albany's WROW, the host was talking about the looming invasion. Stark phoned the program, got on the air, and began saying out loud what he had been thinking to himself for weeks about the inherent dangers of invading Iraq.

That's how Stark got hooked on political talk radio. The next day he tuned in to the same station and for the first time heard the voice of Bill O'Reilly. Initially struck by how the host's voice carried an aura of reasonableness that sucked listeners in, it didn't take Stark long to decide that O'Reilly was full of shit. So Stark phoned in. But it was much more difficult to get past these call screeners and on to the nationally syndicated program. After a lot of trial and error, Stark figured out the talk radio code for successful callers:

> Tip No. 1: Call five minutes after the top of each hour; that's when producers clear the phone lines.
>
> Tip No. 2: Sound reasonable and articulate when being interviewed by the show's screeners, who select which calls get on the air.

Around the same time in late 2002, Stark fell in love with the Howard Dean campaign and talked up Dean's candidacy on right-wing radio. That was the year he read about blogs in *Newsweek,* discovered Daily Kos, and realized how much news and information wasn't getting out into the mainstream.

He started writing up his raucous right-wing radio encounters at Daily Kos, where his diaries became a hit. In 2005 he spent a few hundred dollars on some software that turned his computer into a radio as well as a microphone and created a website, Calling All Wingnuts, where he posted the audio from his freewheeling radio encounters. Scanning the dial often paid off in productive and unexpected ways for an activist like Stark, who was always searching for ways to disrupt the other side. A perfect example came on March 26, 2007.

Driving to law school classes at the University of Virginia, Stark, unlike every other liberal blogger on the planet, was listening to Bill Bennett's *Morning in America* syndicated conservative radio show as the host interviewed presidential hopeful Sen. John McCain, who was scheduled to visit Baghdad within a few days. As McCain's call-in wound down, Bennett asked the candidate to quickly pass along a few nuggets of good news about Iraq as a way to show that the situation on the ground wasn't nearly as dire as the American media made it out to be.

McCain eagerly obliged: "There are neighborhoods in Baghdad where you and I could walk through those neighborhoods, today."

Whoa! Did Stark hear that right? McCain, who prefaced his presidential run on his expertise in international affairs, and specifically the war in Iraq, just announced that everyday Americans, not to mention U.S. senators and radio talk show hosts, were suddenly free to stroll through neighborhoods of Baghdad without fear? It was true that the recently deployed military build-up in 2007 had helped curtail the level of violence in the Iraqi capital. But Americans just wandering along the streets of Baghdad, taking in the sights, outside the secure and heavily fortified Green Zone, where roadside bombs and suicide detonations were commonplace? That seemed preposterous, simply based on bloody news accounts Stark had been reading involving innocent Iraqis, let alone Americans, in the days just prior to McCain's radio interview:

March 26, 2007: Fifteen unidentified bodies are found in Baghdad.

March 26, 2007: A mortar round lands on a residential district in southern Baghdad, killing one man and wounding three others.

March 26, 2007: A suicide bomber kills two civilians and wounds five others in central Baghdad.

March 26, 2007: Gunmen kill a Sunni religious leader, along with two of his employees, in a drive-by shooting in Baghdad.

With his let's-go-for-a-stroll comment, McCain seemed to be describing Baghdad as it existed in some sort of parallel, GOP universe. When Stark returned home from UVA classes that night he saw that the McCain quote had not been highlighted anywhere in the press. Excited about the prospects of tripping up the Republican front-runner, he grabbed the audio from Bennett's show and posted it online at Calling All Wingnuts.

His item got picked up by Raw Story, a popular, left-leaning online news source. The item then ricocheted around the Internet as the sheer absurdity of McCain's comment grabbed people's attention. The next day, when McCain appeared on CNN, Wolf Blitzer read the "neighborhoods" quote from the Bennett show back to the candidate and asked if his description was accurate. McCain said that of course it was accurate and insisted that the U.S. commander in Iraq, Gen. David Petraeus, himself ventured outside the Green Zone nearly every day in an unarmed Humvee.

CNN's Michael Ware, who had been covering Iraq for four years, claimed that his military sources broke out in laughter when they heard McCain's description of Petraeus driving around Baghdad in an unarmed Humvee. "To suggest that there's any neighborhood in this city where an American can walk freely is beyond ludicrous. I'd love Senator McCain to tell me where that neighborhood is, and he and I can go for a stroll."

When the candidate traveled as scheduled to Baghdad on April 1, he ventured out to the local open-air marketplace known as Shorja to show just how safe the capital city had become and prove that Americans weren't learning the real truth about Baghdad from the biased American media. At a Green Zone press conference immediately afterward, a reporter in Baghdad, picking up on the seed Stark had planted that morning while driving to class, pressed McCain: "I just read in the Internet that you said there are areas in Baghdad that you can walk around freely."

"Yeah, I just came from one," McCain snapped.

But in order to travel beyond the Green Zone and into that Baghdad neighborhood, McCain had to a wear a bulletproof vest and was surrounded by 100 American soldiers, 10 armored Humvees, and three Blackhawk helicopters and two Apache gunships hovering overhead. Not to mention the U.S. Army sharpshooters posted on nearby roofs. Back home, McCain's marketplace visit—"The Baghdad Stroll," as it was dubbed online—made the Republican something of a laughingstock and pulled back the curtain on the widely held assumption that McCain, the former military man, enjoyed a mastery of knowledge about Iraq. Soon the embarrassing "Baghdad Stroll" morphed into a larger metaphor for McCain's struggling presidential campaign, which found itself stuck in the political ditch throughout the summer of 2007 as donors abandoned him and his popularity plummeted.

McCain's comeuppance was thanks to Stark, who caught his throw-away line about Baghdad neighborhoods, posted the audio online at his website, and helped push the story out to the larger blogosphere, which then caught the attention of the mainstream media.

BY CONTRAST, THE resolution from Stark's FISA activism wasn't nearly as satisfying. He was thrilled by the outpouring of support the MyBarack Obama.com group generated. And yes, the anti-FISA-legislation group did force Obama to respond publicly and to acknowledge the anger felt by many of his grassroots supporters. To see the Democratic nominee use the Internet with such ease to communicate directly with his supporters represented a revolutionary stop; a thrilling one for online vets who had long dreamed of marrying the grassroots energy of the Internet with the power of the Democratic Party. Those points were all posted in the win column. But for many of the 24,000 group members, Obama's online response to FISA tasted like some pretty weak tea.

The candidate posted his 852-word outreach effort on the Huffington Post around 4 p.m. on July 3, just as most people were preparing for the Fourth of July break. The statement came just hours before Obama attended a $28,500-per-person fund-raiser at the D.C. home of Sen. Jay Rockefeller, who led the pro-immunity charge on behalf of the telecoms during the Senate FISA fight.

Obama's FISA explanation left lots of bloggers shaking their heads. To be honest, after Obama signaled his support for the Bush-friendly FISA bill on June 20, Stark never expected the candidate to change his mind for the bill's final vote, held on July 9. The real point of the FISA group was to let the candidate know his supporters were watching him with a critical eye. But it was the way Obama defended his vote, and the way he never really explained why he had changed course so dramatically on the issue, that bummed out the bloggers.

That nagging sense of disappointment followed bloggers and progressives down to Austin in mid-July, where they met for the annual Netroots Nation conference. Formerly known as YearlyKos, named after the site that inspired the first gathering of the tribes in 2006, where 1,200 progressives converged in Las Vegas, Netroots Nation ballooned to 2,000 attendees in 2008.

A collection of bloggers, their readers, and netroots activists who attended an impossibly wide array of panel discussions, including "The Recipe for Change in America's Food System" and "Creating Political Community around Film," the conference had quickly become *the* progressive meet-up of the year. In Austin, with Democratic Party Chairman Howard Dean roaming the convention halls along with Speaker of the House Nancy Pelosi, former vice president Al Gore, the Internet campaign guru Joe Trippi, and congressional hopefuls in search of some online buzz, the Netroots Nation continued to expand its influence. Even some Republicans wanted in. Former GOP congressman and Clinton impeachment general Bob Barr stopped by the convention center one afternoon, and a former Bush adviser and Austin local, Matthew Dowd, was seen chomping on a cigar at a three-meat blogger BBQ hosted by the unlikely blogger sponsor, *GQ* magazine. (As a rule, the blogosphere, like most newspaper newsrooms, remains a fashion-free zone.)

Despite its instant heavy-hitter status, the conference, a sea of iPhones and backpacks descending on Austin, still retained an air of new-kid mischief. For instance, you could smell pockets of marijuana smoke floating across the convention center's second-story outdoor balcony in the middle of the afternoon as a small group of attendees took a between-session break. And Mike Stark teamed up with the theater professor Lee Papa, aka the Rude Pundit, and videotaped a recon mission they staged across town at the smaller, right-wing media conference at the Renaissance Austin Hotel, where conservatives gathered to try to play catch-up with the netroots revolution. Stark and Papa were promptly tossed out by hotel security officers after creating a disturbance at the registration table.

As for the Netroots Nation itself, the mood was at times surprisingly somber. As the *New York Times* reported, "The energy quotient in Austin seemed more diffuse" than at previous gatherings. Democrats were on track for historic gains in November, but some of the passion and excitement about the White House seemed to be absent from Austin. One A-list blogger joked privately that if the Netroots Nation convention had been held six weeks earlier, before the FISA fracas, there would have been communal, six-times-a-day bowing in Obama's direction. But instead of bowing in Austin, there were bouts of head shaking.

When a lunchtime panel discussion between Daily Kos's Markos and former centrist Democratic congressman Harold Ford was opened to the floor for questions, the FISA queries came early and often. Trying to move the debate beyond the thorny topic, Markos, after conceding that the Obama vote had been a "cluster fuck," insisted that everyone would soon get over it. But when Ford defended the FISA legislation and noted that lots of Democrats had voted for it, the influential blogger Matt Stoller could be heard booing loudly from the audience.

Sitting inside the lobby of the Hilton Austin and across from the increasingly loud hotel bar as happy hour approached on the third Friday in July, the blogger and ardent Obama supporter Martin Longman wasn't buying the campaign's FISA spin. Obama's vote was by no means a dealbreaker for the 39-year-old, Philadelphia-based Longman; he had once worked for the Sarnoff Corporation, which makes microchips for F-16 fighter planes, before becoming a Philadelphia area community organizer and then a full-time blogger in 2005. But the FISA debacle made it much harder, at least during the summer of 2008, for Longman to champion Obama online without reservation at his site Booman Tribune, which was named after his Newfoundland dog. The vote, specifically the hawkish rhetoric Obama used to justify the vote, certainly made it impossible for Longman to look away, not if he wanted to retain any integrity online.

"If you've been telling your audience for almost two and a half years that this FISA thing is wrong, that it's a serious crime—if you write about that stuff over and over again, then you have no credibility left if you just shrug your shoulders [after the Obama vote] and say, 'It's not a big deal,'" he told me.

Also awkward was the fact that the FISA vote came just weeks after the conclusion of the bruising Democratic primary season, when bloggers like Longman had loudly and often aggressively proclaimed Obama's superiority to Sen. Hillary Clinton and insisted that Obama represented the activists' future in the Democratic Party, whereas Clinton stood for the safe, old triangulating ways. In Austin just weeks after the FISA vote, in which Clinton had *supported* the bloggers and Obama had triangulated on the wiretapping issue, Longman conceded, "There's a sense of, 'You just made me look bad. Thanks a lot.'"

twelve

STILL WAITING FOR THE RIGHTROOTS MOVEMENT

Ethan Winner realized trouble was looming right before midnight on September 21, 2008. At home with his wife and sleeping child in a suburb of Los Angeles, the 40-year-old, who works as a vice president at the PR firm founded by his family, wasn't thinking much about the unfolding presidential contest or his support for Barack Obama. He certainly wasn't thinking about a video clip he had produced 10 days earlier and posted online at YouTube, which attacked the Republicans' newly unveiled vice presidential candidate, Sarah Palin, for her previous political support of the separatist Alaskan Independence Party (AIP).

The 30-second video looked like a standard attack ad, filled with ominous images and presented by a narrator's foreboding warnings. The clip had been a modest hit online, viewed approximately 15,000 times thanks to some key links it received from a handful of liberal blogs and news communities. Winner had never done anything like it before. He and his family had been active in Democratic politics for decades. His father once worked for John F. Kennedy and his maternal grandfather was the first Asian American elected to the California Legislature. For years the Winners had given generously to the Democratic Party, the way so many successful 213 area code donors did.

But as the 2008 campaign entered its final, post–Labor Day stage, Winner, like countless other Obama supporters, wanted to contribute in more substantive and creative ways. He didn't just want to write checks;

he wanted to lend his hand and leave his fingerprints. The Internet represented the obvious forum for Winner to generate his own campaign media. The same impulse had led Philip de Vellis to create his "Vote Different" mash-up clip on behalf of Obama in the winter of 2007.

In early September, before the Wall Street crash, when Sen. John McCain moved slightly ahead in the national polls and nervous Democrats brooded about the Republicans' ability to perfect the art of hardball politics, Winner thought YouTube would be a great way to add more of an edge to the Democratic message. If he produced a clip about Palin and the AIP and crafted it with plenty of attitude, it might gain a larger audience and go viral, boosting that new aggressive progressive message.

So he made his own attack ad. The script looked like this:

NARRATOR: "My hatred for the American government. I've got no use for America." These are quotes from the founder of the Alaskan Independence Party. Sarah Palin and her husband were members of this anti-American organization which supported separation of their state from the United States.

ARCHIVAL VIDEO CLIP OF PALIN: I'm Governor Sarah Palin and I am delighted to welcome you to the 2008 Alaskan Independence Party convention.

NARRATOR: Does this represent your view? Your America? Sarah Palin, a heartbeat away from the presidency.

Winner hired a voice-over artist for $700. With volunteer help from some Winner & Associate employees who used the firm's editing machines (he reimbursed the firm for the time used), he produced "Sarah Palin, a Heartbeat Away" for about $1,000 in half a day. The clip went up on YouTube on September 11. (The video inaccurately claims that Palin had been a member of the AIP, rather than simply a supporter.) He would have loved it if the clip had logged 30,000 to 40,000 views, but he was happy that it had been seen at all and that it conveyed a message he thought was important about Palin. By the night of September 21, the video's life seemed to be winding down.

That's the night a colleague called Winner at home, just before midnight. The coworker had listed the firm's name as a Google News alert, which meant that every time "Winner & Associates" appeared on the Internet, all-knowing Google fired out an email with a description of the mention as well as a link. Right before midnight, "Winner & Associates" mentions started popping up at an alarming rate.

Winner & Associates specializes in crisis management, and its core clients come from the energy and gaming sectors, which means that the company is in the discretion business and is not accustomed to having its name tossed around the Internet with any regularity. Even more unusual, the mentions that night came almost exclusively from the far-right corner of the political blogosphere, and they were nasty and accusatory. Something had exploded online. After scanning the links, Ethan Winner, a heretofore anonymous marketing executive with an MBA and a passion for triathlons, realized he had been publicly tagged as a campaign villain. Suddenly the crisis management specialist found himself managing his own media crisis.

During the next week rabid conservative bloggers attacked Winner, his company, and his family for their involvement in the Palin video. Led by a site dubbed the Jawa Report, the online masses became completely fixated, almost fanatically obsessed, with revealing Winner's identity as the creator of the video, which they deemed to be a "vicious" and "malicious" "smear" because he mistakenly claimed Palin had been a member of the AIP. For some reason, unmasking Winner became a paramount pursuit, so much so that the Jawa blogger announced ominously that he had applied the same online detective work to root out the YouTube creator as he had previously used to uncover the identity of "terrorist supporters."

As part of their cyber deep-dive aimed at outing Winner and then unraveling the larger (alleged) conspiracy in play, bloggers quickly posted Winner's photo online, his email address, information from his Facebook page, his cell phone number, and even details about a boat he sometimes chartered. Out of their respect for privacy, his pursuers announced that they would not post pictures of Winner children.

But bloggers didn't stop with uncovering Winner's identity. They suggested that because his YouTube clip looked and sounded so professional, it must have been bankrolled by an outside group. They suggested that the

Obama campaign, or some other nefarious, left-leaning outside entity, "likely" helped Winner's PR firm peddle the video. In fact, Obama himself may have "funded or knowingly supported" the online effort, according to one breathless online allegation.

Dazed, Winner read the laundry list of allegations and every one of them completely bogus, like the claim that his amateur clip had been part of a vast conspiracy, or that he had cloaked its creation in deep secrecy. In truth, Ethan Winner posted the video under the YouTube username "eswinner," which made it pretty clear that he didn't really care who found out about his identity. That's why, when the GOP bloggers announced the findings of their YouTube "investigation," Winner quickly copped to creating the video. Winner had "confessed," Jawa dramatically announced.

Nobody from the Obama campaign had been involved in the Palin clip on YouTube; Winner wasn't even sure anybody there had even *seen* it. This was confirmed when Obama aides quickly issued a blanket denial in response to the right-wing crusade: "This one ranks as one of the most outlandish conspiracy theories in a campaign that has had its share of them. Neither our campaign nor any of our consultants had any involvement with this YouTube video."

Indeed, the bloggers' "investigation," built on layers of guilt by association, failed to prove that anyone except Winner had paid for the Palin video. They failed to prove that anyone associated with the Obama campaign helped to create the clip. And they failed to prove that Winner had long, deep ties with Obama's media consultant David Axelrod. In fact, Winner had never met, spoken to, or communicated with the man. No connection between Winner and the Obama campaign existed. Nobody had paid him to make the video, and nobody had planted the idea in his brain. "It was entirely my own," he said of his modest project. Why was this even a story? Winner kept asking himself.

Given all of that, Winner couldn't believe that, in the middle of a presidential campaign revolving around a massive, unfolding global credit crisis, his modest attempt at amateur campaign advocacy could, or even should, have been considered newsworthy. His right-wing blog critics certainly never nailed down any facts, let alone put the video story in any kind of context. Weren't there hundreds, if not thousands of amateur-

style campaign clips on YouTube? Why single him out for critical examination? Why was he being portrayed as the villain? Was this modestly
successful YouTube clip really what conservative bloggers wanted to focus
their time and attention on during the closing weeks of the historic White
House campaign season?

Much to his amazement, the right-wing collective answer during the
third week in September was an emphatic Yes! On the morning of September 22, just hours after receiving the first heads-up at home about the
brewing controversy, Winner arrived at his Los Angeles office to find that
right-wing blogs all over the Internet had picked up the YouTube caper
and were making wild, sweeping accusations about him:

- "It certainly appears that Barack Obama's campaign manager is
  involved if not orchestrating these efforts," announced the blogger
  Bob Owens at Confederate Yankee.
- "It looks . . . suspicious. And, do you know something? Right now
  [Jawa's] suspicions are pretty damn credible," cheered RedState
  .com, an anchor of the conservative blogosphere.
- "If all of this is true and the Obama campaign can be connected to
  it, it would represent a massive set of FEC violations," proclaimed
  the blogger Ed Morrissey. (False: even if the Obama campaign had
  paid for the YouTube clip, that wouldn't have violated any FEC
  laws.)

That Monday morning at the office, Winner had phone messages waiting for him from *Los Angeles Times* and *Washington Post* reporters intrigued by the developing story. Soon the right-wing blogger Michelle
Malkin appeared on Fox News hyping the Ethan Winner thriller. The PR
man panicked that if the YouTube story got picked up by the major newspapers, nervous clients would start weighing in with votes of no confidence. In the crisis management business, there's no such thing as good
publicity.

Worse, the abusive emails and letters from blog readers started streaming in to Winner's office and his email account. "Ethan Winner, congrat-
ulations," began one correspondence. "You have been voted King of all

Assholes, Queen of All Scumbags and Prick of the Year." Another concluded, "Nigger Dick Sucker!" One especially poisonous handwritten note mailed to Winner opened, "When jew folks like yourself wonder why your kike asses were tossed into ovens by the glorious 3rd Reich . . ." At one right-wing website a commenter cheered that a friend had vowed to "beat the living shinola out of at least one member of the Winner family."

In late September, as the White House campaign hit its peak, the contrast between the liberal and conservative blogospheres could not have been more stark. As the netroots worked hard to elect the next president and cement even bigger Democratic gains in Congress, while also altering the media landscape, conservative bloggers, busy hounding peripheral, innocent players like Ethan Winner, worked hard at becoming irrelevant.

WHAT A DIFFERENCE four years made.

In September 2004 A-list conservative bloggers, like the ones at Power Line and Little Green Footballs, were basking in the glow of their most famous campaign achievement: taking down CBS's Dan Rather for using questionable documents in a *60 Minutes* report on George Bush's leaky service record in the Texas Air National Guard during the Vietnam War. Convinced that they had uncovered forgeries, the bloggers hatched Memogate and watched CBS clumsily try to answer questions that piled up about the *60 Minutes* report.

The collateral damage was widespread. By early 2005 several CBS News executives had been fired and Dan Rather, who for years represented to conservative critics the epitome of the biased liberal media, no longer sat in the network's nightly anchor chair. Toasted in the mainstream press for their dogged detective work and tapped as the next great resource of the conservative movement in America, right-wing bloggers not only helped get a Republican reelected to the White House in 2004, but they enjoyed an enthusiasm advantage over liberal blogs, many of which were still in their formative stage.

But rather than using the CBS story as a stepping stone to launch serious online investigative work and to grow the right side of the blogosphere into an alternative and insightful news-gathering source or a netrootslike hotbed for political activism, the bloggers let their credibility slip away and embraced a kind of strategic mendacity.

In terms of influence and impact, by 2008 liberal bloggers had completely lapped their conservative counterparts. By the campaign's conclusion, Mary Mapes, who served as Rather's producer on the National Guard story and lost her job because of the controversy, took special delight in noting that the A-list bloggers on the right had been forced to the sidelines as the campaign passed them by. "They just don't matter anymore," wrote Mapes at the Huffington Post.

Going into the White House campaign season conservatives already trailed badly online. "For the most part Republicans are stuck in Internet circa 2000," a former Republican aide turned blogger complained to the *Washington Post* in 2007. The Republican operative in charge of Internet strategy for President Bush's 2004 campaign conceded, "We're losing the Web right now." The conservative writer Dean Barrett noted in the *Weekly Standard* that year, "The right-wing blogosphere doesn't hold conventions, doesn't win the attention of candidates, and more important, doesn't move voters the way the progressive blogosphere does."

By November 2008 Republicans were losing the Web race by even wider margins. At the campaign's conclusion, one GOP operative conceded online that "most [Republican] campaigns know absolutely nothing about blogs and do nothing with them." That's why the electoral influence of Republican bloggers during the campaign was so negligible. That's why, during the primary season, right-wing bloggers and websites all across the Internet, as well as Rush Limbaugh and Sean Hannity on AM radio, announced that John McCain was not fit to be the Party's nominee and urged—demanded!—that voters reject his candidacy.

- "Conservatives have to know that Senator McCain is the anti-conservative."—Hugh Hewitt
- "John McCain cannot fairly be called a conservative."—Right Wing News
- "He is richly despised by a lot of people on the Right."—Power Line

What did Republican voters, including millions of conservatives, do in response? They dutifully ignored the online dictates and handed McCain an easy nomination victory.

Rather than raising money for hand-picked candidates or launching policy initiatives the way the netroots did, right-wing blogs effectively marched themselves into a corner by routinely chasing thin conspiracy theories, like the Ethan Winner caper, that led nowhere except occasionally through the looking glass. The silly and mean-spirited Winner "investigation" represented just one of many dead ends bloggers feverishly chased in 2008.

As compiled by the blogger Jon Swift, these were just some of the Obama conspiracies that prominent conservative bloggers and weblogs pursued and hyped, at times relentlessly, during the campaign:

- While attending Columbia University in the early 1980s and interested in the South African divestiture movement, Obama was involved in violent protests, including domestic terrorist bombings, that erupted when a South African rugby team toured America. —Just One Minute, Ace of Spades
- Obama had an affair with a young female staffer who was promptly exiled to a Caribbean island by an angry Michelle Obama, who discovered the blossoming relationship.—Ace of Spades, Say Anything, Right Voices, Protein Wisdom, Hill Buzz, Black Five
- Obama's deeply personal memoir, *Dreams from My Father,* was actually ghost-written by Bill Ayers, the former '60s radical turned college professor who befriended Obama in Chicago in the 1990s. —American Thinker, Ann Althouse, Powerline, Flopping Aces
- Obama was not born in the United States, and therefore is not eligible to be president. The birth certificate his campaign posted online to debunk that story is actually a forgery. He was born in Kenya.—Atlas Shrugs, Right Wing News, Andrew McCarthy, Gateway Pundit, WorldNetDaily
- When Obama went to visit his ailing grandmother in Hawaii in October, he was really traveling there in order to deal with controversy about his bogus birth certificate.—Stop the ACLU

- When he was nine years old, Obama may have had sex with a
  grown man who was "a suspected commie pervert."—Dan Riehl,
  Confederate Yankee, Jules Crittenden
- A Minnesota man claimed that he took cocaine in 1999 with
  Obama and participated in homosexual acts with him.
  —Jawa Report, WND
- Obama was getting answers in the first presidential debate through
  a clear plastic hearing aid in his ear.—Ann Althouse
- Obama is the illegitimate son of Malcolm X.—Atlas Shrugs

As Swift noted, "Just because there is no evidence that something is
true, that doesn't mean it isn't true," which seemed to capture the conservative bloggers' motto for much of the election season.

CONSERVATIVE BLOGGERS STRUGGLED online in part because they
were permanently tied to and spent untold hours trying to defend Republican policies that became universally unpopular. Not to mention an outgoing Republican president who set historic marks in terms of being
disliked by Americans. But that explained just a small part of the conservative blogosphere's failures as compared to the new heights liberals
reached in 2008.

In truth, the two blogospheres had distinctly different DNA because
they were born in different political environments. In the late 1990s and
early 2000s conservatives had already established their own alternative,
movement-based media: the Republican Noise Machine. Built around
talk radio, Fox News, and partisan print outlets, they were part of a political movement first and part of the media landscape second. They had a
clear allegiance to the GOP and they eagerly embraced propaganda: end-
lessly repeating ideas, phrases, and images.

So when the Internet began to emerge as a political force at the turn of
the decade, it wasn't as if a vacuum existed among conservatives when it
came to political discourse. They already had an abundance of established
outlets where their voices could be heard and promoted. That's one reason
they were slower to embrace the Internet.

Consequently, when the conservative blogosphere matured, it did so within the framework of the established, GOP-friendly alternative media system. Right-wing bloggers such as Michelle Malkin and Hugh Hewitt simply joined in the same conversations that were already being heard on talk radio and Fox News and in the pages of the *Weekly Standard*. Bloggers brought another microphone to an already crowded GOP media table and became an appendage of talk radio. (They also adopted the same deficient editorial standards in the style of Rush Limbaugh.) They embraced the old-fashioned model of experts dispensing wisdom to their loyal readers. For years, many of the major conservative blogs didn't even allow readers to post comments, which meant that the conversation flowed from the blogger, that is, the pundit, to the reader. Interaction was limited, as was the sense of a shared community. Consequently, because lots of prominent conservative bloggers showed no interest in leading a larger movement, comparatively little organizing, fund-raising, or policymaking sprang from the conservative blogs. After all, that's what well-funded conservative think tanks were for.

By contrast, at the turn of the decade lots of liberals were anxious to find new, emerging media voices for political discussion, and when they spotted the possibilities online they flocked to the Internet. They were searching, they were desperate, for an alternative; because no, they didn't view the *Washington Post*'s pro-war editorial and opinion pages as a bastion of liberalism. Ironically, liberals were simply trying to duplicate online what conservatives had already built off-line: a powerful message machine, albeit, a more factually accurate one. But in the process liberals swung open their doors and created a far more democratic, organic, and interactive online environment than found at the top-down, pundit-speak conservative outposts.

The conservative blogosphere, or the rightroots, as it was sometimes known, was also cursed with bad leadership. Early pioneers failed to adapt to the ever changing online environment. Free Republic and the Drudge Report represent two perfect examples. The early online anchors that came of age during the Clinton impeachment years provided Republicans with a prime Internet foothold, but over time both sites refused to adapt and ended up actually stifling conservative growth online.

As the conservative online commentator Patrick Ruffini noted, the founders of Free Republic, once the Daily Kos of the rightroots in terms of size and influence and home to some of the most rabid Republican supporters, known as Freepers, "made the decision that they were going to hoard as much [Web] traffic on their servers as possible. Early on, links to blogs were verboten. If you expressed your own opinion when starting a thread, that was a 'vanity' and it was frowned upon. And fundraising for candidates was strictly forbidden, except for those pet causes approved by the site's owner." A frustrated Ruffini wrote in 2007, "Imagine how the history of the rightroots could have been different if Free Republic wasn't still stuck in 1996?"

At the Drudge Report a similar lack of foresight prevented any sort of political community from taking shape there. The influential news site, with an enormous readership and its eagerness to emphasize Republican attacks during campaign seasons, also shuns all interactivity. Readers simply arrive at the site, scan the headlines, and either click on the links or exit. By contrast, the liberal answer to Drudge, the Huffington Post, operates as the antithesis of the conservative bulletin board's time-capsule approach. Where Drudge's site consists almost entirely of headlines promoted by staid, black-and-white links, the Huffington Post, always reinventing its editorial product and presentation using the latest in Web technology, features an eye-popping look as well as an enormous stable of personal opinions from bloggers. Its exploding community of commenters regularly drown the site in daily debates and running conversations.

The Huffington Post embraces all that was new and interactive and personal about the blogosphere, celebrating cooperative networking practices and freewheeling activism, while the Drudge Report purposefully shuns them. It isn't surprising that it took just three years for the Huffington Post to surpass Drudge's Web traffic. In fact, in September 2008 the Huffington Post *doubled* Drudge's monthly traffic. During the general election's autumn season, Drudge proved completely ineffective in influencing the campaign storylines. His nearly daily insistence that McCain remained poised for a "comeback" became something of a running joke online.

For years liberals bemoaned the fact that conservatives dominated talk radio and there seemed to be something in the DNA of liberal listeners that prevented them from tuning in to like-minded radio hosts for hours on end. With the Internet the tables were turned. Conservatives scratched their heads trying to understand the chasm and why there seemed to be a natural disposition on the left to embrace the nonhierarchical style of the Web and turn it into an oversized organizing tool, while so many Republicans simply demurred.

Asking why there wasn't a conservative Daily Kos became the right-roots' Groundhog Day debate: the question got asked over and over and over. Even after McCain's lopsided, Internet-fueled defeat, nobody on the Right could really answer the riddle.

Whatever the reason for the online apathy, the results for conservatives were often gruesome. In 2006 the Republican National Committee set up MyGOP as a next-generation social-networking site designed to generate small-dollar donations via a people-powered movement, the kind the liberal blogosphere had mastered. To launch MyGOP, the RNC announced that the site's top five fund-raisers would win an iPod. It turned out that the top five MyGOP fund-raisers collected just over $1,000 combined, which, as one MyDD blogger calculated, meant that after covering its iPod costs, the RNC likely *lost* money with its online fund-raising initiative.

"Republicans seem to have created an army of zombies that can't think for themselves," noted the blogger Chris Bowers. "In the past, I have been reluctant to apply the term dittohead to the Republican rank and file, but their continuing failures to conduct any self-starting activism whatsoever is making the word more apt all the time."

During the 2008 campaign conservatives still dominated talk radio in terms of hours broadcast each week. But looking ahead to future campaigns and acknowledging the explosion of growth and influence of politics on the Web, which would Party strategists prefer: a lasting advantage online or perennial dominance on the AM band? In 1998 the answer to that question was radio. By 2008 the answer was equally obvious: the Internet. Fact: Talk radio remained a nonentity when it came to fund-raising for candidates.

The conservative blogosphere suffered bad leadership in another way:

Lots of its A-list writers embraced conspiracies. Back in 2002, when Markos at Daily Kos and Jerome Armstrong at MyDD helped lay the foundation for online political activism among liberals, they could have built their pioneer sites around elaborate conspiracy theories about who "really" controls American power or who "really" plotted the 9/11 attacks, and at the time they would have attracted a sizable online following. But they didn't take that tack; they understood that would have meant forfeiting actual political power. Instead, the duo focused on what Democrats needed to do in 2002 to grow a backbone and win elections again.

Many Republican bloggers proved unable to show similar restraint and foresight. Instead, they seemed to leap at every chance to hype what-if stories, only to routinely embarrass themselves when the stories, often built around unraveling an identity like Ethan Winner's, inevitably collapsed. Not only couldn't right-wing bloggers resist chasing conspiracy theories, but they were often the ones hatching the half-baked plots.

IN TERMS OF red-faced humiliation, the right-leaning blogs likely bottomed out in October of the general election campaign season when they let themselves be duped by an Internet tale built around Michelle Obama.

Unable to spot the obvious telltale signs of an outlandish story, scores of prominent conservative bloggers got fooled into promoting a "bombshell" that "caused a political firestorm not seen since the Jeremiah Wright tapes," as bloggers advertised it. With sneering headlines they excitedly claimed that the story about Michelle Obama's alleged "temper tantrum" revealed the truth about her and her Afro-radical leanings. In fact, the uproar revealed much more about the bloggers and their diminished role on the electoral landscape than it did about the future first lady.

The unbelievable story broke online on October 15, when the overseas outlet African Press International announced that it had scored a campaign scoop when Michelle Obama placed an unsolicited "direct telephone" call to the Norway-based operation to condemn it for attacking her husband and for spreading rumors to "damage a black man's name." Specifically, the report claimed that Michelle Obama

- Accused API of colluding with American bloggers in an effort to bring down her husband.
- Condemned "American white racists" who were bringing up issues of Obama's citizenship.
- Urged the African media to give unwavering support to her husband.
- Offered bribes to the API editors in the form of inauguration invitations if they would "write a good story" about the Democratic candidate.
- Claimed there was "no [citizenship] law" that would stop Obama from becoming president.

The obvious red flags surrounding the article were almost too numerous to count. First, the odds of a site as obscure as API landing a huge campaign scoop weeks before Election Day were almost negligible. Second, the idea that Michelle Obama would give an unsolicited interview to rant about "American white racists" was ludicrous. Third, the Obama campaign, and certainly Michelle Obama herself in 2008, had little history of directly engaging with the blogosphere and no history of engaging with unknown entities making wild charges, such as API.

Nonetheless, prominent conservative political websites (Word Net Daily), communities (freerepublic.com), and bloggers (Gateway Pundit) immediately hyped the Michelle Obama story, since it seemed to capture what they thought Michelle was really like: an angry radical. "She's not happy with those who aren't marching in lock-step with the demands of blind racial loyalty," wrote Bob Owens at Confederate Yankee. "This is a shocking rant, even for someone as extreme as Michelle Obama," the site announced.

As the too-good-to-be-true controversy whipped around the Internet (Why wasn't the mainstream media covering the story? angry bloggers demanded), the API site posted a follow-up by an editor who stood by the Michelle Obama story. The site announced that it had an audiotape of its conversation and would release it soon, which set conservative bloggers into an even more frenzied state as they furiously updated their sites and employed lots of exclamation points for their Michelle Obama–related items ("Double WOW!").

In response to the overwhelming interest in its scoop, the API then posted an overseas phone number where editors could be contacted to verify the story; bloggers eagerly phoned but found no useful information on the other end. Still, that didn't calm the rightroots fury. "I just got off the phone with a very reputable source that says there is absolutely, positively an audiotape showing that Michelle Obama did in fact say what she said," wrote one overexcited conservative blogger with Brent Bozell's Media Research Center. "Perhaps [mainstream reporters] don't want to check out this story because Michelle Obama comes off with an extreme case of bad temper."

After letting the story brew online for a while, Obama campaign officials shot it down. "It's bogus, she didn't call, it's all a lie," senior adviser Robert Gibbs told ABC News. Yet still the story persisted. The following day, API called on Michelle Obama to "come clean" about the story even though the campaign had already explained that she never spoke with the online outlet. Once again, API's editor promised that tapes of Michelle Obama's phone conversation would be released, but only after attorneys cleared them for publication. The API even claimed that Obama's campaign manager had offered editors a $3 million bribe to not produce the audiotape of Michelle Obama denouncing "American white racists."

By week's end, even the right-wing blogs had pretty much given up hope that any confirming audiotape would materialize. Just as they had eventually given up hope trying to prove that Obama had been involved in domestic terrorism while at Columbia University, or had had gay sex or an affair with a female staffer, or had asked a former '60s radical to ghost-write his memoir, or had lied about his birth certificate and was therefore ineligible to become president. Well, not so much the last one; bloggers pursued that claim well beyond Election Day.

Liberals laughed that "gullible morons" on the right were taken in by an obviously bogus API story that was so full of holes it made spam email from wealthy Nigerian princes look like the real deal. Some GOP-friendly blogs, such as Atlas Shrugs, at least pulled their original Michelle Obama items when questions about API's claims arose. But most of the early on-line boosters of the story refused to acknowledge their missteps or apologize to Michelle Obama for propagating the bogus story.

Back in Los Angeles, Ethan Winner could relate. He never saw any apologies from right-wing bloggers who baselessly accused him of being a party to election fraud. His online pursuers just moved on in search of another target. And though Winner didn't lose any clients because of the controversy the bloggers manufactured about his PR firm in their pursuit of Obama, lasting damage was done.

"There's no question that this will have a lingering effect and will impact my future," said Winner, who is still stunned by the bloggers' mob-like lack of fairness and common sense while tagging him as a campaign crook. "When somebody wants to learn a little bit more about me or about Winner & Associates and they run a Google search, they're going to see a lot of hateful things. That's never good when you're trying to run a business. That's a negative shadow that's going to follow me for many years."

thirteen

SARADISE LOST

"**I**t's Sarah."

Phil Munger, a college professor of music (low brass), progressive blogger, and Wasilla, Alaska, resident, broke the news about John McCain's vice presidential pick to his wife, Judy.

"It's Sarah."

Judy didn't believe him. Wasilla's former mayor? No way.

"It's Sarah."

No, really, who did McCain pick?

"It's Sarah."

For almost a full minute on the morning of August 29 the "No, really" game played out in the kitchen of Munger's house, which looks out over Neklason Lake in the Talkeetna Mountains, where large white Trumpeter swans take off and land and where, on that late August a-day-that-would-live-in-Alaskan-infamy morning, the outdoor temperature hovered around 40 degrees.

Judy kept protesting, but the answer kept coming back the same: "It's Sarah."

Everywhere else in the Lower 48, stunned political observers buzzed about McCain's shocking pick and asked, Who is the Tina Fey lookalike? But in Wasilla, and in every inhabited corner of the Last Frontier, "It's Sarah" was all locals had to say to convey the stupefying news about the popular governor of a state whose population and square mileage perfectly match: 600,000 people and 600,000 square miles. Sarah might become the vice president of the United States? Not possible, Munger's wife announced.

Just minutes earlier, Munger had felt the same sense of shock wash over him when he learned of the political lightning bolt and had nearly simultaneous panicked thoughts. First, with her strident fundamentalist, anti-science, End of Days far-right Christian beliefs, there was no way that Sarah Palin should be allowed anywhere near the button that set off U.S. nuclear missiles. Second, the McCain campaign hadn't vetted Palin. It just wasn't possible, thought Munger. And what did that say about McCain's judgment?

During the previous weeks, when fleeting rumors surfaced among Alaskans politically obsessed about Palin's being considered for the GOP's number two spot, Munger dismissed them as faint chatter. He didn't even bother to blog about it at his site, Progressive Alaska. Most of the state's other key bloggers also ignored the far-fetched what-if talk. Munger figured the McCain camp simply had to perform a rudimentary political background check on Palin and they'd realized they couldn't tap her for the VP slot. He assumed that if anybody had bothered to vet Palin they would have learned that she had been caught up in a scandal that summer surrounding the firing of her Department of Public Safety chief, Walt Monegan, the story that would become known as Troopergate. Munger didn't see how a seasoned Beltway strategist could look at the tangled facts surrounding that case, along with Palin's ever-changing explanations, and decide to elevate Palin to the national stage.

So he blogged it. "I wanted to warn people," Munger recalled weeks later. When he sat down to write his first impressions about Palin's meteoric ascent, he headlined the post "Saradise Lost," in part because "Saradise" was Alaskan slang describing the idyllic frontier realm populated by Palin's most fervent Republican supporters, the Sarabots.

That same morning, liberal bloggers all over Alaska tapped away on their keyboards wearing the same stunned expression that Munger had stuck to his face. They didn't realize it then, but within just a matter of days Alaskan bloggers would emerge as one of the most important local newsgathering sources of the entire election season. Collectively, they wrote a new chapter in campaign journalism. In the right place—4,300 miles and 74 hours by car from the Beltway—and at the right time and boasting unmatched knowledge about Palin and Alaska politics, the bloggers served an invaluable function.

While major media organizations scrambled to even *get* reporters to Alaska to start their background reporting on the star governor, the bloggers were teeing up all kinds of meaty morsels from the minute the Palin news first broke. That, combined with Munger's hunch being proven accurate, that Palin hadn't been vetted by the McCain camp, meant there existed an avalanche of information for bloggers to push out to eager readers nationwide who were suddenly afflicted with an unquenchable thirst for Palin news and commentary. (Because of the Palin pick, Daily Kos's online traffic that Labor Day weekend reached unprecedented heights.)

The Bridge to Nowhere, Troopergate, Palin's unorthodox religious beliefs, her former love affair with federal earmarks, her antiscience beliefs, and her dubious claim to being "commander-in-chief" of the Alaska National Guard: it was a smorgasbord for local bloggers like Munger operating with clear-eyed skepticism, who for long stretches of time *owned* the Palin story.

Alaska bloggers, including previously little-known entities such as Celtic Diva's Blue Oasis, Kodiak Konfidential, Mudflats, Own the Sidewalk, AndrewHalcro, What Do I Know?, Alaska Real, Immoral Minority, and Just a Girl from Homer, effectively formed their own organic all-Palin-all-the-time news collective, their own de facto reporting pool, that often rivaled traditional outlets when it came to output and insight. "Alaska Bloggers Breaking Palin News," acknowledged a *Time* headline in September. They were progressive pioneers sending back dispatches from the frontier.

While the Beltway press's initial Day 1 and Day 2 response to the Palin pick featured praise for McCain and his return to his bold, maverick roots, the Alaska bloggers were relentless in posting serious hometown analysis and background checks about Palin's little-known past. Their due diligence became a key reason why, one month after her VP selection, 6 out of 10 voters thought Palin lacked the experience for the job and why she eventually became a drag on the Republican ticket.

The only online demerit from the Palin coverage came from a small group of netroots residents, almost all of them outside Alaska, who fell in love with a Palin conspiracy theory, flew a little too close to the politics-of-personal-destruction flame, and threatened to tarnish all the smart reporting done by hard-working bloggers up north. Bloggers like Phil Munger.

ON THE MORNING of August 29 Munger could tell big news had broken when he checked his iPhone and saw that producers for the nationally syndicated *Thom Hartmann Program* had been trying for hours to reach him. Munger had turned the ringer off that morning because it was his first day off in almost two weeks. His real job was teaching tuba and music appreciation at the University of Alaska at Anchorage. But his other job that year had been as a nearly full-time volunteer for Diane Benson, a local progressive who tried to wrestle away the Democratic Party's nomination for the state's lone congressional seat. On August 26 Benson went down to defeat, outspent 8 to 1 by the more Party-friendly candidate. Munger still felt his hundreds of volunteer hours had been time well spent.

The plan for that Friday was to relax and disengage from politics a bit. Maybe he'd tend to his bedraggled garden. He couldn't remember a more inhospitable summer; just two days in the entire month of July broke past the 70-degree mark. And forget about August; lots of days didn't even make it past 50. During the valley's 100-day growing season, Munger's green beans didn't make it and the red cabbages were the size of softballs instead of beach balls.

But he couldn't really complain. In June he got to take his son and daughter on a 22-hour, round-trip net-dip fishing excursion up on Copper River for the world's best-tasting salmon. They drove all night and through the upper Matanuska canyons and into the high country near Gunsite Mountain, where they boarded boats at 5 a.m. and powered down the river into Wood Canyon. By day's end they had snagged 85 world-famous Copper River salmon, including a couple of jumbo,

30-pound King salmon. Back home they smoked and then vacuum-sealed the salmon and packed them away at 20 below so they'd last the long winter.

That's what Munger loved about Alaska and why he fell in love with the place three decades earlier. A textbook Baby Boomer in many ways, Munger grew up in the Seattle area and studied music at Ohio's Oberlin Conservatory in the mid-1960s. When a marine buddy of his got killed in Vietnam, Munger felt waves of guilt. After a drunken night in Oberlin, he woke up the next morning and sent a letter to his local draft board asking that his 2F status be changed to 1A, making him eligible for the draft. When he later realized the foolishness of his noble gesture, Munger wrote a desperate second letter asking his draft board to ignore his first request. The draft board claimed it never received his second letter. So at the end of the semester in 1966, Munger packed up his college gear and reported for duty. He hated the army and never actually made it to Vietnam. A helicopter mishap cut his military duty to two years, and after he won an honorable discharge in 1968 he studied music composition at the University of Washington. He also helped slip Pacific Northwest draft dodgers over the Canadian border aboard unmarked fishing vessels in the middle of the night. Four decades later, Munger would volunteer his musical talents and play the bugle at veterans' ceremonies around south-central Alaska.

In 1973 he moved to Alaska for the adventure, to maybe make some money, and to reevaluate his life. He became enchanted with the place. His initial plan to work construction fell through, so he ended up doing what people in Alaska do: a little bit of everything. He ran a radio station in Cordova, at the foot of the Chugach Mountains. Then he moved on to Whittier, a tiny, remote port town on the western edge of Prince William Sound that received no direct sunlight between the months of November and February because the sun didn't rise high enough in the sky to get above looming Maynard Mountain. Cars have to drive through a 2.5-mile tunnel through the mountain to access the town of a few hundred inhabitants. In Whittier, Munger worked as the town's harbormaster. His wife taught school.

Then they moved to Wasilla to start a family. For years Munger worked to rehabilitate criminals while running Alaska's largest halfway house. In 1993 the state of Alaska awarded Munger a fellowship to write classical music. Within a decade his work was performed all over Alaska, as well as at Lincoln Center, the Kennedy Center, Juilliard, the National Gallery, and the National Cathedral.

In March 2003 two events clicked for Munger and sparked his semi-dormant Baby Boom political activism. The first was the U.S.–led invasion of Iraq, which Munger saw as an act of pure evil reminiscent of the Vietnam War. The second was the death of the American activist Rachel Corrie in the Gaza Strip.

A 23-year-old senior at Evergreen College in Washington State, Corrie was killed on March 16, 2003, in the Palestinian town of Rafah after being run over by an armored D9 Caterpillar bulldozer manned by the Israeli Defense Force, in the process of demolishing local Palestinian homes. Protesting the destruction, Corrie refused to get out of the bull-dozer's way. That March, with the drums of war with Iraq beating so loudly in America, Munger hadn't followed the news of Corrie's death. But when he Googled in search of antiwar poems for a song cycle he wanted to write, he came across a site that hosted poems written in Corrie's memory. Most of the efforts, he thought, were sort of shallow, Jewel-wannabe expressions of regret. But a couple struck a chord, including one written by a Sri Lanka–born computer engineer named Thushara Wijer-atna, who worked for Microsoft in Washington State. Titled "The Skies Are Weeping," the poem was based on Sri Lankan Buddhist imagery. "That's what got me hooked," Munger recalled.

Thirteen months later the University of Alaska at Anchorage issued a press release announcing the world premiere of Munger's seven-movement cantata, *The Skies Are Weeping,* to be performed at the university's recital hall on April 27, 2004.

The announcement sparked intense political opposition. Critics ac-cused Munger, who previewed the text of the cantata with community leaders prior to the premiere, of presenting unbalanced attacks on Israel and not taking into account the Israeli women and children who were killed by Palestinian suicide bombs. As the rhetoric escalated and email threats poured in, Munger, fearing for the safety of the student musicians involved, canceled the performance. Subsequent attempts to stage *The Skies Are Weeping* in New York and Toronto fell through. Finally, in London in 2005, with Corrie's parents in attendance, the cantata was performed.

During the yearlong controversy, Munger, who had spent his adult life happily cloaked in Alaskan anonymity, got denounced as a terrorist sympathizer, received constant hate mail, and was labeled an anti-Semite during a joint session of the Alaska Legislature. "I wasn't surprised there was pushback, but I was surprised at the vehemence," he told me. He felt that one of the few places where he received support, or at least a fair hearing, was online. Thanks to the cantata controversy, Munger became exposed to the netroots, where he quickly became a Valerie Plame–case aficionado and an ardent fan of Firedoglake, which live-blogged the Scooter Libby trial.

Prodded into action by several Firedoglake contributors who urged Munger to start his own blog, he launched Progressive Alaska on November 4, 2007, and picked up a small but influential audience of daily readers from the world of Alaska politics, including the former Wasilla mayor and now governor, Sarah Palin, who read the blog each morning. Munger was quickly tapped as the first blogger asked to serve on the board of the Alaska Press Club.

Progressive Alaska gave Munger a forum to air his opinions about hometown politics, but he also did some original reporting, blogger-style, by picking up scraps of information here and there. One great source of political scuttlebutt was Munger's cab-driving buddy in Anchorage, who heard all kinds of tidbits shuttling people between the airport and downtown government buildings.

In the summer of 2008 Palin dismissed the state's top cop, Walt Monegan, after he refused to fire her former brother-in-law, a state trooper whose marriage to Palin's sister ended in acrimony and allegations of lawbreaking. The story morphed into Troopergate after discrepancies emerged surrounding the firing. Munger scored a nifty scoop at one of his son's cross-country meets. It came when Palin announced that Chuck Kopp, the chief of police for the town of Kenai, was her pick to replace Monegan as the state's Department of Public Safety chief. Munger recalled that months earlier, at the cross-country meet, he had talked to one of the dads who worked for the city of Kenai; the dad mentioned that Kopp had been involved in a sexual harassment inquiry and had to be reassigned. As soon as Munger heard that Palin had picked Kopp to replace Monegan, he knew Kopp hadn't been properly vetted and wrote that the guy didn't stand a chance, that his nomination was DMOA: dead meat on arrival. Ten days later Kopp withdrew his name from consideration. "Alaska is the biggest fucking small town in the world," Munger laughed. It's where overlapping relationships are based on two degrees of separation, not six.

To be honest, though, the number of people who read Munger's miniscoop on Kopp could have filled a small section of the bleachers at Wasilla High School. The Palin pick changed all that. Overnight the audience eager for Alaska political news mushroomed into the tens of millions. August 29 kicked off Palin-palooza, and the band of liberal Alaskan bloggers starred as unlikely headliners for the festival.

After Palin got picked, Munger's Alaska Progressive went from a couple of thousand unique visitors for the entire week to tens of thousands logging on during the middle of the night to read the site and its ongoing "Saradise Lost" installments. He went from 2,800 readers the week before the Palin announcement to 92,000 the week of the big event. (By Election Day, Munger had posted his 181st "Saradise Lost" entry.)

The downside? Munger became chained to his computer and spent eight hours a day on the Palin blogging patrol. That came on top of his full-time teaching job, which meant there just weren't enough hours in the day to chronicle "Saradise Lost" *and* write melodies on his upright piano to accompany Shakespeare sonnets for his choral students to practice. And Munger was hardly alone, or even the most read of the Alaska bloggers who shot to prominence following Palin's selection.

Maia Nolan, the witty 29-year-old writer behind the quirky blog Own the Sidewalk, had been way ahead of the fashion curve when she dressed up as Sarah Palin for Halloween back in 2006. She enjoyed a steady readership that numbered in the hundreds as she used her blog to semi-stalk Mark Begich, Anchorage's boyish mayor, as he ran for the U.S. Senate. That's when she wasn't busy posting details from her team's weekly pub trivia quiz outings at Humpy's Great Alaskan Alehouse in Anchorage. But on the night Wasilla's former mayor debuted as McCain's running mate, Nolan posted "Palin Myths Dispelled." Example: "She was never Miss Alaska. She was Miss Wasilla. She lost the state pageant to Miss South Central, Maryline Blackburn." The item scored 60,000 clicks.

That figure paled in comparison to the overnight sensation experienced by Mudflats, a site launched just three months prior to Palin's pick and run by the anonymous blogger AKMuckraker. With a pair of yellow galoshes posted in place of her photo, the Anchorage-based blogger was actually an East Coast transplant with a New England liberal arts background. She arrived in Alaska in the early 1990s with $300 in her pocket and did not know a single person in the Last Frontier. She took her first drink at an Alaskan bar in Wasilla's infamous Mug-Shot Saloon.

Still reeling from the Palin VP announcement on the morning of the 29th, AKMuckraker that night posted her thoughts under the headline "What Is McCain Thinking? One Alaskan's Perspective," where she spelled out her sweeping reservations about the Palin pick: "Frankly, I don't even know if she's ever been out of the country." The post also offered newcomers the most concise cheat sheet regarding Troopergate. After she posted the item, AKMuckraker wondered if it might attract a little extra traffic. People would be curious to learn more about Palin's past, and who better to tell her tale than local bloggers? On her nascent site, where posted items normally generated between two and four reader responses, "What Is McCain Thinking?" logged more than 1,200 comments from readers around the world. In the three weeks following the Palin-as-VP pick, the overwhelmed Muckraker counted 2.5 million page hits on her site and 25,000 posted comments. AKMuckraker's preferred meal during the Palin insanity of September was cereal, simply because it took so little time to prepare and she could eat it while sitting in front of her computer screen.

There was the relentless Linda Kellen Biegel, who blogged at Celtic Diva's Blue Oasis, and Anchorage native Andrew Halcro, a car rental executive who ran against Palin for the governorship in 2006 and started blogging about Alaska politics. Together, according to Munger, they were really the ones who broke the Troopergate case wide open in the summer of 2008. "If they hadn't been there the [Anchorage] *Daily News* would have just let it go by, I'm one hundred percent certain of that," Munger claimed.

Meanwhile, it was local bloggers, including Munger, who flagged the fact that videos of sermons from Palin's former pastor had been quickly yanked off the Wasilla Assembly of God website, perhaps because in the past the provocative pastor had suggested that critics of President Bush would be banished to Hell and that people who voted for Sen. John Kerry in 2004 wouldn't be accepted into Heaven.

The local bloggers were among the first to fact-check Palin's claim about the Bridge to Nowhere, the state's infamous earmark, which asked the federal government for nearly $400 million to build a span the size of the Golden Gate Bridge to connect the city of Ketchikan to the Ketchikan International Airport on Gravina Island, which had a population of 50. During her Republican coming-out party at the Dayton Rally on August 29, when McCain first introduced her as his running mate, and again at the GOP National Convention in St. Paul, Palin cheerfully announced that she had said "Thanks but no thanks" to the Bridge to Nowhere. It became Palin's money line. But it wasn't true. Alaska bloggers quickly wrote that Palin had been on the record during the 2006 governor's race supporting the construction of the bridge. Only after it became a national laughingstock did she back off the proposal. Besides that, she was never in a position to say "no thanks" to the bridge since the funding got yanked before she took office.

Outside of Alaska, however, not all the netroots Palin investigations produced such stellar results.

HEADLINED "PALIN'S FAKED 'Pregnancy'? Covering for Teen Daughter?," the Daily Kos diary, written by Inky99 and posted on the evening

Palin was introduced as McCain's VP pick, claimed, "Palin's last child, a baby with Down's syndrome, may not be hers. It may be that of her teenage daughter." In other words, Palin had faked being the mother of her four-month-old son, Trig, because Trig was actually born to Palin's unwed teenage daughter, Bristol. Palin faked the birth to cover up any controversy the news would have created for the sitting governor with close ties to the evangelical community, which looked down on premarital sex and teenage pregnancy.

As proof of the conspiracy, the brief Daily Kos item linked to an *Anchorage Daily News* article from April, which detailed how surprised people around Palin had been to discover she was pregnant in 2008 because she didn't look pregnant. It also linked to a photo of Palin just prior to her pregnancy, when she did not appear to be pregnant. From that, and the fact that Palin's teenage daughter "apparently" had been out of school for months at the time when Sarah Palin gave birth to Trig, Inky99 suggested that Trig was not Palin's son, but Bristol's.

Inky99's post from Saturday created some buzz online, but it was the following day's jaw-dropping Daily Kos post by ArcXIX that created the firestorm, as the entry raced up the site's recommended list, thanks to so many Daily Kos readers who gave the post an electronic thumbs-up. Much more detailed in terms of photographic and video evidence in support of the conspiracy claim that Palin had faked her pregnancy, the new diary, "Sarah Palin Is NOT the Mother," also dripped with personal disdain:

> Now, I've known liars in my life. Their single core problem is not with themselves, but those around them. If they're never called out on their twisting of truths and fabrications, they simply continue to make larger lies.
>
> Sarah, I'm calling you a liar. And not even a good one. Trig Paxson Van Palin is not your son. He is your grandson. The sooner you come forward with this revelation to the public, the better.

Dissecting the physical evidence in search of clues, the diarist paid particular attention to the physiques of Palin and her daughter, noting that

"Sarah's waistline never changed [during the pregnancy]. Her wardrobe still remained tight and professional." As for 17-year-old Bristol, photos in early 2007 convinced the diarist that she was pregnant. "She is not carrying belly fat, which grows outwardly wide, and does not become dome-shaped. That's because fat is generally evenly distributed around the abdomen and a fetus is not. Bristol's chest is sticking out, a normal body reaction when sucking in stomach muscles."

That Saturday, the story enjoyed pickup around the Web on sites like the Moderate Voice, Comments from Left Field, and 23/6. Netroots readers were devouring the post, but most top bloggers wouldn't touch the story. John Aravosis at AmericaBlog wrote back to a reader who emailed him a link to the Daily Kos firecracker, "I've seen the story, but I'd like to see more facts before even considering writing about it. I just don't like publishing this kind of thing without firm evidence that something is awry." Martin Longman at the pro-Obama site Booman Tribune later blogged that, "We didn't want to touch the Sarah Palin pregnancy story with a 10-foot pole and the overwhelming consensus [among bloggers] was to strongly discourage anyone that was running with the rumors. We stifled the story as much as we could without deleting people's diaries."

But on the Sunday evening of Labor Day weekend, the high-profile *Atlantic* blogger and Obama cheerleader Andrew Sullivan embraced the fake pregnancy claim, suggesting that the Daily Kos diaries posed intriguing questions that needed to be addressed by the McCain campaign. With a loyal following among Beltway journalists, Sullivan's post signaled to the press (incorrectly) that the fake pregnancy story represented a serious matter of inquiry among liberal bloggers. That same night, the Drudge Report tagged the story, although with a different spin: "Lefty Bloggers Go After Palin's 16 year old [*sic*] Daughter."

And just like that, for better or worse, the blogosphere was assigned ownership of the fake pregnancy story, the most infamous online conspiracy theory concocted during the general election season.

•   •   •

FROM HIS BURBANK, California, apartment, Lee Stranahan watched in dismay as the fake pregnancy story detonated at Daily Kos on Friday and Saturday. A self-described recovering libertarian, Stranahan had become a registered Democrat and was anxiously awaiting his chance to vote for Barack Obama in November. He'd spent years as an erotic photographer, and in 2008 his day job was working as a graphic artist for the celebrity-worship show *Access Hollywood.* But his real interests were politics and the Internet. He'd been online forever, nearly two decades, and was among AOL's earliest subscribers.

Recently he'd been creating satirical video clips and posting them online. His spoof of a Mike Huckabee campaign ad posted on YouTube in 2007 received 250,000 views, and Markos at Daily Kos hailed it as one of the year's best efforts. Eager to make a name for himself online— "I'd rather not be doing graphics at *Access Hollywood*," he conceded— Stranahan figured that the best way to do that as a writer was to plant some flags early on, to get out in front of a story or two and be the person saying "Here's what it is." And hopefully, of course, get the story right.

Sometimes that strategy required that he play the contrarian. In July 2008 Stranahan definitely stood out at the Huffington Post when he admonished the liberal blogosphere for remaining silent about the just-published reports in the *National Enquirer* that John Edwards had had an affair and that he'd been caught inside the Beverly Hills Hilton after a rendezvous with his lover, Rielle Hunter. The tabloid claimed that Edwards may have fathered a baby with Hunter.

After looking into the story himself, doing some original reporting, talking with *Enquirer* editors, and noting that the tabloid had published firsthand accounts of the hotel ambush, not the usual secondhand rumors, Stranahan became convinced that the story was true and that the truth about Edwards's affair would quickly tumble out. But as he searched his favorite blogs he saw virtually no discussion of the story. So he went online to warn progressives, who appeared to be in a state of denial about their favorite son. He warned them that they were ignoring the story at their own peril, because when it broke big it would have larger implications for the Democratic brand. Stranahan wrote up his Edwards post and logged on to the Huffington Post, but he still had doubts about hitting the *save* button, which would publish the item live online. He remembered thinking, "Why the hell isn't anybody else talking about this?"

Stranahan cross-posted his warning on Daily Kos, and over the course of 10 days wrote three other scandal-related diaries, belittling Edwards apologists for refusing to admit the truth and for refusing to debate the potential political fallout for all Democrats if the Edwards allegation was true. His claims touched a nerve at Daily Kos, where Edwards had been highly regarded as a populist candidate. The Kossaks mostly hurled insults at Stranahan—"You're a moron," "An idiot opportunistic jerk"—and accused him of being a Republican troll bent on embarrassing Edwards.

Then one day in early August, when Stranahan logged on to his Daily Kos account to respond to one of the many comments posted beneath one of his Edwards-related diaries, he realized he didn't have a *reply* button. Then he realized that he didn't have a button to create a new diary either. And then he realized that he'd been banned from Daily Kos. His posting privileges had been revoked.

"If you're an Apple fan and Apple goes and does something stupid and you criticize them, you're going to be viciously attacked by people who think Apple can do no wrong. This was exactly the same thing," was how Stranahan interpreted his banishment.

Less than one week later, Stranahan watched breaking reports as the suddenly chaste John Edwards admitted his affair with Hunter. (He denied being the baby's daddy.) Appealing to Daily Kos to be reinstated in light of the fact that he'd been right about Edwards all along, Stranahan never received a response. He did notice that Edwards's wife, Elizabeth, made her only public statement about the affair on Daily Kos, which generated lots of extra publicity for the site. Three days later Daily Kos's founder, Markos, warmly thanked the community for the sensitive way it handled the Edwards saga. Stranahan thought that was strange: the Daily Kos community toasted for turning a blind eye to a breaking news story that involved a prominent Democrat?

Now, just three weeks after the embarrassing Edwards revelation, Stranahan thought it odd that so many within the Daily Kos community who had remained silent about the story regarding Edwards's personal life, a story brimming with established facts, suddenly embraced the Palin pregnancy story, which seemed to him to be barren of facts. If Stranahan was banned by Daily Kos readers for his (accurate) posts about the Edwards affair, why wasn't ArcXIX being driven from the online community? (ArcXIX would eventually take the Palin diary down voluntarily.)

Perhaps even more troubling were the speculative personal attacks in the Daily Kos pregnancy diaries, attacks Stranahan thought had no place in the blogosphere or any kind of progressive political community. He wasn't allergic to hardball tactics in the name of a bump in the polls, but this obvious attempt to dehumanize Palin struck him as desperate. Besides, even if the far-fetched pregnancy story were true, wouldn't that just make Palin appear to be some sort of martyr when headlines like "Supermom Shields Daughter from Life's Unexpected Turns" started appearing? What was the upside for Democrats in unmasking this extremely murky whodunit?

In terms of the diaries themselves, Stranahan thought the ArcXIX post in particular was just bat-shit crazy. Since when did anonymous strangers accuse other people, let alone public officials, of *faking* pregnancies? Since when did progressives try to win elections by concocting conspiracy theories about a woman's reproductive history? To Stranahan, the diary embarrassed not only Daily Kos, but the larger progressive community. It hand-delivered potent ammunition to long-time netroots critics on the Right, who immediately began typing up howls of protest about the Palin conspiracy theory and how the Loony Left was at it again. "Journalism by mob rule," "Despicable, sexist trash," and "the worst kind of putrid mudslinging" were just some of the posted condemnations. Conservatives also accused the Obama campaign of pushing the rumors to friendly blogs in hopes they would air the accusations.

It's true that hundreds of readers at Daily Kos posted angry comments in response to the ArcXIX diary and urged that it be taken down. But that didn't stop the diary from racing up the site's recommended list after so many Daily Kos readers voted it one of the day's best posts. Plus,

Inky99 had attached an interactive poll to the first Daily Kos pregnancy diary, asking readers to vote on the rumor's worthiness. More than 20,000 people responded, and a robust 63 percent believed that the fake pregnancy story was a legitimate one worth chasing. Just 23 percent deemed it to be off-limits.

Stranahan was disturbed by the controversy, and by the larger silence within the netroots community as the Daily Kos diary came to life. He wondered why so few people came forward to shout the story down or to point out that it represented a political loser. He was sure that the allegations would simply engender sympathy for Palin from most news consumers.

On Sunday morning, August 31, he logged on to the Huffington Post, where he'd been contributing since April, and posted an essay that ridiculed both the Palin story and Daily Kos: "It's the wackiest rumor about Sarah Palin or any other politician so far this election. It's making its way all through the internet. And of course it came from DailyKos." But Stranahan felt awfully lonely, as he did when he posted his first critique of the Edwards story. He felt like the loner at the beach on a beautiful day with nobody else around. He kept thinking to himself, "Why am I the only person here?"

Stranahan hoped his denunciation of the gossip-mongering story would be echoed and embraced around the blogosphere. Instead, most of the links he picked up that day came from *conservative* bloggers, who used it to bash the netroots community for either hyping the pregnancy story or failing to condemn it. In fact, less than six hours after Stranahan's salvo, the fake pregnancy story landed its most influential online sponsor when Andrew Sullivan, blogging at the *Atlantic,* picked up the story and urged readers, and reporters, to investigate it further.

Stranahan was dumbfounded.

Sullivan was one of Stranahan's favorite bloggers. He'd been reading the British-born writer for years. Because Sullivan was a self-described conservative who voted for Bush in 2000, warned after 9/11 that "decadent left enclaves on the coasts may well mount a fifth column," and stood out as a cheerleader for the Iraq war in 2003, Sullivan was never going to be an official member of the liberal blogosphere. But his political reversal, which soon included relentless attacks on the Bush administration, as well as his vocal cheerleading for Obama, had won Sullivan a legion of progressive fans online in 2008. During the final weekend in August Sullivan became by far the highest profile Obama supporter online to link to the fake pregnancy story and suggest that it required serious attention, that it represented a legitimate line of inquiry for traditional reporters to pursue.

Under the headline "Things That Make You Go Hmmm" on August 31, Sullivan announced, "The noise around this [pregnancy] story is now deafening." (The post marked the beginning of something of an obsession for Sullivan, who continued to push the Palin pregnancy story even *after* Election Day.) Less than one hour later, in response to hostile reader feedback that accused the blogger of lobbing a smear, Sullivan defended the post, claiming that he just wanted clear answers, including medical records, from the McCain camp regarding Palin's most recent pregnancy. "The job of a blogger is to get facts straight," stressed Sullivan, who blogged again and again that night about the fake pregnancy story.

But to Stranahan, the facts *were* straight. Asking the governor of Alaska to prove that she gave birth to her own son just four months earlier and demanding that the McCain camp produce medical records to prove the Palin family wasn't living out an episode of *Desperate Housewives* did not represent "good faith questions" that anyone "with common sense would ask," as Sullivan suggested. Stranahan was surprised that the high-profile blogger posted a link to ArcXIX, suggesting that the Daily Kos diary raised "legitimate questions." And he was puzzled by Sullivan's claim that answers about Trig's birth could "easily be provided" by the McCain campaign. If that were suddenly the campaign standard for lodging allegations, wouldn't that just encourage right-wing critics to concoct some heinous story about Barack Obama and then demand that answers could "easily be provided" by his campaign to show the candidate had never, for instance, beaten his wife?

Stranahan wasn't alone that night in feeling a sense of dread about the gathering online momentum behind the fake pregnancy story. Back in

Alaska, the liberal blogger Linda Kellen Biegel begged readers, for the sake of credibility, to turn away from the distracting Trig story. The same Palin rumor had been floating around Alaska for months, but nobody took it seriously. Right before midnight on August 31, the Daily Kos diarist known as The Red Pen posted an April 13, 2008, photo, taken on the final day of Alaska's legislative session and just days before Trig's premature birth, in which a clearly pregnant-looking Palin was interviewed by a local television reporter. The Red Pen posted the image at Daily Kos, announced that the pregnancy story had officially been debunked, and chastised the community: "We can drop this crap now. We look stupid pushing this rumor."

Stranahan appreciated that some members of the Daily Kos community corrected ArcXIX's claims. In theory, that's what the netroots did best: police its own. But he was concerned that the damage had already been done. The mere fact that a large chunk of Daily Kos readers thought the fake pregnancy hoax was worth pushing signaled to Stranahan that something had gone seriously wrong online, that a very important track had been jumped during the heated campaign season.

Around the netroots many bloggers privately wrestled with what to do about the fake pregnancy story. "This whole thing is making me queasy and questioning whether the netroots have any sense," one veteran blogger conceded off-line. Caught up in the passion of the campaign, spooked by McCain's staying power in the polls, and startled by the wave of good early press the Palin pick had generated (i.e., McCain's a maverick!), the netroots did cast a wide opposition research net that first weekend following the VP announcement. Liberal bloggers had adopted a "shoot first, ask questions later" mentality about checking out Palin. In that hothouse environment some of them read the Daily Kos pregnancy diaries and were genuinely intrigued by the timeline, the posted photos, and the political ramifications if the story were true.

But it was only late August. Obama had just completed a wildly successful nominating convention, he remained (slightly) ahead in the polls, and there were already scores of solid, substantive Palin leads to follow up. There was no reason to hit the panic button and suddenly cast aside editorial guidelines to hype anonymous Daily Kos diaries that seemed to ex-emplify the definition of "fantastic."

Then again, blogging is an hourly game in which editorial choices can't be delayed forever. If a topic or a particular blog post blew up online, no-body wanted to be the last one to acknowledge something that turned out to be a game-changing event. Bloggers weren't completely opposed to rais-ing uncomfortable questions about Palin's family, as long as it was done under the guise of highlighting how poor a job the McCain camp had done in vetting its VP pick. Still, virtually none of the A-list liberal blog-gers touched the fake pregnancy story or suggested that the Daily Kos di-aries raised serious, substantial questions about Palin.

That, for Stranahan, was the good news. The bad news? Virtually none of the A-list liberal bloggers touched the fake pregnancy story. In other words, not enough netroots leaders stepped forward to call bullshit on the Daily Kos diaries or stressed that the netroots had better Palin stories to tackle than spinning conspiracy theories about her birthing history.

Truth is, most bloggers don't really think that way. Outsiders might view the netroots as a fully formed community overseen by some sort of governing body. But that just isn't the case. For bloggers, simply main-taining their own site and posting new content—feeding the beast—is time-consuming enough. They don't have the hours or the energy to con-stantly take the blogosphere's temperature and comment on the larger goings-on. Most don't consider themselves blogger cops whose job it is to tell people what to write and what not to link to. The major blogs are run by big boys and girls who can make their own editorial decisions. After all, one of the allures of the blogosphere is that inhabitants trust each other to be sufficiently smart and insightful to make the right deci-sions day after day, month after month. The high-wire act—Look ma, no editors!—has strong appeal.

On Labor Day weekend in 2008, just hours after the Palin blockbuster story broke, and with bloggers scrambling to quickly define Palin, the idea of stepping up onto a cyber soap box while traffic whizzed by and blowing a whistle to call time-out on the fake pregnancy story just wasn't at the top of many people's to-do list. In hindsight, maybe it should have been, but in real time it just was not. Al Giordano, writing at his blog, the Field, represented an exception: "Too many bloggers and their commenters have jumped on rumors—about pregnancies and other matters—that turned out to be false, and have harmed the messengers' own credibility by stating them as fact," he warned on September 3.

Nine times out of 10 the kooky stuff posted online that couldn't withstand serious scrutiny collapsed under its own weight, as the fake pregnancy tale eventually did. But the circumstances surrounding the Palin pregnancy diaries were so extraordinary and so high-profile that partisan critics easily latched on to the story as a way to target and demote the netroots.

The McCain campaign made sure of that on September 1, when it announced that Palin's 17-year-old daughter, Bristol, was five months pregnant, planned to have the baby, and would soon be marrying the baby's daddy. Of course, the Republican camp had to make that announcement at some point during the campaign since by Election Day Bristol would be eight months pregnant. But using the fake pregnancy rumor published at Daily Kos to its advantage, McCain's aides claimed they had to rush out the Bristol announcement to silence the ugly Internet innuendos, and that's the story the press told. The *New York Times* and Reuters were just two key news outlets that inaccurately reported that "liberal bloggers" had pushed the fake Palin pregnancy story. In truth, liberal bloggers' *readers* had pushed the story; there's a big difference. It would be like blaming radio talk show hosts for a conspiracy theory that listeners keep bringing up on the air, even though hosts refuse to discuss it.

And of course, the announcement that Bristol's due date was just four months away only further undercut the fake pregnancy theory. Since Trig was born in April and Bristol was due in December, for the conspiracy theory to be accurate, Bristol would have to give birth twice in an eight-month span.

The Palin episode highlighted the inherent risks for any decentralized, bottom-up community like the netroots. Up in Alaska, bloggers like Phil Munger put that freedom to good use and helped change campaign journalism for the better while reporting on Palin. Elsewhere, some overeager diarists took advantage of the autonomy and created opposition research without a filter.

Said Stranahan, "It's like that old cliché: With freedom comes responsibility."

fourteen

THE OBAMA NATION

With a MacBook in her lap and perched on the couch in her row house apartment in south Philadelphia, where empty Coke bottles lingered nearby, Stephanie Craig was in her usual 5 p.m. spot on October 17, counting down the days of the general election: in front of her TV watching *Hardball* on MSNBC.

A recent creative writing graduate from the University of Kansas who arrived in Philadelphia to be part of the Teach America initiative, Craig taught math at William Penn High School. But she wanted to find a way to incorporate the politics of the primary campaign into her students' curriculum, both because she was obsessed by it and because she wanted to make sure her kids fully understood what was happening across the country. Soon her students were combing polling data and sample sizes and doing delegate math. The students were also put in charge of a schoolwide primary, in which voters picked which party they wanted to participate in. With a student body of more than 1,000, just 26 voted in the GOP contest.

Obama won with nearly 90 percent of the student vote, and Craig's kids thought they had her pegged. "Because I was a twenty-three-year-old white girl from the Midwest they assumed that I was voting for Hillary," she remembered with a laugh.

Instead, Craig brought in Obama posters and buttons for her teacher friends at work who requested them. She first became a fan when she saw the young Illinois politician deliver his prime-time speech at the 2004 Democratic National Convention. When returns came back on Election

Day and John Kerry's chances slipped away, Craig and her campus friends took solace in Obama's senatorial win. Soon she read his books and by 2008 had become addicted to all things Obama.

Craig wanted to help out as much as she could with the campaign, especially since the Pennsylvania primary would be so pivotal. But she was jammed with prep work for her William Penn class, as well as keeping up with the education courses she took at the University of Pennsylvania. So instead of showing up at a local campaign office to make calls alongside rows of volunteers, the way she'd done in previous Democratic contests, Craig logged on to MyBarackObama.com and accessed a script as well as a list of targeted voters to call on behalf of the campaign. In Craig's case, the voters lived in Mississippi. After telecanvassing, she uploaded the results of her outreach and fed it to the Obama campaign. The proactive exercise made her feel she was doing her part to elect the Democrat.

The organic emphasis of the Obama grassroots campaign called for Craig, and volunteers like her all around the country, to talk to her neighbors, to make personal contact with friends and family, to speak with them directly about Obama, and to do it in an informal setting. The idea was to make those conversations natural and to expand beyond the model of knocking on doors and handing out pamphlets that campaigns had used for decades. The Obama team urged supporters to be proactive and independent, knowing that undecided voters would be more receptive to information when it came from a friend or a family member rather than from a surrogate appearing on cable TV or a 30-second television ad.

For Craig, that meant chatting with her stubborn Italian neighbor who wanted to vote for John McCain. And it meant that when she went to her corner store wearing her Obama button she was ready and willing to talk to the man behind the counter about Obama's candidacy. Those day-to-day interactions made Craig feel she was helping the campaign and that she was part of something bigger. "People on my street and in my community knew I was crazy for Obama," she told me.

Craig had been a political junkie since high school and an active Democrat since the ninth grade. That's when, growing up in Edmond, Oklahoma, just outside of Oklahoma City, she experienced a political epiphany. Up until the ninth grade in the late 1990s, she thought she was a Republican and she thought she hated Bill Clinton because her parents were Republicans and they hated Bill Clinton. But during her first year of high school, after some careful examination of the issues of the day, Craig realized that she was a Democrat, that she didn't hate Bill Clinton, and that she couldn't ignore either fact no matter how mad her mom and dad got.

In high school Craig served as president of the school's Young Democrats club, which in Edmond was like being the captain of the badminton team; it was often tough to field a starting lineup. At the University of Kansas she found other liberal activists on campus and ran for student senate vice president. Over the years, she did everything she could to help Democrats. She volunteered for the Kansas Democratic State Party, she canvassed, and in 2004 she hosted a house party for John Kerry, where her cash-strapped college pals helped raised $200 for the Democrat.

Craig sent the check off to Kerry headquarters, but she never really sensed a connection with the Kerry campaign or what it was trying to accomplish. "I didn't feel like we were a part of anything. I just thought that [because] other people are raising money we could do it too. But I didn't feel like we could do this together," she remembered.

Four years later, though, the Obama campaign felt all-encompassing, like a lifestyle. That was thanks to how the Internet had grown up around Obama's candidacy. The Internet helped Craig feel more attached to the larger progressive movement, the movement beyond Democratic Party politics, in a way that simply did not exist in 2004.

LIKE MOST POLITICAL junkies just out of college in 2008, Craig got her campaign news online. But during the primaries she became obsessed with watching the cable coverage as the battle progressed. There were just so many amazing personalities involved in the drama that she felt the story really had to be watched on television to be appreciated.

MSNBC's *Hardball* had become a permanent part of Craig's media diet. Host Chris Matthews had come a long way since January and February, when his on-air behavior toward Democrats had raised the ire of lots of partisan viewers, especially Hillary Clinton supporters, who launched a blogswarm against his sexist ways and his habit of routinely undercutting

Democrats for being out of touch with the "regular folks." By the campaign's conclusion, Matthews had remade himself on the air, and lots of liberals and Democrats came to see him as a media ally and looked forward to his interviews, especially when he faced off with Republican campaign surrogates. Increasingly, the *Hardball* confrontations made for entertaining television.

On October 17, as Craig tuned in from Philly while her boyfriend napped, Matthews's first guest was Minnesota Congresswoman Michele Bachmann, that day's surrogate sent over by the McCain campaign to discuss the Republican's increasingly aggressive, and personal, attacks on Obama.

Craig couldn't stand watching Bachmann, who had become a rising star of the GOP's far-right wing. "She's a special brand of crazy," said the math teacher. The 47-year-old Bachmann, a former Methodist minister who once sermonized about being "hot for Jesus," had been in Congress only two years. But thanks to her relentless campaign to publicize herself via nonstop cable TV appearances (she logged 23 guest slots during a six-week election season stretch), she had already fashioned herself into a spokesperson for the Party's far-right, "Drill, baby, drill" wing.

In the wake of Sarah Palin's campaign proclamation that small towns represented "the real America" and the "pro-America areas of this great nation," Matthews asked Bachmann what that Republican rhetoric implied. Did it mean Democrats and liberals were not pro-American? The MSNBC host kept pressing the Republican, until finally this exchange unfolded:

> **MATTHEWS:** Do you believe that Barack Obama may have anti-American views?
>
> **BACHMANN:** Absolutely. I'm very concerned that he may have anti-American views.

Moments later came this:

> **MATTHEWS:** How many people in the Congress of the United States do you think are anti-American?

BACHMANN: What I would say is that the news media should do a penetrating exposé and take a look. I wish they would. I wish the American media would take a great look at the views of the people in Congress and find out, are they pro-America or anti-America? I think people would be, would love to see an exposé like that.

Obama had "anti-American views" and there ought to be an investigation to find out who else serving in Congress was not sufficiently "pro-American." For Craig, questioning people's pro-American leanings did not belong in any campaign. It should be assumed that if candidates were running for president they either wanted to help America and make it better, or, on the dark side, they were selfish and just wanted to be in power. But not that they wanted to *hurt* the country. Not that they were anti-American. Craig knew Bachmann was extreme; she'd just never seen anyone on television hand the congresswoman quite as much rope as Matthews did. "It was just spectacular," she said.

Because *Hardball* aired twice each weeknight, Craig wanted to give progressives a heads-up about Bachmann's jaw-dropping performance so everyone could catch her during the show's encore at 7 p.m. So she logged on to Daily Kos as Stiffa (her old college nickname), and less than 10 minutes after Matthews had thanked his GOP guest for appearing on the program, Craig posted her item: "Chris Matthews Wades Deep into Michelle Bachmann's Mind."

Her original item didn't include any video of Bachmann's appearance, but Craig knew that in a matter of minutes somebody, somewhere within the netroots universe, would post her appearance on YouTube, just because it was that strange. So Craig hit the *refresh* button at YouTube every two minutes, and pretty soon the *Hardball* clip she wanted appeared, and she added it to Daily Kos.

Craig figured that the collective response among online Kossaks would be "Oh my God, this woman's crazy." Not "This woman is crazy and we must vote her out of office now!" Craig just wanted to spotlight the unhinged attack on Obama and let Republicans, as well as the press, know that the days of attacking Democratic leaders as being anti-American were over. Really, Craig just wanted to vent at Daily Kos. But activists there immediately decided that the best way to fight back was to raise a ton of money for Bachmann's opponent, whoever that was.

Craig actually knew who: Elwyn Tinklenberg. That's not a political name you quickly forget. Craig had been listening to a podcast of the liberal talk show host Stephanie Miller the week before and heard an interview with Tinklenberg, who had been wallowing in obscurity prior to Bachmann's meltdown on MSNBC since he was challenging a Republican incumbent in a reliably red congressional district. When Craig heard Tinklenberg on Miller's podcast, she liked what she heard from the Minnesota candidate. Now she had a perfect opportunity to support him.

Soon, spurred on by Craig's alert about Bachmann, money started streaming into Tinklenberg's campaign. The collective response stunned Craig. She'd given (modestly) to lots of Democrats over the years. But she'd never pledged $50, $100, or $150 based solely on watching a three-minute YouTube clip that didn't even feature the candidate. But that's what progressives all across the netroots nation did after watching Bachmann's *Hardball* performance.

Craig watched the Tinklenberg tally rise all night on his ActBlue page. That's where progressive candidates set up online profiles that allowed liberals across the country to contribute with a click of the mouse to their favorite candidates, no matter what district they were running in. When Craig first checked Tinklenberg's ActBlue page right after *Hardball* that night, his online haul for his entire campaign season stood at a very modest $2,600. Just half an hour later it jumped to $5,000.

If supporters could push him over the $10,000 mark that night, Craig thought, if online progressives in Pennsylvania and Florida and Georgia could help quadruple Tinklenberg's Internet treasure chest in a matter of hours, that would send a potent signal about liberals' commitment. For hours that night donations poured in to the Minnesota Democrat's campaign. Just before midnight, Tinklenberg himself logged on to Daily Kos and thanked everyone for the surge in support.

The next morning Craig stared at her computer screen in disbelief. Tinklenberg's online tally stood at $100,000, 10 times what she had hoped for. Of that $100,000, $97,400 had been raised after Craig's Daily Kos post about Bachmann's *Hardball* debacle.

That was the Saturday tally. On Monday the Tinklenberg camp announced that since Bachmann's *Hardball* appearance, the Minnesota Democrat had netted nearly $900,000 in donations—nearly 100 times what Craig first hoped for—and almost all of it had been given online. Within days new Minnesota polling data showed that Bachmann's once comfortable reelection lead had evaporated.

The episode combined the netroots' two great strengths: monitoring the media and marrying that activism with candidate advocacy. With Tinklenberg, bloggers came this close to electing a long-shot Democrat to Congress based on nothing more than a three-minute YouTube'd interview from cable television that didn't even feature the Democratic candidate, an interview that just one or two election cycles earlier would have gone completely undetected and unremarked upon. Bachmann's comments would have simply vanished into the ether. But in 2008 the comments were pounced on by an army of Obama supporters on the lookout for GOP smears against their candidate, an army that had access to a loud, liberal echo chamber to spread the news. That news was then met with an avalanche of online donations.

That was the Obama Nation. And Stephanie Craig represented a model foot soldier.

Young, college-educated, and a big Obama fan, Craig spoke passionately and incessantly about Obama's candidacy with neighbors and coworkers. She listened to her favorite liberal talk radio show via podcasts. She checked out campaign updates on her bookmarked sites: MyDD, Talking Points Memo, Fivethirtyeight, and the Washington Monthly's Political Animal. She tweeted with Obama-fanatic friends and touched base with the campaign via MyBarackObama.com. She watched *Hardball* with her laptop in front of her and logged on to Daily Kos when she wanted to document a political or media atrocity. And if she needed accompanying video clips to make her case, she just refreshed YouTube until she got what she wanted.

In the end, Stephanie Craig couldn't get Elwyn Tinklenberg elected;

he lost by less than 3 percentage points. But she did help Barack Obama. The Obama campaign, via the Internet, helped inspire and empower Craig and the army she volunteered to join. In the end, she helped get the Illinois senator elected the forty-fourth president of the United States. It really was that revolutionary.

THE KEY TO the Obama campaign's embrace of the Internet was that his team urged supporters to actually *do* something, besides donate money. His campaign empowered them with lots of online tools, especially social-networking tools, and helped them organize among themselves. In the process, through the connective tissue of the Internet, Obama's candidacy changed the face of grassroots activism.

"We've tried to bring two principles to this campaign," Joe Rospars, Obama's director of new media, told the *Atlantic* during the campaign. "One is lowering the barriers to entry and making it as easy as possible for folks who come to our Web site. The other is raising the expectation of what it means to be a supporter. It's not enough to have a bumper sticker. We want you to give five dollars, make some calls, host an event. If you look at the messages we send to people over time, there's a presumption that they will organize."

The allure of the Internet as a campaign tool was obvious: the Web made it easier for supporters to let the campaign know that they wanted to help, and it made it easier for the campaign to communicate with supporters about how they could help. The Internet was about connecting people in the fastest, easiest, and most specific way possible. And it was about expanding the participation of people in the process.

In previous election cycles, campaigns simply provided information about their candidate and asked supporters to volunteer and to donate. With the decentralized Obama push, supporters immediately connected online with like-minded fans and began coordinating events in their own communities. The potential for what supporters could achieve expanded dramatically as volunteers seized the initiative.

Nationally the campaign collected more than 10 million email addresses from supporters who helped register 1.9 million new voters and made 13.3 million voter contacts. As the Daily Kos diarist Populista noted, that meant 1 out of every 10 voters on Election Day had been personally contacted, had been personally spoken to, by the Obama campaign or an Obama supporter. That's why the tech bible, *Wired* magazine, toasted Obama's push as "the most sophisticated organizing apparatus of any presidential campaign in history."

Still, the point wasn't to make Obama's an Internet candidacy, it was to use the Internet to reinforce what volunteers and supporters were doing on the ground. The goal was to tie the off-line world to the online world. The whole idea, according to Obama's social-networking architect, Chris Hughes, revolved around creating an environment in which supporters left their computers and went to a locally sponsored Obama house party, interacted with other supporters face-to-face, and then returned to their computers to share stories about the event, sign up for the next event, donate money, or all of the above. The key for the campaign was to accentuate the connection between the offline and the online. Hughes's goal in building the Obama brand in 2008 revolved around using online tools to make real-world connections.

For Hughes, that refrain had a familiar ring to it; he had used the same mantra to help build the Facebook brand into a social-networking phenomenon that changed the way people communicate. Hughes is one of Facebook's three cofounders who launched the landmark Web 2.0 site from their Harvard dormitory in 2004. By combining the connectivity of Facebook with the natural appeal of Obama, Hughes made sure the Democrat lapped the competition online in 2008.

In this way, Hughes emerged as the key, transformative campaign figure in the election cycle. Unlike previous campaign stars, such as Karl Rove, James Carville, and Lee Atwater, who all put their stamp on White House runs, Hughes didn't do politics per se. He didn't talk to the press much, either. What Hughes did was social networking and organizing. And he was arguably the central reason Obama won the way he did.

All the more amazing is the fact that on Election Day 2008 Hughes was just 24 years old and the Obama campaign was the first one he ever worked on. Hughes represented a new generation of campaign wizards who had little in common with those previous middle-aged male strategists. In fact, in 2008 Aaron Sorkin, the creator of *West Wing,* signed on with Columbia Pictures to write a screenplay about the Facebook phenomenon and the people behind it. If Disney's Zac Efron, the pinup star of the fourth-grade franchise, *High School Musical,* signed on to play the sandy-haired Hughes in the Facebook movie, it would not be a stretch.

In other words, James Carville he is not.

Hughes grew up in Hickory, North Carolina, whose national claim to fame in recent years was a massive 40-foot-deep sinkhole that swallowed a Corvette whole in the parking lot of Buffalo's Southwest Cafe. In high school he began plotting his escape from small-town conservative life and set his sights on Phillips Academy boarding school in Andover, Massachusetts, which he liked because it was progressive and secular. Hughes was accepted but needed financial aid because his working-class Republican parents—his dad sold graphic arts paper and his mom taught math—couldn't afford the annual $30,000 tuition. When the school initially refused financial aid, it was the 14-year-old Hughes who personally contacted school administrators to press his case. They relented.

At Phillips Academy Hughes joined the Democratic Club and then became its president. In the fall of 2002 he arrived at Harvard ready to study French history, literature, and political theory. Living in Harvard's Kirkland House, famous for its drunken, in-house-only "Incestfest" winter dance, Hughes roomed with Mark Zuckerberg and Dustin Moskovitz, a pair of computer-loving, code-writing prodigies.

In late 2003 Zuckerberg zeroed in on the university-issued facebook, the printed yearbook for incoming Harvard students that featured bad ID photos as well as a few crumbs of bio information doled out by the administration (hometown, birth date, high school, etc.). Harvard administrators had been saying for years that they would get around to posting the facebook online. But Zuckerberg, Moskovitz, and Hughes all thought it should be done immediately and that it should be interactive. The key was that students should decide how much and what kind of information about themselves they wanted to give out to each other. Answer: They wanted to give out a lot, everything from cell phone numbers to relationship status. The idea was to combine the university online database with an interactive social-networking component.

During the January break between semesters in 2004, Zuckerberg hunkered down in the common room of his Kirkland House dorm suite and created the software framework for Facebook. The free site allowed students with a Harvard email address to create their own Facebook profile, where they could post photos as well as list their major and favorite books and movies. They could also create every imaginable interest group and friendship network by inviting in friends as well as befriending friends of friends.

On February 4, 2004, the Massachusetts Supreme Court made history in downtown Boston when it ruled that gay marriage should be legal in the commonwealth. Three miles away and across the Charles River in Cambridge, a different kind of social and cultural history unfolded that same day: Facebook was launched out of Harvard's Kirkland House, and sophomore Chris Hughes ranked among its first three members. Within three weeks, thousands of Harvard students logged on and created profiles. Within 12 months, after expanding to several hundred campuses nationwide, Facebook had revolutionized campus social life and boasted one million, often addicted members. By the end of 2008, when the membership door had been thrown wide open to nonstudents, 150 million users worldwide were part of Facebook; nearly 350,000 new members signed up every day.

The genius of Facebook was that it connected real-life communities, such as real students and real campuses, and translated them on the Internet for people to learn more about their peers and to join them. Users weren't going online to meet some random member 5,000 miles away; they were getting information about real people they already cared about. And the information about friends spread virally and socially among users. For millions of college students Facebook became the new cup of morning joe, that first, addictive act of every new day. It became habit-forming and impossible to break. Like trying to quit using email, it just wasn't possible. YouTube and Facebook soon emerged as the procrastinator's ultimate refuge.

After earning his Harvard degree in 2006, Hughes joined the Facebook team, established in Palo Alto. That year, Obama's staff wanted to set up a Facebook page for the new senator, who was already attracting lots of attention, especially from college-age supporters. Hughes responded to an email from an Obama aide and offered to help build the senator's Facebook profile. (Favorite movies: *The Godfather* and *Casablanca*.)

When Obama announced his presidential candidacy in early 2007, Hughes met for coffee at Union Station in Washington with Jim Brayton, who oversaw the senator's Internet operation. Asked about his ideas for the campaign's online initiative, Hughes "basically went on for an hour," Brayton told a reporter. Ten months after graduating college, Hughes took leave from the privately held, multibillion-dollar company he helped found and accepted a $44,000-a-year job with the Obama campaign as the online technology coordinator, or "online organizing guru," as the position was known internally. Tapped to oversee a Facebook-like social-networking hub for the campaign and to build on the existing Internet habits of college kids, Hughes wanted to spread that pattern of behavior to a larger audience, to use those new routines to spark political activism and to invite participation.

The vehicle Hughes drove onto the campaign racetrack, with the help of the online architects at Blue State Digital, was MyBarackObama.com, or MyBO, as it was affectionately known. MyBO allowed supporters to build lists of like-minded friends, contribute blog posts, share photos, and, most important, meet supporters in their area and organize local events as well as mobilize fund-raising efforts for their candidate. At MyBO fans could register to vote, get text-message updates on their mobile phone, pick from a dozen Obama-themed ring tones ("Yes we can!"), and download an Obama news widget to stay current on campaign events. MyBO, with its Facebook-friendly feel, was how the campaign distributed online phone banks for volunteers so they could telecanvass from home and allowed supporters to set up every conceivable kind of local and national group (e.g., Texas Business Women for Obama).

Just as with Facebook, MyBO invited friends to join friends online, which meant that recruitment for the campaign spread on a local level as peers recruited peers in their own way. The site became a campaign phenomenon. Within the first 24 hours of launching MyBO, the site boasted more than 1,000 user-generated, localized groups. By the end of the campaign, 35,000 MyBO groups were started by two million users, who hosted more than 200,000 Obama events.

By embracing online technologies, especially the social networking of MyBO, the Obama campaign put old-fashioned, block-by-block movement building on steroids. That was the magic: Obama's team married the power of an overflowing online community with real on-the-ground field operations to create the kind of voter army no other Democratic candidate had ever commanded before.

"The way the campaign worked volunteers into a system orchestrated by professional organizers was staggering both in its scope and its efficiency," marveled the blogger Jane Hamsher. "It's taking advantage of the way people communicate in order to fundamentally change the architecture of modern politics."

None of that would have been possible without genuine passion for the candidate, though. Just ask the Hillary Clinton campaign, which put all kinds of bells and whistles on her website and built Web communities for her supporters to spread the word about the candidate and to spark a bottom-up grassroots movement. For long periods, that passion just didn't materialize online, at least not among Clinton's core base of older, middle-class female supporters. It wasn't there until February and March, when her candidacy lurched from crisis to crisis and each week brought the possibility that she might be knocked out of the race for good. It wasn't until her campaign fell into panic mode that Clinton benefited from a genuine grassroots uprising, when voters and supporters belatedly went online and became activists and donors. That's when the Internet became the fundraising engine for her entire campaign. Without that engine she never would have been able to carry on into March, April, May, and June.

That is the great irony of the Democratic battle and the role the Internet played. Without the Internet as a revolutionary fund-raising tool, Obama never would have been able to match Clinton's donor firepower early on in the campaign. Unlike the experience of previous insurgent candidates, such as Howard Dean and Bill Bradley and Gary Hart, the Internet changed the way Obama could finance his challenge and allowed him to translate his grassroots support into tens of millions of dollars of early donations. Obama pocketed $28 million in online contributions during the month of January, and a staggering $500 million during the entire campaign. If it hadn't been for the Internet, Obama would not have been in such a strong position to battle for the nomination at the outset of 2008.

At the same time, if it hadn't been for the Internet and the fund-raising power it represented, there was no way that under the old, traditional donor model Clinton would have been able to soldier on beyond February. After losing a dozen straight primary and caucus contests, she never would have been able to tap a traditional money source to keep her campaign alive. Instead, the Internet—that is, everyday supporters—bankrolled her campaign for at least the final three months. The online fund-raising tools that Clinton's campaign eventually used to capture the tens of millions of dollars that flooded in had been in place for months. It was the bottom-up energy and passion for Clinton that had, until then, been missing.

In many ways Clinton was the AOL to Obama's Google during the campaign season. Online, she represented the more lumbering, established giant, and he was the nimble newcomer. Poor John McCain. He was the CompuServe of 2008.

THAT A McCAIN aide had to reassure attendees at a tech conference in the summer of 2008 that the candidate was "aware of the Internet" just highlighted how far behind Republicans lagged in the online world, and how little community building the GOP did in 2008. McCain's Internet fund-raising effort was anemic compared to Obama's bonanza. Libertarian candidate Ron Paul was the only Republican who figured out how to tap into the Internet's money machine in 2008, and his candidacy was completely shunned by the GOP establishment.

The ease with which Obama bested McCain online simply reflected the ease with which Obama bested McCain at the ballot box, as the Democrat rolled up an electoral landslide win in November. It was at times as if Obama and McCain were running campaigns from two different decades. Following Election Day, the blogger Pete Quily compiled the statistics from key online forums and highlighted how decisively Obama had beat McCain online:

- At Facebook, where the Democrat landed 400,000 new friends in just the last two weeks of the campaign, Obama received 3,032 percent more hits than McCain did over the course of the election.
- At MySpace, Obama garnered nearly four times the number of friends as McCain, and 269 percent more search results were done for Obama's name.
- At Flickr, the photo-sharing site featured nearly five times more search results for Obama than for McCain and hosted more than 50,000 photos on Obama's Flickr page. McCain did not have a page.
- At Twitter, McCain barely had a presence at the micro-blogging service. Obama sent out nearly 10 times more mini-messages than the Republican. He had 2,254 percent more Twitter followers, and there were 1,029 percent more Obama searches conducted there.
- At YouTube, Obama generated twice as many search results as McCain, posted five times as many videos, and boasted 117,000 YouTube subscribers along with 25,000 friends.

In fact, the Obama campaign completely revolutionized how YouTube is used and made it much more substantive. Prior to the 2008 cycle, the user-generated video hub had been best known in campaign circles for catching candidates midgaffe, such as when Virginia Republican George Allen disparaged a staffer from his opponent's campaign with the little-known pejorative epithet "macaca." The homemade video clip of that race-based put-down took flight on the Web and likely cost Allen a seat in the U.S. Senate.

Obama's campaign not only created its own channel on YouTube, where supporters could become subscribers; it also inundated the site with content, posting thousands of hours of Obama-related clips, which were created by a small army of Obama campaign videographers who documented his every move. With an insatiable appetite to hear from the candidate directly, people watched and watched and watched. Sure, they clicked on the funny and entertaining videos posted online by supporters, including clips of celebrities such as the rapper Jay-Z and the actress Natalie Portman. But they also watched longer, meatier Obama videos that often ran 10, 15, and 20 minutes. His supporters could not get enough. Obama's 2007 YouTube response to President Bush's State of the Union speech attracted more than 700,000 views in just two days.

In March 2008, when Obama, spurred on by the Rev. Jeremiah Wright controversy, gave his speech about race in America, the 37-minute address became a YouTube sensation. Within a week of being posted online, it had been watched more than four million times. As Ari Melber at the *Nation* noted, that represented one million *more* than the total audience of cable news viewers who tuned in to watch the address the day it was given. By November Obama's race speech had been viewed more than seven million times on YouTube.

By the height of the general election season, Obama's official YouTube channel attracted two million views *each day*. By November 4 the site, loaded with more than 1,800 clips uploaded by the Obama team, had logged a total of 96 million views during the course of the campaign. And yes, after watching any one of those videos on Obama's YouTube channel, viewers had the option of clicking on the *contribute* button and donating to the campaign by using a credit card and Google Checkout.

TO VETERAN ONLINE progressives who felt as though they had been shouting in the wilderness for years, especially those who joined the blogosphere during the nascent, dark days between 2002 and 2004, when Bush enjoyed the height of his power and popularity, watching Chris Hughes and the rest of the Obama campaign harness new technology and use it for Democratic good was like a vision realized.

In many ways it was the blogosphere's culmination to see the Obama team recruit new voters and build a national and largely youth-based political coalition that embraced minorities and labor, shattered records for voter turnout, and sparked a generational political awakening. When it was unfurled, the coalition boasted enough firepower to dent any remaining vestiges of a permanent Republican majority, the kind Karl Rove had dreamed about since Bush's 2004 reelection.

That was the good news: Democrats took back the country in 2008 and they did it thanks to an unprecedented grassroots movement made possible by new technology and the political embrace of a bottom-up, Internet-friendly approach. Obama activists built on and added to Howard Dean's netroots model, which embraced the Internet as an organizing tool, and they benefited from heavy youth support and a record-breaking number of small donors. "The political zeitgeist that the progressive blogosphere first seized upon five or six years ago was released into the population at large and came back, unexpectedly, as the Barack Obama campaign," wrote the blogger Chris Bowers.

The bad news for liberal bloggers was that as the Obama campaign unfolded, as his new community-based coalition was being built and celebrated, it became obvious that bloggers were never really invited to the party. Liberal bloggers simply never became active partners with Obama in the way they had been with the Dean insurgency four years earlier, and the way they had been with scores of Democratic politicians in skirmishes throughout the Bush years. Why? Mostly because Obama didn't seem to want the bloggers around.

In other words, in 2008 Obama clearly harnessed the Internet, but he ignored the blogosphere, that vocal subset where activists congregated and plotted. It's true that Obama captured lots of fierce loyalty within the blogosphere, as Hillary Clinton could attest to. But he managed to achieve that without actually directly engaging the community.

Collectively the netroots did everything it could to get Obama elected, including playing defense for him. For instance, using vigilant fact-checking, the netroots pillar Media Matters for America almost single-handedly demolished the anti-Obama book, *The Obama Nation,* released in August by the right-wing author responsible for the Swift Boat Veterans for Truth smear campaign that helped derail Democrat John Kerry in 2004.

Still, Obama maintained a pronounced distance from the netroots. "There's clearly no one in the Obama campaign who is communicating with us," the online activist Matt Stoller complained to me in early 2008.

"They don't care what we think. They have other channels they care about, including a whole network of grassroots organizers," he noted in late April. "That's fine. That's their choice. They've made it, there's not much any of us can do. Just know that their logistical operations are remarkable, their campaign structure is phenomenal, and we're not a part of it."

During the campaign both Hillary Clinton and John McCain sponsored blogger conference calls in which the candidates fielded questions from netroots writers. But Obama never did that. It wasn't until late August, when McCain was still hanging around the polls and Democrats nationwide began expressing an uneasy feeling about another blown chance at the White House, that the Obama campaign made a real, sustained effort to reach out. But when Obama surged back into the lead in late September, that sustained outreach evaporated, according to bloggers.

The Obama team's lack of blogger outreach remained a constant, mostly off-line topic of conversation throughout the campaign. Blogger outreach simply meant having someone on the campaign staff, preferably somebody with some internal clout, who kept bloggers up to date on events, answered their questions, fed them information, and schmoozed them off the record. Basically, a blogger liaison played the same role as a traditional campaign spokesperson, except this person dealt only with the bloggers and understood the world of the netroots.

In 2007 Democratic candidates Hillary Clinton, Chris Dodd, and John Edwards all tapped netroots veterans to fill blogger liaison positions. That same year the Obama campaign hired 26-year-old Josh Orton, a former Air America producer, to be deputy director of new media. Among his duties was staying in touch with A-list bloggers, and according to netroots veterans, Orton did a solid job. But following an internal turf conflict with his similarly young, 26-year-old campaign boss, Joe Rospars, Orton left the campaign that October.

"There seems to be a debate in town whether Josh wanted to do more outreach but wasn't allowed to," the AmericaBlog founder and Obama fan John Aravosis mentioned during the primary season. "It's pretty clear the campaign does not want to do a lot of outreach to the blogs." Long after Orton left the campaign in 2007, bloggers still emailed and called him, trying to figure out who handled Obama's blogger duties. Orton told them he didn't think the campaign had anyone doing that. (By 2008, the Obama team did.)

"I just don't think they like the blogs," concluded Chris Bowers during an NPR interview just weeks after Election Day. "They just do not seem to like the entire ethos of the outsider blogosphere." Bowers sensed "more of a Beltway attitude" among the Obama team. During the campaign it had become clear to Bowers that Obama's campaign preferred circumventing the blogosphere in order to build up its own, independent grassroots infrastructure and on-the-ground volunteer field team. Equally clear was the fact that Obama was building a movement that, in sheer numbers, dwarfed what the blogosphere had been able to create. And he was building a movement that was noticeably less partisan than the blogosphere.

During the campaign the implicit message from Obama's supporters, who were never asked to rally around specific liberal policies, was that they had faith in the candidate's ability and judgment, and that once he became president he would choose the correct course for the country. It was a campaign built on inspiration and change. But did that represent a sustainable movement? And, bloggers asked, was that going to help non-Obama Democrats win elections in the near future?

One warning flag went up on December 2, 2008, during Georgia's runoff election for its U.S. Senate seat between Democrat John Martin and Republican incumbent Saxby Chambliss. Just weeks earlier, when Obama's name appeared atop the ballot, extraordinary high voter turnout in Georgia helped keep the Martin-Chambliss race too close to call. During the December runoff, though, with Obama absent from the ballot and turnout way down, Chambliss won with ease, trouncing the Democrat by 16 percentage points.

Questions also arose about whether Obama's expansive movement and the netroots were on the same page. Election Day exit polling data indicated that African American voters, who turned out in historic numbers, voted heavily not only in favor of the Democrat, but also in favor of ballot initiatives in Florida and California to ban gay marriage, bans that were widely condemned within the liberal blogosphere.

Deep down, lots of bloggers understood that what they had built over the previous five years had been bypassed to a certain degree during the presidential push. They realized that Obama simply reinvented the wheel and built his own, more powerful and more densely populated online movement. It was a movement less vocally liberal and less politically active than the blogosphere. Rather than embracing the existing netroots infrastructure, Obama's team created new institutions, such as MyBO, and tapped the social-networking and fund-raising aspects of the liberal Internet, while leaving mostly undisturbed the political activism that had defined the netroots for years. In other words, Obama went over the bloggers' heads. And truthfully, not many of them complained as they supported his march toward an Election Day victory.

But in terms of governing, it became clear that Obama's maneuvering had political implications beyond the campaign. In the wake of the sweeping electoral victory, the famed community organizer and Harvard University professor Marshall Ganz, who worked closely with the Obama campaign to train 23,000 local organizers in three-day "Camp Obama" training sessions, marveled that Obama would be the first president to take the office as the leader of a movement.

Bloggers were certainly in awe of the grassroots energy that propelled Obama's run. But they were also political pragmatists, and some wondered what, exactly, the "movement" behind Obama stood for in the long term. What did it signify beyond getting Barack Obama elected president? After all, Obama himself represented the central organizing principle behind the movement. And Obama did not run as a liberal ideologue, which was why some of his early centrist cabinet selections drew praise from unlikely sources, such as the conservative mouthpieces Karl Rove and Rush Limbaugh.

Bloggers quietly stewed over that fact, as well as when the netroots hero and outgoing Democratic National Committee chairman Howard Dean was snubbed and reportedly told to stay away from the press conference in which Obama introduced the new DNC chief in January. But bloggers shared a collective, and very vocal, "WTF?" moment when Obama turned to Rick Warren, the far-right, antigay evangelical pastor who compared gay marriage to incest, and asked him to give the invocation at the president-elect's inauguration. Obama's nod to Warren highlighted the distance that existed between the online progressive movement and his new, more centrist-leaning administration.

Still, even with that intramural jockeying among Democrats, there was no taking away from the bigger blogger accomplishment. To see how the netroots, in just a few years' time, had helped change the face of American politics as well as alter the media landscape, and to note how a ragtag band of volunteer activists had fought back against a hard-right, Bush-led political turn in Washington, and won, was to acknowledge a transformation.

For the bloggers, Obama's sweeping victory, as well as the Democrats' expanded majority in Congress, represented a very personal vindication. "I had a Crooks and Liars party on Election Night in Los Angeles," recalled John Amato, who created his video blog in the summer of 2004 in order to oppose Bush. "And when I was driving to the party, tears were actually welling up in my eyes as I thought about what Crooks and Liars had become and to see where my life had gone. But also the fact that we were on the verge of electing a Democratic president, and who was an African American, it was very overwhelming. We worked for four years to try to expose the Bush administration for the fraud that it was. And to now have a chance to right the ship, it was quite emotional. Just the sheer impact of the day."

Added Howie Klein, the retired record-executive-turned-blogger who epitomized the completely unlikely lineup of netroots players who helped bring the blogosphere to life, "When historians look back they'll say, 'Well, the election was a natural pendulum swing away from the Republicans because of their excesses.' But the blogosphere played a big role. The work done by Markos, the work done by Matt Stoller, the work done by MoveOn, the work done by both Robert and Glenn Greenwald. The work done by John Amato and Jane Hamsher, who have certainly built up tremendous sites with huge numbers of very sophisticated readers. There are so many people working so hard, it's just mind-boggling. It's such an inspiration."

INDEX

ABOUT THE AUTHOR

ERIC BOEHLERT, an award-winning journalist who writes extensively about media and politics, is a Senior Fellow for Media Matters for America and a former writer for *Salon* and *Rolling Stone*. He is the author of *Lapdogs: How the Press Rolled Over for Bush* and lives in Montclair, New Jersey, with his wife and two children.